ADI SHANKARACHARYA

ADI SHANKARACHARYA

Hinduism's Greatest Thinker

PAVAN K. VARMA

First published by Tranquebar Press, an imprint of Westland Publications Private Limited in 2018
61, 2nd Floor, Silverline Building, Alapakkam Main Road, Maduravoyal, Chennai 600095

Westland, the Westland logo, Tranquebar and the Tranquebar logo are the trademarks of Westland Publications Private Limited, or its affiliates.

ISBN: 9788193655610
10 9 8 7 6 5 4 3 2

Typeset by Ram Das Lal, New Delhi, NCR
Printed at Manipal Technologies Limited, Manipal

In deep obeisance to our great seers and sages and thinkers whose philosophical vision has made Hinduism one of the greatest religions in the world.

Contents

PREFACE

Hinduism, for most within its fold, is a way of life. It has no one Pope, no one text, no inflexibly prescriptive ritual, no mandatory congregation, and no one presiding temple. It is precisely for this reason that it has continued to flourish from time immemorial, sanatan and anant, because what is ubiquitous but not constrained by the brittleness of form, is by definition imperishable.

But it is precisely for this reason too, that most Hindus, while practicing their faith in their own way, are often largely uninformed about the remarkable philosophical foundations of their religion. Hinduism, as a religion, is inseparable from Hinduism as a philosophy. If Hindus are adrift from the deep philosophical moorings of the religion they practice, they are deliberately choosing the shell for the great treasure that lies within. When religions are largely reduced to rituals, there is always the danger that the form will become more important than the substance. That, I believe, will be a great disservice to Hinduism itself, and to the great seers and sages and thinkers—to whom this book is humbly dedicated—who gave to this sanatan dharma some of the most profound philosophical insights the world has seen.

It is for this reason that I wrote this book. Jagad Guru Adi Shankaracharya was, undoubtedly, one of the greatest minds in Hinduism's unrelenting quest for the ultimate truth. His short life of but thirty-two years is as fascinating as the Advaita philosophy he so meticulously crafted. My purpose was to discover this remarkable man and his life, and I travelled from Kaladi in Kerala where he was born, to Kedarnath, where he obtained samadhi—and to most other places which are associated with his life—in this pursuit.

Apart from physically traversing the length and breadth of Bharat in the footsteps of the Jagad Guru, I was deeply involved in the cerebral voyage of immersing myself in his philosophy, and its correlation to what we know about ourselves and the universe today. In fact, my research on the correspondence between his philosophical tenets, and the discoveries of contemporary science, especially in the fields of cosmology, quantum physics and neurology, has been one of the most rewarding aspects of my research.

There are too many people to whom I owe my gratitude in the writing of this book, but I would be unforgivably remiss if I do not mention a few names specifically. Mani Shanker Dvivedi, an exceptionally bright young scholar of Sanskrit who has done his doctorate from Jawaharlal Nehru University in New Delhi, was of indispensable help in locating elusive books, assisting with Sanskrit texts, and in putting together the Select Anthology. His perennial willingness to help, and his belief in my project is something that I can never ever reciprocate.

I have spent many hours with scholar-statesman Dr. Murli Manohar Joshi, discussing abstruse aspects of Hindu philosophy and the correspondence of many aspects of Shankaracharya's work with contemporary science. Doctor Saheb, as he is universally and lovably known, was also of great help in facilitating many arrangements during my extensive travels. I owe a deep debt of gratitude to him. My genuine thanks are due also to N.N. Vohra, Governor of Jammu & Kashmir, who was of immense help during my visit to Srinagar, and enabled my meetings with scholars on Hindu philosophy and, in particular, with those knowledgeable on Kashmir Shaivism. The many hours I have spent over the years with Dr Karan Singh, so learned in both Sanskrit and Hindu philosophy, is also something I will always cherish.

I must record my sincere appreciation to H.H. Bharati Tirtha Mahaswamiji, the Shankaracharya of Sringeri, H.H. Swami Nischalananda Saraswati, Shankaracharya of Puri, and to H.H Swami Swarupananda, Shankaracharya of Dwaraka. Each of them graciously received me and blessed the book I was researching. I must also profusely thank M.P. Veerendra Kumar, Member of Parliament and publisher of Mathrubhumi, for his help during my visit to Kaladi. My old friend, Pinaki Mishra, Member of Parliament from Puri, provided valuable assistance during my visit to the matha there. Shobha Karandlaje and Poonam Ben, both Members of Parliament, went out of their way to render support for my visit to Sringeri and Dwaraka respectively. Legislator Om Prakash Saklecha provided vital logistical support for my visit to Omkareshwar and Maheshwar.

My heartfelt thanks are also due to Manish Pushkale, the talented artist, and my guide and mentor, who accompanied me to Omkareshwar and Maheshwar; to Ashok Kapur for his unstinting care in Varanasi; to Ghulab Singh who made my visit to Kedarnath, Badrinath and Joshimath possible; to Professor Subramania Iyer who showed me around in Kaladi; to Tirupati Khemka in Chennai for facilitating my visit to Kanchipuram; and, last but not the least, to Manish Tiwari, my dedicated secretary, but for whose constant coordinating support I would have found it impossible to complete this book.

I cannot but especially mention two key friends who are directly involved in this book being written: Mita Kapur, my literary agent who runs Siyahi, and Sudha Sadhanand, Managing Editor of my publishers, Westland Publications. Mita works diligently for the author she represents. Sudha was my editor when I published my first book in 1989, which was a biography of Ghalib, and

Shankaracharya. Thank you very much Mita and Sudha for the faith you reposed in me.

My wife, Renuka, travelled with me from Kaladi to Kedarnath. She is an inseparable part of the books I write, and there is little more I can say than to reiterate that but for her—and this should be not held against her—I would not have written any of my books!

Finally—and this may seem odd to some readers—I must bow deep in gratitude to the Jagad Guru himself. There were countless occasions when I felt he was directly there to give me hope and strength, and find solutions to what appeared to be intractable obstacles. As a human being, I have felt his benevolent presence throughout the writing of this book, and while I take full responsibility for any shortcomings in the writing, I feel, at a deeply personal level, that this book would never have been written but for his aashirvad or blessings.

LIFE—A PERSONAL JOURNEY

The Periyar river shimmers like molten silver as the plane descends to land at Kochi airport. The landscape is a lush tapestry of coconut trees, banana plantations and fruit orchards, interspersed with applique work of green vegetable patches. Kochi airport is built in traditional Kerala architecture, modern but reminiscent of another time.

I have come to Kochi to visit Kaladi, the birthplace of Jagad Guru Bhagwad Adi Shankaracharya, which is but a short twenty-minute drive from the airport, just off the Mahatma Gandhi Marg that leads out of Kochi.

In 788 CE, when Shankaracharya was born, Kaladi must have been a small but distinct village not too far from the town of Kochi. But now, urbanisation has swallowed such distinctions, and Kaladi is, for all practical purposes, a suburb of Kochi. There is nothing much to distinguish it from the urban sprawl of all Indian towns—shops, dust, cars, motorcycles, scooters, concrete and noise—except that this is the place where a millennium and two hundred years ago, a child was born who was destined to change the course of Hinduism and to elevate philosophy and metaphysics to a level that has hardly been equalled since.

A nine-storied octagonal tower, right on the main road, is the first sign of this momentous association. It is the Sri Adi Shankaracharya Paduka Mandapam with a statue of the great seer. The building is disappointing, with no great distinguishing aesthetic features, a soulless effort in concrete, far removed from the intellectual lucidity of the man to whom it is dedicated. Two black elephants in concrete greet the visitor at the entrance, with a collapsible metal grill on the gate. The main shrine consists of a small statue of Shankaracharya dressed in a white sanyasin's cape, and surrounded by his four main disciples, Sureshvara, Totakacharya, Hastamalaka, and Padmapada. Somewhat incongruously, on the adjacent wall is a picture of tenth class students of the Sri Kanchi Shankara Public School who secured 98 per cent or more marks in their exam.

A short drive from here, on the banks of the river Periyar, is the actual birthplace of Shankara. The Periyar is also called Purna. In Sanskrit, it means 'full'; in Malayalam, it translates as Periyar. By contrast to the Paduka Mandapam, this place has an aesthetic serenity that immediately evokes the spiritual mood. A pond with lotus flowers leads to a traditional Kerala mandapam (hall) paved with cool slate-coloured granite. On the western corner is a shrine commemorating Shankaracharya; on the eastern side is a temple dedicated to Brahmi, the wife of Brahma, which is another name for Saraswati, the Goddess of Learning. The parikrama around the sanctum sanctorum has idols of the Saptamata, the seven incarnations of Devi, representing the power of Shakti (which, as we shall see, is a constant association with Shankara), viz., Maheshwari, Kaumari, Vaishnavi, Varahi, Indrani and Chamunda.

Professor Subramania Iyer, a gentle, wizened man with an unkempt beard and white hair, dressed in the traditional mundu and white shirt, welcomes us into the mandapam. He is in charge of the Sanskrit College at Kaladi run by the Shankaracharya Peeth at Sringeri. Kaladi, he says, was forgotten for many centuries, until in the late nineteenth century, the 33rd pontiff at Sringeri (the first matha set up by Shankaracharya), Sacchidananda Sivabhinava Bharathi, began a search for the janmabhoomi or birthplace of the great sage-philosopher. The problem was that there were three villages in Kerala with the name of Kaladi. But, there was only one Kaladi on the banks of the Purna and that was a significant pointer, since all the traditional biographies of Shankaracharya were unanimous that his family's home was on the Purna.

There was another bit of clinching evidence. When the research team entered the house purported to be that of Shankara, they found a group of ladies lighting a lamp on a stone pillar in a corner of the home. When asked, they said this was the spot where Aryamba, Shankara's mother, was cremated.

Shankara's parents, Shivaguru and Aryamba, were Nambudiri Brahmins. This placed them at the pinnacle of the social order, although Shivaguru is not known to have distinguished himself in any other way. The couple led a life of pious conformity to prescribed religious ritual and scriptural learning. The void in their lives was the absence of a progeny. Legend has it that one night Shiva, who was the couple's family deity, appeared in Aryamba's dream and answered her plea for a child. Interestingly, Shiva is said to have given Aryamba a choice. She could either give birth to a fool who would live long or be blessed with a genius who would die young. Aryamba, so the legend says, chose the second option.

According to modern historians, Shankara was born on the fifth day of the waxing moon in April–May 788 CE.[1] However,

1 Anandagiri's biography, *Shankaravijaya*, believes he was born in Chidambaram in 44 BCE and died in 12 BCE. Dr R.G. Bhandarkar believes his birth date to be 680 CE. The most accepted view, however, is that, based on Shankara's reference to Kumarila Bhatta, who lived in 700 CE, and his refutation of the doctrines of Asanga, Nagarjuna and Ashvaghosha, who are known to have lived not earlier than the 3rd century CE, as also the fact that he came later than Bhartrihari whose dates are around 600 CE on the authority of I-Tsing, the dates of his life

many others dispute this date, assigning to him a much earlier period. According to the Guruparamparas (records kept by gurus or pontiffs of mathas) in the Dwaraka, Puri and Kanchi mathas, he lived around 500 BCE, while the Sringeri Matha takes him back to 44 BCE.

The truth is that direct evidence about Shankara's dates is practically non-existent, and modern historians who argue on the basis of credible cross-inferences from his writings and references to contemporaries or other well known personages who preceded him, that he was born in 778 CE, have to contend with other traditions that posit faith (and its associated arguments) as against historiography.

The controversy about his date of birth notwithstanding, other details of his life can be pieced together from his extant biographies and collateral evidence. We know that the young Shankara began to display very early all the signs of being a prodigy. When not yet three, he is said to have memorised the Vedas and the basic Sanskrit texts, his extraordinary memory allowing him to remember what he heard but once, *eka shruti dhara*.

It is almost certain that from the very beginning he showed an inclination to lead a life of renunciation, shunning the conventional pleasures easily accessible to a bright child from his social background. This was, not surprisingly, a cause of worry for his mother. While she revelled in her son's intellectual precocity, which was the talk of the village and beyond, she did not want him to become a recluse or an ascetic. Like any mother, she wanted him to marry and have children and be with her, especially since her husband, Shivaguru, had died when Shankara was very young and she was a widow with no other family members.

Shankara, however, seemed to be unrelenting in his decision to renounce life and lead the life of an ascetic. There must have been

---

span are 788 to 820 CE. These dates have the support of Max Mueller, Paul Deussen, and Dr S. Radhakrishnan.

considerable tension between mother and son, but matters were brought to a head by an incident that straddles both mythology and fact. It is said that once when Shankara was bathing in the river, a crocodile caught his leg. He shouted out to his mother: 'Mother! Save me! A crocodile has caught me and I cannot be saved until you give me permission to become a sanyasin. Please mother, don't delay, otherwise it will be too late!' Aryamba hesitated for a moment, but her son was being dragged into the swirling waters, and she had little choice but to say yes. The moment she gave her permission, the crocodile is said to have released Shankara and disappeared.

Did such an incident actually take place, or was it some biographer's anecdotal flourish? It is difficult to give a definitive answer. In all probability, there must have been some dramatic incident that forced Aryamba to give her consent, since in the normal course she, as a widow, would not have allowed her son to abandon her. It could also be that Shankara played a ruse on his mother to force her to acquiesce.

On the other hand, the crocodile could quite well be a metaphor for the perils of worldly life, from which Shankara found release, a resort to symbolism by an imaginative chronicler. Fact, legend, myth and symbolism coalesce in such stories, but this much is true that even today, right next to Shankara's home, there is a Crocodile Ghat that commemorates this pivotal moment, and hosts an annual festival in its memory.

Aryamba may have given her consent under duress, but she was still worried about living alone. There was also the traditional worry about who would perform her funeral rites. Shankara assured her he would return whenever his mother, conscious, unconscious or burdened by sorrow, needed him. He further made the commitment that on her death he would perform the final rites, even though this was contrary to the conventional code of the ascetic order. With this vow given, he bade farewell and left home, still a child, in search of the right guru or teacher.

This search took him across the Deccan plateau and the Satpura ranges to the city of Omkareshwar, situated on the river Narmada, a little south of Indore, in the Vindhyas. The hill that comprises the city resembles the figure Om, and the shape of the Narmada, as it skirts the city, also looks like Om. In fact, Omkareshwar is an island, encircled on one side by the Narmada and on the other side by a tributary of the Narmada—the Rewa. Both rivers, which part just before Omkareshwar, come together after crossing the city.

For centuries prior to Shankara's arrival, Omkareshwar was known as a holy city housing one of the twelve jyotirlingas symbolising Shiva. But, the temple was not the primary reason why Shankara trekked hundreds of miles across dense jungles to come to Omkareshwar. His search was for the right guru, and he knew that in this city resided the learned Vedantic scholar, Govindapada, disciple and son of the famous Gaudapada, the author of the *Karika*, a seminal commentary on the *Mandukya Upanishad*.

According to most accounts, corroborated also by local belief, Govindapada was deep in meditation inside a cave when Shankara arrived to meet him. Shankara waited outside the cave, and when Govindapada broke his meditation, he asked the young boy: 'Who are you?'

To this, according to lore, Shankara recited a shloka: 'I am neither the earth, nor water, nor fire, nor air, nor sky, nor any other properties. I am not the senses and not even the mind. I am Shiva, the undivided essence of consciousness.'

Hearing such a profound reply, Govindapada took Shankara under his tutelage. Some accounts aver that to indicate his acceptance, Govindapada simply extended one of his feet outside the cave and Shankara reverentially bowed and touched it.

It is not certain how long Shankara stayed at Govindapada's hermitage. We can assume that it must have been somewhere between eighteen months to three years, during which he mastered the non-dual Advaita philosophy. In the eye of one's mind, one can picture what Omkareshwar must have been like twelve hundred years ago: an island hill, verdant and green, surrounded by the crystal clear waters of the Narmada and the Rewa, an ancient temple on the hill slopes, and adjacent to it the hermitage of Govindapada. How much has it changed today? And, of what remains, how much corroborates the facts of Shankara's visit and sojourn here?

To find out I flew to Indore from Delhi. With me were my wife, Renuka, and the talented and intrepid artist, Manish Pushkale, who hails from this region. Omkareshwar is a two-hour drive from Indore but before we set out, we had arranged to meet two renowned Sanskrit scholars in Indore. Our first stop was at the simple middle class home of Dr Mangal Yeshwant Mishra, Principal of the Shri Cloth Market Girl's Commerce College and his wife, Chhaya. Although he teaches Commerce, he is fluent in Sanskrit. His visiting card makes for interesting reading: Dr Mangal Yeshwant Mishra, BCom, MCom, MA (Economics), MA (History), MA (Sociology), MA (Public Administration), MBA, PhD (Commerce), PhD (Political Science), PhD (History), PhD (Sociology), PhD (Economics), PhD (Business Administration), DLitt. I venture to tell him that he should apply to the *Guinness World Records* for the maximum number of degrees. He accepts the suggestion as a compliment, missing out the gentle sarcasm. However, there are endearing qualities about him. His innate humility, and the care and concern of his wife, Chhaya—who also teaches at the Shri Cloth Market Girl's Commerce College—wins our hearts.

We are served a simple homemade lunch of daphla (a local wheat specialty) with dal, rice, kadhi and vegetables, and halwa as dessert.

Dressed in a simple dhoti, and a vest hugging his ample belly, Dr Mishra spoke to us over lunch about Omkareshwar. He is in no doubt that Shankara stayed at Omkareshwar in the ashram of Govindapada and cites several accounts of the sage's life to prove his point. Mythology and fact overlap in his narrative. The cave where Shankara met with Govindpada is still very much there, he says. So is the temple, at Mamaleshwara, across the Narmada, which Shankara built for the benefit of pilgrims unable to visit the main Shiva temple at Omkareshwar when the river was in spate during the monsoons. The temple at Mamaleshwara is identical to the one on the island. The original is called sankalp, or resolve, and the replica built across the river, is its vikalp, or alternative.

We did not learn anything very new from the much-educated Dr Mishra except to internalise his personal belief in Shankara's association with Omkareshwar. As we left, he placed a small stone in my hands in the shape of the Shivalinga, adding that every such stone found in the Narmada represents the joint blessings of both Shiva and Shankaracharya.

Our next stop was the residence of Mithilesh Prasad Tripathi, who was a different kettle of fish from the humble Mishraji. A red tilak adorned his forehead; his rotund and large presence conveyed that he wished to be taken seriously, and would not suffer fools gladly; proud of his lifelong study of Sanskrit, he was dismissive of mimic scholars; he made it clear that he was impatient with conventional thinking, and annoyed with pandits who practiced rituals without knowing the meanings behind them.

Tripathiji reiterated that all evidence points to Shankara coming to Omkareshwar, and joining the hermitage of Govindpada. He said that it was Govindapada, and the Advaita teachings of his father, Gaudapada, that Shankara internalised in Omkareshwar, and these had a lasting influence on his young mind. In his sojourn here, Shankara must be seen as a student, eager to learn the intricacies of the Vedantic school of thought. His passion to learn was beyond doubt, and, the gurukul of Govindapada, where the teacher conversed with his students in a relentless schedule of study, enquiry and contemplation provided the ideal atmosphere to do so.

There was a great deal of *obiter dicta* in our freewheeling conversation, as Tripathiji, sitting cross-legged on the diwan of his small living room, was prone to digress into acerbic commentaries on some of his peers in the area of the study of Sanskrit. But, there was an important point to which he drew my attention. Don't focus, he told me, only on Shankara's philosophy and its intellectual tapestry. That, of course, is important, but equally important is what Shankara learnt in Gaudapada's matha in terms of service to the people, and the creation of centres where the Advaitic philosophy could be taught and preserved. Even though Shankara was against the *karmakanda* (the performance, as per Vedic instructions, of rites and rituals) ritualism of the mimamshaks, he approved of this kind of selfless service, and the foundations of his thinking in this respect was laid at Omkareshwar.

For all his arrogance, Tripathiji had warmed up sufficiently to us by the time we left, and came right up to our car to see us off. As we left, he said that he liked to live alone. His wife, he said, was visiting his children in America, and his nephew took care of him. He came across as something of a recluse, absorbed in his study of Sanskrit and Hindu philosophy, quite content to be left alone among his thousands of books, but combative and argumentative if anybody challenged his views.

Our drive to Omkareshwar took us through the Vindhya ranges. The road was winding, the terrain hilly and full of sagon trees withering in the hot sun, their paper-dry leaves strewn all over. It took us two hours to reach the Gajanan Maharaj Ashram in Omkareshwar where our stay had been arranged. The ashram, a stone's throw away from the Narmada, was an oasis of calm, full of greenery, with a serene temple intricately carved in stone at the centre of the complex. Joshiji, the administrator, welcomed us with tea and biscuits and showed us to our rooms, which were spartan but clean, air-conditioned, and with modern bathrooms. We learn that Gajanan Maharaj was from Sheogaon in Maharashtra, a contemporary of Shirdi Sai Baba, and had a great following. His pictures were ubiquitously put up all over the ashram, a lean and tall man, with an unkempt beard and piercing eyes, a chillum in his hands, and, in some photographs, with not a stitch on his body.

In the evening we set out for our visit to the Omkareshwar temple and the cave where Shankaracharya is said to have met with Govindapada. To do so, we crossed the Narmada by foot over a newly-constructed bridge that led to the temple. It was a full moon night, and also Hanuman Jayanti; aartis were on at several ghats along the river; bhajans in invocation to Rama and Shiva filled the silence; the rays of the moon bathed the Narmada in a silvery glow—a truly ethereal sight.

The temple is built into the hillside. Originally it must have been a cave, but now, outside, there is a mandapam with intricate carvings on pillars and arches. The sanctum sanctorum has a Shivalinga that is just a stone rock jutting from the ground. It is supposed to be svayambhu, born on its own, one of the twelve jyotirlingas established by Shiva himself. Behind the linga is an idol of Parvati, Shiva's consort. It is said that of the twelve jyotirlingas, this is the only one where Parvati is part of the sanctum santorum. An akhand jyot or perennial wick lamp burns here throughout the day.

We witnessed the *shayan* or bedtime aarti at 9 p.m., after which Shiva and Parvati are left alone for the night. The arrangements for this aarti are a tribute to both faith and human imagination. A swing or jhoola is richly decorated in rich pink brocade for the divine couple. A checkered cloth for the game of *chaupad-pansa* (something akin to Chinese Checkers) is spread out on the jhoola for their entertainment. There are twelve counters in the game, each shaped like a linga, representing the twelve jyotirlingas. Nobody is allowed to disturb the God and Goddess at night. It is believed that when the pujari enters the temple in the morning, the counters have moved.

A few steps away from the temple is the cave where Shankara met with Govindapada. Although decorative brickwork has been added outside the entrance, the cave is clearly marked out. Inside the cave is a statue of Shankara in black stone. It shows him seated cross-legged on an elevated pedestal, holding his familiar mendicant's staff in his left hand. Above him, is a stone mural depicting a popular legend about Shankara's supra-human powers. Once, when the Narmada was in spate, its waters threatened to enter the cave where Govindapada was in deep contemplation. To prevent his guru from being disturbed, Shankara held out his hand and the waters of the river receded. Another variation of this legend speaks of him holding out his kalash or mendicant's bowl, and all the waters of the river being subsumed in it. The stone mural shows Govindapada meditating inside the cave, and Shankara, his feet in the rising waters, keeping at bay the river.

There is another very interesting idol inside this cave. It is that of Kali, the Mother Goddess, but in a tantric depiction, the body draped in a red sari, the face bereft of definitive features except a fiery red tilak on the forehead. The most compelling feature of this depiction is the eyes of the Goddess, piercingly black, that follow you almost hauntingly in any direction you move. The chief pujari of the temple tells me that this idol was made and put in the cave following Shankara's visit to Bengal. There he met with a great number of tantrics, and was unable to defeat them in *shastrartha* or debate because of his inadequate knowledge of tantrism. He, therefore, returned to Omkareshwar and learnt tantra in the form of Kali siddhi. This idol of the Goddess was installed at that time. Having made himself adept in tantrism, Shankara, so the belief goes, went back to Bengal and worsted his tantric opponents.

The Narmada is a beautiful river. Although now its flow at

Omkareshwar is tamed because of the dams built upstream, it is still a majestic river, quite unique for several reasons. It is the only major river in India that flows from east to west; also the only river where temples have been built on both banks, giving it the name of Ubhay Tat Tirtha. The name Narmada also has a special significance. Nar stands for male, and mada for female: the river symbolises the powers of both, or even a fusion of the powers of both as depicted in the unisex concept of Ardhanarishwara, an androgynous deity very much a part of Hindu mythology.

Next morning, as we left Omkareshwar after a dip in the Narmada, I kept thinking about Shankara's association with this town. How would he have walked through dense jungles to reach this place from far away Kaladi in Kerala? Was there a known route to this holy town, or did he take the help of traditional navigational methods? In an age when communication was primitive, how did he know of Govindapada, and of his father, Gaudapada? There were no printing presses at this time. How then was he familiar with the seminal work of Gaudapada on Advaita philosophy? Did he come to know of his *Karika* on the *Mandukya Upanishad* only through oral recitation disseminated from one disciple to another, and in what manner did this reach all the way to Kaladi? What informal networks of learning and teaching prevailed at that time to enable this flow of information?

The interplay between the rarefied pursuit of philosophy and the rituals of religious practice also struck me. It is said that Govindapada and Shankaracharya began the day by a visit to the nearby jyotirlinga. In the cave where Govindapada lived, the intellectual pursuit was about the non-dual, attribute-less Brahman, beyond all human description, transcendent of human worship, formless and oblivious to all ritual. But once they entered the temple, they paid obeisance to Shiva and Parvati, and countenanced all the rituals of worship to a personalised god, including the preparation for Shiva and Parvati to spend the night in conjugal bliss with a game of chaupad-pansa laid out for their additional entertainment. The extravagant humanisation of divinity, and the contemplative enquiry into what lay behind the pageantry of ritual and worship, must have co-existed seamlessly.

After a few years of stay in Omkareshwar, and after he had mastered the intricacies of the Advaita doctrine at the feet of Govindapada, Shankaracharya took his permission to leave for Varanasi. It must have taken him several months to complete this long journey on foot, through dense forests, and unchartered territory, with all the attendant dangers of attack by robbers and brigands. In Varanasi, he stayed for several years, and this is where he wrote some of his most important works, including the *Shankara Bhashya*, his commentary on the *Brahma Sutra*, as also his commentaries on the *Bhagavad Gita*, and the principal Upanishads. Why did Shankara decide to go to Varanasi? Quite clearly, the city was even then, the capital of the Hindu faith, where saints and philosophers took up abode on the banks of the Ganga, and carried on a vibrant dialogue on the many aspects of Hindu philosophy. It was the ultimate stage for any scholar of Hindu thought to establish his credentials, through discussion, debate and interaction with other philosophical luminaries and scholars. It was, therefore, but natural that Shankara, whose fame as a philosophical genius had spread far and wide, would want to take up residence in Varanasi.

I visited Varanasi to try and find more about Shankara's sojourn there. My old friend, Ashok Kapoor received me at the airport. He is a cultural activist of prominence in Varanasi, and now the convener of INTACH for the city, with a deep interest in restoring the many crumbling or neglected historical landmarks that abound in one of the most ancient cities in the world. Varanasi, also known as Banaras and Kashi, is congealed in a massive labyrinth of narrow alleyways (*galis*) and temples along the western bank of the Ganga. Within these galis, heaves a density of population that defies human imagination. Sometimes, one is left wondering how people, temples, motorcycles, scooters, dogs, cows, filth and noise coexist in a situation where there is such an unbelievable disproportion between space and population.

But, Varanasi has defied the unbelievable from times immemorial. The ancient city's interface with modernity, in the form of the town that has come up now beyond the ghats and the galis, is messy, to say the least. The drive from the airport takes much longer than it should because a flyover, that should have been completed much earlier, is still under construction.

The newer city is a cacophony of traffic, noise, pollution and filth, in short, a municipal nightmare with no easy solutions. The amazing thing, though, is that the people of Varanasi take all this in their stride, either because they are born stoics, or congenitally oblivious to the travails of the material world, beyond too much worry about what is wrong today, because, after all, the measure of time is eternal, and much like the millennia-old Ganga, only a speck against the infinite canvas of time.

My first stop in Varanasi is the Sampoornanand Sanskrit University. Professor Hari Prasad Adhikari, who heads the faculty of Philosophy and teaches Comparative Religion, has arranged for me to meet with scholars on Shankara and Hindu philosophy. There are no tables and chairs. We sit on a white sheet on the floor with bolsters for a backrest. The session kicks off with a mangalacharya, an invocatory recital of some *stotras* or devotional hymns, written by Shankara. What follows looks uncannily like a replay of how a shastrartha must have happened in the days of Shankara. Several professors of different aspects of Hindu philosophy are present. Each of them is a passionate believer in his viewpoint and interpretation. All of them accept the primacy of the Advaita doctrine developed by Shankara, but all of them have a different take on it, and evaluate it from the point of view of their own philosophical 'loyalties'.

A robust disputation follows, with Sanskrit shlokas being thrown about with abandon, as each speaker stresses a different point of view on such esoteric matters as the difference between *shabda* or word knowledge, *pratyaksha jnana* or direct intuition, the validity of *shruti* or the revealed word, the influence of Buddhist thought on Shankara's thinking, the limitations of Advaitic monism, and the validity of Vishista Advaita or qualified non-dualism as developed by later Hindu philosophers like Ramanuja.

Tempers rise and opinions clash. When someone interrupts a speaker, he protests vehemently that this is contrary to the rules of shastrartha, where each protagonist must be allowed to present his point of view fully before objections are raised. Professor Adhikari tries valiantly to moderate the discussion but is often disregarded. This goes on for more than an hour, until Adhikari brings the meeting to a close by the ceremony of *upa-samhara*, which is in the nature of a summation and vote of thanks.

By this time tempers have cooled down, and I am informed that such displays of embattled ideological confrontations on obscure points of Hindu metaphysics is not uncommon among a small group of Philosophy teachers who have spent a lifetime studying the Sanskrit texts. In fact in a shastrartha some years ago, one professor, who was very highly regarded for his erudition, was so incensed by his adversary's interpretation of Shankara's tenets, that he died of a heart attack while making his rebuttal.

There was something of the surreal in what I had witnessed. Here, in this non-descript room of a university that is visibly in physical neglect, were a handful of people arguing as if their life depended on it, on matters about which the overwhelming bulk of Hindus have no clue! Was there, in what I had just seen, a resurrection of what must have happened on the banks of the Ganga in the time of Shankara? Perhaps yes, but the difference being that then even ordinary people wouldn't have been completely unaware of the subjects being discussed, and actually lived the Hindu philosophical experience of ideas and arguments.

The Sampoornanand Sanskrit University is among India's oldest educational institutions. It was set up in 1791, ironically by an Englishman, Jonathan Duncan, who persuaded Governor General Lord Cornwallis on the need for a Sanskrit college to translate important texts, including those needed for administrative needs. An annual budget of Rs 20,000 was sanctioned, and John Muir was appointed the first principal of the college. In 1857, the college began post-graduate teaching, and in 1974 was conferred the status of a university. But, the university languishes now, for most Indians have little time for Sanskrit, or the vast wisdoms contained in its texts. In many ways, thus, the vehemently argumentative professors quoting Sanskrit shlokas to discuss the intricacies of Hindu philosophy have become relics in their own land.

The Saraswati Library of the college, set up as far back as 1894, has one of the most valuable collections of Sanskrit manuscripts, but most of them remain unstudied. The motto of the university is *Srutam Me Gopaya*: Let my Learning be Safe. Unfortunately, it seems that the British—for their own reasons—were more concerned about this, than we are today.

None of the professors were able to tell me historical details about Shankara's stay in Varanasi. Their plea was that in those times, scholars were more concerned about ideas and concepts than about chronology and sites, and so, no details have been left for posterity. What was Banaras like when Shankara lived here? Where did he live? And for how long did he stay? Nobody seemed to know. Certainly, the city must have been much smaller, largely confined to the ghats or river front stone steps and terraces, and settlements along the Ganga. The labyrinth of narrow alleyways, leading to the riverbank, would have been there, but with a lower popular density; it would have been a cleaner city, with a cleaner river, and more space along the bank, where saints and scholars with their entourage could camp.

I visited Kedara Ghat where a branch of the Sringeri Matha was established possibly as far back as the fourteenth century CE. This is what I infer from a plaque inside the 'Shri Jagadguru Shankaracharya Mutt' that reads: 'This ancient Chandramoulishwara Lingam was installed and worshipped by His Holiness Sri Vidyaranya Mahaswamiji Sri Sringeri Sharada Peethadipathi in the year 1346 AD.' Inside the matha is a temple with shrines of Ganesha and Devi Sharada, with the statue of Adi Shankaracharya, similar to the one at Kaladi, placed between them.

Did the Sringeri Matha choose this site because Shankara lived here, or in the vicinity? The area where it is located has a preponderant presence of residents from South India. How old is this regional linkage, and could travellers from the South have come here to stay even a thousand years ago? If so, there is the possibility that Shankara, hailing from Kerala, would have chosen to live here. But again, no one had answers.

The Sringeri Matha wears a dreary look, with no activity that I could see of scholarly research or study. It seems to only serve the purpose of a dharamshala (resthouse) for visitors, and the managers appear to have little interest in anything else. The matha also has an ashram in the city, and there is one too, run by the Kanchi Matha, near the Banaras Hindu University (BHU) campus called the 'Sri Jagat Guru Shankaracharya Ashram'. The last has a large notice board at the gate prohibiting smoking and gutka in the premises, but those who run it have no clue about any historical details regarding the residence in Varanasi of the Jagad Guru himself.

I visit Manikarnika Ghat too, for some people believe that this is where Shankara stayed. Here, everybody is busy with the business of consigning the hitherto living to flames. As I walk through the narrow galis towards the ghat, dead bodies passed by to the chant of '*Ram Naam Satya Hai*', and the living scurried around to fulfill the paraphernalia of disposing them off. There is something incongruous in how frenetically alive the venue to cremate the dead can be. Like the undergrowth in a tropical forest, life burgeons from every crevice of the ghat, and the density of sound, touch, smell and sight are overpowering in their collective effort to dispose off those now lying inert, deprived of such senses.

Dr Rana P.B. Singh is a retired professor of Geography at the BHU, and I meet him at his simple home on the university campus. His unassuming demeanour hides the fact that he is an internationally renowned specialist in examining the scientific reasons why a particular place is chosen to become a holy site. Dr Singh has surveyed the 'sacred geography' and 'cosmic geometries' of Kashi, by studying magnetic forces around its many temples and holy spots, and interfacing the findings of Global Positioning Satellites with the sacred texts and traditions of the city.

He tells me that the word Kashi means 'where the cosmic light concentrates in a circle'. The city, he says, has a well-organised pilgrimage system with four identifiable 'inner sacred journeys' that all verifiably terminate at a single point. This point, the *axis mundi*, as he puts it, is the Gyan Vapi. If this is true, it opens for my search, an interesting possibility. Gyan Vapi, meaning the well of wisdom, is situated at the spot where the Kashi Vishvanath temple, the city's most famous shrine dedicated to Shiva, used to be. The Shivalinga at the temple was one of the twelve such lingas established across India, and had a great antiquity, finding mention in the *Skanda Purana*, and other ancient Hindu texts. In 1194 CE, the temple was destroyed by Qutubuddin Aibak, but was rebuilt by a Gujarati merchant in the thirteenth century. It was again destroyed by either Hussain Shah or Sikander Lodhi in the fifteenth century, but rebuilt yet again by Raja Man Singh during Emperor Akbar's reign.

However, in 1669 CE, Aurangzeb definitively destroyed the temple and built the Gyan Vapi mosque on its ruins. (An idea of the newly built mosque on the ruins of the temple can be gained through James Princep's sketch of 1834.) Finally, in 1780 CE, Ahilya Bai, the Holkar queen, built a new temple on an *adjacent* site.

This history being as it may, the original Vishvanath temple must have stood at its original site, the Gyan Vapi, at the time of Shankara's visit to Varanasi. Now, Shankara's partiality to Shiva is known, and he would have liked to find residence somewhere close by to his favourite divinity, and Kashi's most revered shrine. But there is an additional dimension to this possibility. Gyan Vapi is situated on the Lalita Ghat. Lalita, the symbol of bliss, is synonymous with Shiva's consort, Parvati. The *Lalita Sahasranama*, or the thousand names of Lalita, is a text in the *Brahmanda Purana*, and is a pivotal document for Shakti worshippers. Shankara's inclination towards the Shakti sect, and to the concept of 'Divine Mother', as is evidenced by the fact that all the four mathas he established are called shakti peeths (or the seat of Shakti), is well known.

Moreover, Manikarnika Ghat is but a stone's throw away from here. It is one of the oldest of the eighty odd ghats in Kashi, finding mention in a Gupta period inscription of the fifth century CE. Manikarnika in Sanskrit means, earrings. According to mythology, when Sati immolated herself due to the arrogance shown by her father, Daksha towards herself and her husband, a grief-stricken Shiva is supposed to have picked up her dead body and in a frenzy of rage danced the tandava across the Himalayas. Finally, seeing his unrelenting grief, Vishnu sent the divine chakra and cut Sati's body into fifty-one parts that fell to the ground. Wherever a part of her body or attire fell, became a shakti peeth. As per mythology, Sati's earring fell at Manikarnika, and that is how the ghat got its name. Manikarnika Ghat was, thus, a very important place of worship for the Shakti sect, and was known as Ekannya Shakti Peeth.

The tradition of associating Manikarnika Ghat almost exclusively as a cremation site began, Professor Singh tells me, only around the end of the eighteenth century. To argue, therefore, that Shankara, during his stay at Varanasi, would have liked to be close to the most prominent shrine dedicated to Shiva, the Vishvanath temple, and in the vicinity too of the Lalita and Manikarnika ghats, that were prominent sites of the Shakti cult, to which Shankara (especially as later evidence testifies) was inclined, is not unfounded. But, this is at best a theory, because no confirmatory evidence (except a passing mention in Chidvilasa's biography) is available as definitive proof, a testimony both to our traditional disdain of historiography and, in recent times, to academic research and curiosity.

Whatever the exact location of Shankara's abode in Kashi, there are some incidents of his life there that have been recorded by biographers. There are several biographies, called *Shankara Digvijaya,* but the most popular is that written by Madhavacharya, who later took on the name of Sri Vidyaranya and became the 12th head of the Sringeri Sharada Peetham (1380–1386).

In these traditional accounts, there is a great deal of hyperbole regarding miracles performed by Shankara. If these are discounted as the excesses of biographers, we can still cull out some events that are common to all accounts and must, therefore, have some basis in fact. There is agreement that when in Kashi, Shankara acquired one of his most dedicated devotees, Sanandana. Legend has it that one day, when Sanandana was on the other side of the river, Shankara asked him to return by walking across. Without a thought the pupil, in absolute faith, obeyed the commandment. As he did so, the Ganga put forth a lotus to support him, and so Sanandana actually walked across the river. After this, Shankara renamed him Padmapada (lotus-footed).

But legends apart, there are three incidents at Varanasi that are important for providing an insight into Shankara's thinking, and the texture of his times. The first relates to his meeting with a chandala or 'outcaste', someone traditionally regarded to be from the lowest rungs of society. The encounter took place in the narrow alleyways of the embankment. Apparently, Shankara was going to the Ganga to bathe when he came upon the chandala. In those days, Brahmins were supposed to be 'defiled' by the very presence of those of this caste, and the disciples of Shankara asked the 'outcaste' to move out of the way.

However, the chandala retorted by asking the question: 'How do differences such as, "This is a chandala and this is a Brahmin", arise in the Advaitic doctrine? After all, it is the same Atman that is present in all bodies, irrespective of their castes?'

Shankara was taken aback by this response, and promptly exclaimed that anyone who sees Brahman as the sole reality and recognises the Atman as the same in all is worthy of respect. All other distinctions are false, said Shankara, and the chandala, who has realised the unity of the supreme consciousness, is akin to my guru. It is this thought that is enshrined in Shankara's five-stanza composition, the *Manishapanchakam,* of which a representative stanza reads as follows:

> I am Brahma alone. And, this entire world has been spread out by pure consciousness. All this, without residue, has been superimposed by me through nescience which consists of the three gunas (sattva, rajas and tamas). Thus, he in whom there is firm knowledge in respect of the eternal, blemishless supreme (Brahma) which is unexcellable bliss, is the preceptor, be he a chandala or a brahamana. This is my conclusive view.

Shankara's views on the caste system have been discussed in greater detail in the chapter on his philosophy. What needs to be mentioned here is that some biographers have tried to reassert the validity of the rigid and discriminatory social system by underplaying the wisdom of the chandala. According to their versions, the moment Shankara uttered his thoughts—revolutionary for their explicit denial of social orthodoxy—the chandala disappeared and in his place Shiva and the four Vedas appeared. The attempt here is to marginalise the remarkable assertion for equality of the chandala, and give to the whole incident a sacred gloss, in the form of Shiva and the Vedas.

The scholars at the Sanskrit university whom I met did much the same when they told me that the chandala episode was but a way to demonstrate that even the lowest of the low in Kashi were imbued with philosophical insight. The truth, however, appears to be that for Shankara, consistent with his own philosophical logic, there was, in his meeting with the chandala, the express rejection of social exclusion created by man-made institutions.

The second incident is about Shankara's reaction to a student enthusiastically engaged in learning Sanskrit grammar. Hearing him trying to memorise the rules of grammar by rote loudly, Shankara is supposed to have spontaneously composed one of his most popular hymns, *Bhaja Govindam*, in which the last line of every stanza exclaims: 'Worship Govinda, worship Govinda, worship Govinda, foolish one! Rules of grammar profit nothing once the hour of death draws nigh!'

As an example of devotional or bhakti hymns, *Bhaja Govindam* must rank very high, and is even today sung all over India. It indicates Shankara's impatience with mechanical learning, and his emphasis on the need to use the path of knowledge—the *jnana marga*—for acquiring the wisdom than enables the achievement of moksha through a true understanding of the transience of the empirical world, to which we give so much undue importance.

The third incident is about a disputation he had with an old man on the interpretation of the *Brahma Sutra*. The argumentation went on for almost a week, with neither protagonist willing to yield ground, and, if what I had witnessed in the brief shastrartha at the Sanskrit university was illustrative, it must have involved some degree of frayed tempers, sarcasm and acrimony. Finally, so the story goes, Padmapada, Shankara's disciple, appealed to Vishnu to bring the argument to an end. It was ultimately revealed, so traditional biographies claim, that the old man was an incarnation of Vyasa, the author of the *Brahma Sutra*. This episode, more realistically, is probably indicative of the fact that,

> there was a good deal of wrangling over Shankara's commentary on the *Vedanta Sutra*, and that he was perhaps occasionally forced to give up his earlier positions and meet opponents half-way. The old man here may well represent an opponent of that kind, whom Shankara could not find it quite easy to satisfy and whose acquaintance with the literature of the Vedanta philosophy must have been so good as to entitle him to be looked upon as a reincarnated Vyasa.[2]

After spending several years in Kashi, with occasional trips to Badrinath, Shankara went to Prayaga (modern Allahabad). It is said that Ratan Singh, the then ruler of Banaras, persuaded him to stay on, but Shankara explained that his mission lay in being a peripatetic teacher and to spread his philosophical vision to all parts of Bharat.

At Prayaga he bathed at the Sangam, the holy confluence of the Ganga, the Yamuna and the mythical Saraswati. However, his visit to Prayaga is most remembered for his meeting with the formidable Kumarila Bhatta, an Assamese Brahmin, and one of the greatest exponents of the Purva Mimamsa school of Hindu philosophy. Those of this school of thought believed that the chief aim of life was karmakanda. Shankara, who believed in the validity of the jnana marga, disagreed with this emphasis on ritual, and was keen to debate this difference with Bhatta.

---

2 C.N. Krishnasami Aiyar, *Sri Shankaracharya, His Life and Times*, G.A. Natesan and Co., Chennai, date unknown, pp. 28-29.

This opportunity was denied to him for dramatic reasons. When he did meet with Kumarila Bhatta, the venerable scholar was lying on a burning heap of rice husk in the process of self-immolating himself. He had taken this extreme step as an act of atonement for two sins he believed he had committed. Firstly, in order to demolish some of the tenets of Buddhism, he had joined a Buddhist monastery in the guise of a disciple so as to master the doctrines he wished to counter. Subsequently, he became one of the most influential critics of Buddhist philosophy as propounded by its later theoreticians.

But in this process, he had to live with the guilt of having 'betrayed' the guru at whose feet he had learnt. This betrayal required atonement. Secondly, in expounding the karmakanda philosophy, he had, in preference to Vedic ritual, denied even the existence of god. This, he felt, was taking his philosophy, to an unacceptable extreme.

It is said that Shankara tried to persuade Bhatta to give up his resolve to self-immolate, but the sage was adamant. With his body already half-burnt, he was in no position to enter into a debate with Shankara. But even as he lay dying, he told Shankara that the person he should debate with was his pupil, Mandana Mishra, who lived in Mahishmati.

Many historians believe that Shankara's dramatic meeting with Bhatta is more illustrative than factual. In all probability, Bhatta lived in the second half of seventh century CE, and was thus not a contemporary of Shankara. Yet, the tradition of this meeting is so entrenched, that its purpose must have been to highlight the fact that the differences between the ritualism espoused by the Purva Mimamsha school, of which the most prominent exponent was Kumarila Bhatta, and the knowledge-based Advaita school, of which the most well known proponent was Shankara, were so widely known and debated, that they *required* Bhatta and Shankara to have met. The fact that they were possibly *near* contemporaries would have been sufficient reason for later biographers, not particularly painstaking about chronology or exact dates, to overarch historical fact by the super structure of creative symbolism.

The debate with Mandana Mishra, whom Shankara, on Kumarila Bhatta's advice, went to meet at Mahishmati, occupies a pivotal place in all accounts of his life. There is a sharp division of views on where Mahishmati is. By many accounts, including that of Madhavacharya in his *Shankara Digvijaya,* Mandana Mishra was from the village of Mahishi along the banks of the Kosi in the modern Saharsa district of Bihar. There are families even today in this village who claim they are descendants of Mandana Mishra. According to lore firmly believed by residents here, Mandana Mishra married Kumarila Bhatta's sister, Ubhaya Bharati (later known as Sharada Devi), who was from the village of Bhattapura in the Mithila region of Bihar.

As against this tradition, there are equally strong adherents of the view that Mahishmati was a kingdom on the banks of the Narmada near modern day Maheshwar. In fact, while travelling in this region, I came across at least three sites that lay claim to be the exact place where the famous debate between Shankara and Mandana Mishra took place. The most prominent of these is a temple at Mandleshwar (which is believed to be the new name of Mahishmati), just short of the city of Maheshwar.

A large ceremonial gate announces in bold lettering: 'Shri Gupteshwar Mahadev (Cave) Temple'. On the right side of the gate is a three-dimensional mural in concrete showing the statues of Shankara, Mandana Mishra and Bharati Devi, with a board stating that this is where the famous shastrartha between the two scholars took place.

The temple and its precincts appear to be absolutely deserted. There is not a soul to be seen, not even the priest in-charge of the temple. An unkempt garden without a fence surrounds the temple. On the side of the temple wall is another notice board that says: *Aaj se 1200 varsh pahle Shiv avatar Adi Shankaracharya tatha digvijaya maha pandit Brahma avatar Mandana Mishra ke saath sanatan dharma sansthapan va vishva kalyana ke liye shastrartha, yahin Shri Gupteshwar Mandir se 100 gaj door sthit sthan par hua tha* (1,200 years ago, in order to reestablish the Sanatana Hindu Dharma, and for the welfare of the world, the debate between Shiva incarnation Adi Shankaracharya and Maha Pandit Brahma avatar Mandana Mishra took place a hundred yards from this spot).

There is, indeed, an open space about a hundred yards from the temple under the shade of a guler and barh tree, but on what basis the temple management could claim with this degree of certitude that that was the exact place for the shastrartha is not clear. As we were grappling with this question, the pujari of the temple finally made his appearance.

According to him, the Kolkata Maha Milan Matha had done the research on this subject. In 1984, the then head of the matha, Premananda Kishor, came to Mandaleshwar and built this temple at the place where he believed the shastrartha took place. The pujari was unable to provide the evidence backing this research, nor could we obtain it from the matha itself. The pujari did clarify, though, that this spot used to be earlier on the banks of the Narmada, and while the river has moved away a little today, in the monsoons its waters come right up to this point.

There are at least two other sites in this region that also claim to be the place of the famous debate. One is in Maheshwar, not far from the majestic fort built by the Holkars on the Narmada, where there is nothing left except a small platform with a Shivalinga and a paduka (wooden clogs reproduced in stone). The other, also in Maheshwar, but entailing a short drive from the fort, is a more imposing venue. It is called Kadamba vana, the forest of the kadamba (burflower) tree, although none can be seen now except a large patch of banana plants. The temple has a plaque claiming that this is the *kshetra* or area where the shastrartha took place. On top of the plaque are paintings of Shankaracharya,

Mandana Mishra, and Sharada Bharati. The walls of the temple also have large paintings depicting the debate. In the largest of these paintings, Shankaracharya and Mandana Mishra are seated on low stools facing each other in a posture of animated discussion, with Sharada Bharati looking on, and a large audience in the background.

Whatever the validity of the competing claims of these sites, the fact is that all of them are in the region of the city of Maheshwar, and its suburb, Mandaleshwar, a few kilometres away. It is also undoubted that Mahishmati was an ancient city of prominence in central India, now Madhya Pradesh. Historical texts state that it was the most important city of the ancient Avanti and Anupa kingdoms, and continued to be a thriving urban centre during the rule of the Paramaran dynasty until it was defeated by Allauddin Khilji in 1305 CE. There is evidence in some accounts that Mahishmati was located on the Narmada, with Ujjayani to its south, and Pratishthan to its north. This is exactly where Maheshwar and Mandaleshwar are located today.

It would appear, therefore, that Mahishmati, as the place where the interaction between Shankaracharya and Mandana Mishra took place, could well be where Maheshwar and Mandaleshwar are located today. At least, this is what those who live here believe very strongly. However, we cannot completely negate the other viewpoint that holds Mahishi to be in the Saharsa district of Bihar. The residents here too are passionate about their claim on Mandana Mishra.

It is not for us to adjudicate between two opposed versions of history, both unsupported by clinching proof. From the point of view of history, a middle ground could well be that while Mandana Mishra hailed from Bihar, and was born in the village of Mahish there, he moved to the city of Mahishmati in central India. This would be plausible given that Mahishmati was a bigger and better known city, with a royal court, and—in his capacity as the chief pandit of the court—would have provided a more befitting canvas to a scholar of his eminence. Significantly, Madhava's *Shankara Digvijaya*, although by no means always historically accurate, does say in its eighth chapter that the debate took place along the banks of the river Rewa, which is another name for the Narmada.

Whatever the place, the basic details of the great debate between these two scholars have, thanks to the effusive flourishes of devoted biographers, their fair share of drama and histrionics. Apparently, to Shankara's query as to where he would find Mandana Mishra in Mahishmati, the burning Kumarila Bhatta is supposed to have said: 'You will find a home at whose gates there are a number of caged parrots discussing abstruse topics like, "Do the Vedas have self-validity or do they depend on some external authority? Do karmas yield their fruits directly or do they require God to intervene? Is the world eternal or merely an illusion?" Where you find parrots discussing such complicated philosophical issues, you will know that this is Mandana's house.'

When Shankara walked into Mandana's home, the latter was not pleased to see him. He was busy with the rituals of his father's death anniversary, shraddha, and the sight of a celibate sanyasin was considered inauspicious, for those of his belief, in which leading the life of a householder while performing the prescribed Vedic rituals, was the correct choice to make. Apparently, he was rude to Shankara, who did not, however, rise to the bait, and finally, it was agreed that the debate between the two scholars would commence the next day.

Mandana Mishra asked Shankara to choose an umpire, but was surprised when he said that Sharada Devi, Mandana's wife,[3] could be the arbiter. The learned lady agreed, and put a garland of flowers around the neck of the two contestants, declaring that

3 There is some debate among certain scholars on whether Bharati was Mandana Mishra's wife, but the bulk of academic opinion and popular belief accepts that she was, so this controversy, if one at all, need not detain us.

the person whose garland withers first will be considered to be defeated. It was also decided that whoever loses would become the follower of the other, and adopt the rules of life of his opponent.

As per different accounts of the event, the debate between the two went on for anything between seventeen days to six months. In the end, the garland worn by Mandana Mishra withered away, and it was clear that Shankara had won the argument.

But Ubhaya Bharati was not willing to concede defeat. She said that as the wife of Mishra, she was, one-half of his person, and it had sanction in the acceptance of the androgynous concept of Ardhanarishwara in Hindu thought. Therefore, she too wanted to debate with Shankara. Shankara was reticent to do so, for under the rules of a sanyasin that he followed, debating with a woman was not permissible. But Ubhaya Bharati was insistent, and Shankara had no option but to agree.

At this point we come across a most interesting twist to this narrative. Ubhaya Bharati asked Shankara to answer questions on kama shastra that related to sensuality and eroticism, which she, as a married woman was familiar with, but about which her opponent, as a sanyasin, was clueless. Then Shankara asked to be given a month to learn about this 'science', and return to the debate, to which Ubhaya Bharati agreed. The story goes that Shankara, through his yogic powers, left his body in a cave on the banks of the Narmada, and entered the dead body of the King of Amaruka, which was being taken for cremation. Incidentally, this cave, known as the Gupteshwar cave, is still identified at the eponymous temple at Mandaleshwar referred to earlier. It lies below the temple, and can be accessed by stairs going down. The cave is cramped, its rock walls unornamented, with white tiles at the base. A yoni in stone with a large serpent in copper at its centre is the only image inside.

The resurrection of the King was hailed as a miracle, and Shankara, in the body of the dead potentate, returned to the palace. There, in the company of the dead king's wives, he learnt the art of making love, and became adept in kama shastra. In fact, so his biographers say, Shankara began to so much enjoy his new distractions and the luxuries of the palace that he forgot that he had to within a month reassume his own body kept in the cave. This greatly worried his disciples, who arranged to remind him of who he really was by singing a few philosophical songs in his presence.

Shankara then woke up from his sensual stupor, and hastened back to reenter his body, and apparently, did so just in time because, after lying for a month in the cave, it had been discovered by the King's messengers, and was about to be consigned to the flames. Having mastered kama shastra, he returned to Mahishmati and successfully answered the questions put to him by Ubhaya Bharati. The debate was won. Mandana Mishra donned the robes of a sanyasin and became a disciple of Shankara. On Shankara's persuasion, so did Ubhaya Bharati.

This remarkable narrative has to be assessed beyond merely the colourful details added later by sundry biographers. What the debate actually represented—and that is the reason why it was projected as such an important part of Shankara's life—was to assert the primacy of thought over ritual, at a time when precisely the opposite seemed to have become the accepted way of life for Hindus.

The sixth and the seventh centuries CE saw a revival of Hinduism, and the relative decline of Buddhism. However, this revival was excessively focused on Puranic mythology, blind devotionalism, and, above all, the mechanical performance of Vedic ritualism as propounded by mimamshaks like Kumarila Bhatta.

Somewhere, in all of this, there was a divorce from the loftiness of thought that was the essential substratum of the Hindu vision. In the pursuit of how exactly to perform a ritual as per precise Vedic injunctions, the glorious mystical insights of the Upanishads had been overwhelmed. Temples were flourishing, but there was a disconnect between the motions of worship and the philosophical foundations underlying it. There was the need to once again reassert the jnana marga to salvation, to relink Hinduism to its metaphysical insights, and restore to it the grandeur of thought and contemplation. That was the manifest purpose of Shankara, and there could be no better metaphor to project it than his victory in a debate over Mandana Mishra.

The redoubtable Pandit of Mahishi was a formidable opponent, and was considered an avatar of Brahma himself by his admirers. He was, without doubt, the most well known disciple of Kumarila Bhatta, and the author of several seminal works on mimamsha such as the *Mimamshanukramanika*, the *Bhavanaviveka* and the *Vidhiviveka*. In addition, he had written a significant work on the philosophy of language, the *Sphotasiddhi*, and a book on the theories of error, the *Vibhramaviveka*. His defeat in a debate with Shankara would, therefore, have made a major impact on the beliefs and practice of Hinduism across India. Even without modern means of communication, the progress of the debate and the intricacies of the arguments would have been witnessed by thousands of people, and spread by word of mouth to thousands more across the length and breadth of the country. The debate, when seen in the historical context of the evolution of Hinduism, acquires great importance, and that is also the reason why it has been given such prominence in every account of Shankara's life.

The incident of Shankara acquiring the knowledge of kama shastra is fascinating. Did this really happen, or was it introduced to make a collateral point related to the larger worldview of Hinduism. Rationalists will discount the claim that Shankara could discard his body and enter that of another through his yogic powers. Others will maintain that such powers are not unknown to practitioners of yogic siddhis. However, the fundamental question is why Ubhaya Bharati tested Shankara on issues relating to carnality, and why did Shankara accept this challenge? For a sanyasin, sensuality was equivalent to blasphemy, and even a disavowal of the very vows taken for life. What is even more interesting is that Shankara's biographers admit that, once in the company of the queens of the dead King, and the enticements of the luxurious palace, Shankara was sufficiently seduced to actually forget his commitments as an ascetic, and even wrote a manual on erotica called the *Amaruka Sataka*. Why would he do this, and does this not diminish his towering persona as someone completely above the blandishments of the flesh?

The answer, to my mind, is that the incident was meant to validate the four *purusharthas* or goals in the Hindu worldview: dharma (right conduct), artha (pursuit of material well being), kama (the pursuit of the sensual) and moksha or salvation. As Vatsyayana, the author of the *Kama Sutra* had explained centuries before Shankara, each of the first three goals pursued in proportion, and none in exclusion, leads automatically to the fourth, salvation. In other words, kama has philosophical validity within the framework of a balanced life. Shankara may have chosen an ascetic's life, where artha and kama had no place, but this did not negate their relevance for ordinary mortals. There was a need, therefore, *not* to posit Shankara's personal choice of celibacy and materialistic denial as against the legitimate pursuit of both these goals in the larger Hindu perspective.

By living a life of a householder, Shankara did not reduce his own image as a sanyasin, but enlarged the appeal and reach of his philosophy to those outside the limited cadre of celibate mendicants.

Mandana Mishra became one among the four most important disciples of Shankaracharya, and (although some scholars do not agree on this point) took on the name of Sureshvaracharya. He became a scholar of great repute of the Advaita doctrine, and is credited with being the author of an insightful treatise on this subject, the *Brahmasiddhi*. It is believed that Shankara made him the first head of the matha at Sringeri, although Kanchi makes the same claim. Ubhaya Bharati, considered to be the incarnation of Goddess Saraswati, accompanied Shankara and her husband to Sringeri, where she passed away. Shankara built a temple consecrated to her in the city, which stands even today. In a sense, she represented the central role played by the shakti doctrine in Shankara's philosophy.

Having won the great debate, and with his fame now spread far and wide, Shankara travelled southwards, preaching the Advaita doctrine. In Maharashtra, he is believed to have converted to his thinking the sect of Mallari Brahmins, who believed in primitive animal worship. It was said that it was here that he engaged in a raucous argument with the Kapalika sect, who worshipped the god Bhairava (a fierce manifestation of Shiva), and practiced human sacrifice. Apparently one Kapali almost killed Shankara while he was absorbed in deep meditation. Only the last minute intervention of his disciple, Padmapada, who attacked and killed the Kapali, saved Shankara's life.

Shankara set up a matha at Sringeri (the setting up of mathas will be discussed in greater detail subsequently in the book), a beautiful spot on the river Tunga. There he spent some time with his principal disciples, encouraging them to write commentaries on different facets of the Advaita doctrine, and on his own works relating to it. Padmapada was asked to write a commentary on Shankara's *Brahma Sutra Bhashya*.

A small story relates to this event. As directed, Padmapada wrote his commentary, and took it along on a tour to Rameshwaram. At Srirangam, he left the manuscript with his uncle, who was, apparently, a believer in the karmakanda school of thought, and against the Advaita doctrine. Angered at reading his nephew's exegesis on Vedanta, he burnt the work. Padmapada was heartbroken and with great sorrow informed Shankara of the loss of his manuscript. Shankara, however, told his disciple not to be crestfallen. Before leaving for Rameshwaram, Padmapada had read out his commentary to Shankara. The master remembered it verbatim, and could easily dictate it. The incident, even if apocryphal, is important for emphasising the prodigious intellectual grasp and memory of Shankara. Memorising what he heard was not difficult for him, which is what explains how, at such a young age, he could learn and recite the most lengthy and abstruse Sanskrit shlokas and treatises with ease.

From Sringeri, either because he wanted to meet her, or on learning that she was not well, Shankara set off alone to meet his mother at Kaladi. On reaching home, he found her bedridden, and close to death. The reunion of Shankara and his widowed mother, whom he had left as a child, must have been one of the most emotional moments in his life, especially since she was now terminally ill. At one level, it was a fulfillment of his promise to her that he would be by her side when she needed him. At another, when he finally did return, it was too late, and her mortal life was about to end.

Shankara attempted to speak to her about the Advaita doctrine, but such an abstruse subject hardly interested her. She wanted solace, and assurance, from her son, whom she was overjoyed to see, but would not be with for long. Biographers of Shankara have said that, heeding her request, Shankara sang to her one of his most evocative hymns to Shiva, and then one of Vishnu, and lost in this devotional mood, she breathed her last.

The relationship with his mother had a lasting influence on Shankara's life. As we know, he was an only child, born late to his parents, and his father had died young. While the urge within him to renounce life and become an ascetic was too strong, he must have nursed a guilt all his life that this entailed abandoning his mother, who had no one else except him as family. The importance he gave to the Mother Goddess, in the form of Shakti or Devi, can be traced to this attachment to his mother. That would explain why, when he came back to meet his mother, he broke the vows of a sanyasin and bowed to touch her feet. It must also have been the reason why he decided to perform her last rites, although this too was against the rules of asceticism.

However, his decision to perform his mother's last rites, was met with hostility by his Nambudiri clansmen in Kaladi. They decided to boycott the ceremonies, and even worse, not even to assist him in preparations for the funeral and the pyre. But, Shankara was not one to be shaken from his resolve. He decided to make the arrangements himself, cutting the body into smaller parts, and making a pyre from the banana saplings in his home courtyard. His biographers claim that angry with the behaviour of his community, he prevailed upon the local chief to issue an edict that his Nambudiri relatives henceforth be not allowed to chant the Vedas, and that they would burn their dead in their own courtyards, after having cut the body into pieces. Whether this is true or not, it is a fact that even now, traditional Nambudiri families touch a knife to the joints of their dead, as a symbolic act of cutting the body, and cremate them in the compounds of their home.

After the cremation of his mother, Shankara, the ever-peripatetic preacher set out again on his travels across India.

He returned to Sringeri, collected his disciples, and travelled across central India, through Ujjain, towards Puri on the western coast, where he set up the Govardhan Matha. He then went to the western coast, to Dwaraka, in Gujarat and established a matha there too. It is believed that his travels also took him to Bengal and Assam, where he had discussions with the tantrics and the shakta school, including its most famous exponent, Abhinava Gupta.

Fact and legend both indicate that Shankara also visited

Kashmir, and this arduous journey has a special importance that needs elaboration. What brought Shankara to Srinagar? The city was at that time renowned for its Buddhist and Hindu scholarship. Ever since Ashoka conquered the Valley in third century BCE, Buddhism had flourished here. There is historical evidence that the fourth Buddhist Council was convened here in second century CE and was attended by over five hundred scholars, including Ashvaghosha and Vasumitra.

Along with Buddhism, Kashmir was also—in times more coterminous with that of Shankara—the locus of a specific kind of Shaivite philosophy, whose founder was Vasugupta (800–850 CE), who was the author of *Sivasutras*, a collection of seventy-seven aphorisms also known as *Trika* or *Trika Yoga*, which essayed a specifically Kashmir Advaita tradition. This philosophy echoed Shankara's monism, with the difference that Shiva was seen as the cosmic symbol of Brahman, both immanent and transcendent. All individuals were Shiva incarnate, and only their ignorance veiled their knowledge of their essential identity.

Kashmir Shaivism also introduced the concept of Shakti as an integral part of Shiva worship. The God, formless and omniscient, was Brahman incarnate, but the world emanated from Him due to the powers of Shakti. This worship of the Goddess was the basis of a vibrant tantric tradition, wherein she, representing the female principle, was venerated as an intrinsic part of Shiva, but also separately for her causal role in the creation of the phenomenal world.

Shankara must have been aware of this powerful Kashmiri tradition, and would have travelled to meet first hand its chief votary, Vasugupta, who, in all probability was his contemporary. Undoubtedly, Shankara would have read Vasugupta's *Sivasutras*; Advaitic non-dualism would have been their common ideological meeting ground; and in all likelihood, Shankara and Vasugupta must have met in Srinagar.

Local legend has it that when Shankara arrived in Srinagar,

his entourage camped just outside the city. The teacher and his disciples were hungry and weary after their long travel, but had failed to light a fire to cook some food. A young Kashmiri girl then came to their help. Taking two pieces of wood, she rubbed them while chanting a mantra, and the spark that emerged from the friction lighted the fire. The wood, the girl explained, is Brahman. The fire that sprang forth from it is Shakti, the power inherent in Brahman.

It is also believed that at the very outset of his advent into the Valley, Shankara entered into a shastrartha with a Kashmiri lady on the concept of shakti. The debate lasted for seventeen days, at the end of which Shankara conceded defeat. This apocryphal story signifies his acceptance of shakti worship, and his association with tantric interpretations of Advaita philosophy.

The famous Shankaracharya temple in Srinagar is located on the Gopadri hill (part of the Zabarwan Mountain overlooking Srinagar) a thousand feet above the Valley. It is also known as the Jyeteshwara temple, and was earlier called Pas Bahar by the Buddhists. Kalhana, the great historian of Kashmir says that it was first built by King Gopaditya (426–365 BCE), and later repaired by King Lalitaditya (697–734 CE). The interesting thing is that Sikander, the sixth Sultan of the Shah Miri dynasty in Kashmir (1389–1413 CE), who was called Butshikan for his propensity to destroy idols, did not destroy this temple. In fact, two Muslim rulers in later times—Zain-ul-Abideen in the fifteenth century, and Sheikh Mohinuddin, who was the Governor of this region when Kashmir was under Sikh rule—renovated the temple. All of this provides evidence of the great sanctity of the temple, and of the fact that this was the place where Shankara chose to stay when in Srinagar.

I travelled to the temple by car, on a road built in 1974 by the state government. The drive is surrounded by a forest rich in deodar trees, and one can only imagine how much denser this beautiful forest must have been more than a thousand years ago. The road takes you up to the hilltop, but there is a further climb of 243 steep steps, constructed by Dogra ruler Gulab Singh in the nineteenth century, to reach the temple proper. There were a great many tourists from all parts of India, and as I trekked up the steps, one could hear Tamil, Gujarati and Bengali in voluble abundance. About half way up is a halting point where Hoja Singh, a Sikh, has a small outlet for the sale of books and pamphlets on the temple's history, Shankara and Hindu philosophy, and other touristic trinkets. I asked Hoja how he happened to set up this improvised outlet here. He said that he belonged to Kashmir and earlier worked with the Archaelogical Survery of India (ASI); after retirement, instead of getting bored sitting at home, he had come upon this idea, and greatly enjoyed his new vocation.

The temple is a rock structure. It has a large Shivalinga surrounded by smaller idols of Parvati, Kartikeya and Ganesha. A tall trishul, with a drum balanced on the top of it, stands behind the linga. The small sanctum sanctorum was crowded with tourists from all parts of India, but my wife and I managed to participate in the *abhisheka* (ceremonial anointment) of the linga. Set into an alcove on the outside wall of the temple is a portrait in marble of Shankaracharya, his forehead smeared with sandal paste, his eyes looking far into the distant horizon. The Shankaracharya of Dwaraka installed this statue in 1961.

Next to the temple, at a lower level, is the cave where Shankara is said to have stayed in and meditated. A notice board outside identifies it as 'Jagad Guru Shankarcharya Tapasya Sthal'. The entrance to the cave is through a narrow and low entrance. Inside is a large portrait of Shankara, seated on a low *peedha* or stool, with two open books on a bookstand in front of him. The portrait is in the Thanjavur style, which shows the influence of the artistic traditions of South India. Next to the portrait is a large copper replica of a snake with its hood spread out in a protective posture. The three-pronged trishul also stands adjacent, like a sentinel on guard. The cave is cramped, but I sat, alone, on a rug spread alongside, to meditate for a while.

It is believed that Shankara wrote the *Saundarya Lahari*, his passionate ode to Shakti, while he lived in this cave. This work clearly shows the influence on him of the Kashmiri tantric tradition. It can reasonably be posited that following the interaction with Vasugupta, Shankara would have studied in depth the tantric associations with Kashmir Shaivism, leading to his writing of the *Saundarya Lahari.*

The view of Srinagar from the temple is truly breathtaking. The breadth of the Valley, surrounded by towering snow-clad peaks, the pellucid Dal Lake, the river Jhelum in the distance, the cluster of house boats, red roof top homes reflecting the sun, overlooked by the mountain slopes lush with deodar trees, makes one's spirits soar. Living here, studying the Shaiva tradition of Kashmir and imbibing the principles behind its strong Shakti worship, must have been an ethereal experience for Shankara, especially since at that time the Valley would have been much quieter, much greener and the waters of the Dal Lake and the Jhelum much cleaner.

It is not known how long Shankara stayed in Srinagar, but it is unlikely that it would have been more than a year. What is certain is that key elements of Kashmir Shaivism, and of its tantric offshoot, had a major influence on his thinking.

While in Srinagar, N.N. Vohra, the Governor of Jammu and Kashmir, arranged for me to meet Maroof Shah, reputed to be a scholar of Kashmir Shaivism, and of Hindu philosophy. The reputation, I soon found out, was entirely justified. I spent an afternoon discussing with him the intricacies of Shankara's thoughts and their overlap with Kashmir Shaivism. Maroof, a diminutive man with a heavy Kashmiri accent, works, improbably enough, in the state veterinary department. Philosophy, however, is his passion. According to him, Shankara's Advaita, and Kashmir Shaivism, have more similarities than differences. Both are non-dualistic; both believe that Brahman is the only ontological reality; both accept that the world is real at one level but illusory and impermanent at the real level; and, both argue that ignorance is the cause for our mistaking the ephemeral for the real.

The difference is only on emphasis. Kashmir Shaivism, especially as elaborated upon later by Abhinava Gupta, believed that Shiva was Brahman incarnate, and his potentiality to create the phenomenal world was due to the power of Shakti within him. The worship of Shakti, along with its tantric associations, thus became one of the key distinguishing features of Kashmir Shaivism, and were taken on board by Shankara. Mythology, Maroof said, was only meant to illustrate, at a commonly comprehensible level, the substance of metaphysics. The dialogue Shankara supposedly had with a Kashmiri lady, where he was compelled to accept defeat, could be a mythological construct to prove the point that Shankara accepted the powerfully devotional aspects of Shakti worship, which, Maroof said, signified an affirmative monism and took into account the senses and the sensual. As we ended our conversation, Maroof said ruefully, that very little work is being done now on Kashmir Shaivism within Kashmir. The interest in this aspect of Hindu philosophy is far greater abroad. Not even Kashmiri Pandits—with the exception perhaps of the great scholar Laxman Joo in the twentieth century—are aware of the greatness of this tradition, or of its link with Shankaracharya.

The Shankaracharya temple is a tourist spot for most visitors, and Kashmir's sole integral link with Hindu philosophy. The irony of a devout Kashmiri Muslim, who happened to be keeping the Ramzan fast when we met, making this point, was not lost on me.

Any recreation of Shankara's life is incomplete without a special word about the mathas or monastic orders he set up. The Dakshinamnaya Sri Sringeri Sharada Peetham was the first matha set up by him. What strikes a visitor about this matha is its scenic location. Nestled on the Mysore plateau on the Western Ghats, it is situated on the river Tunga, and surrounded by the mountain ranges of the Rishyasringa Parvata. Lore has it that Shankara chose this place because he saw an unusual sight on the banks of the Tunga: a cobra had spread out its hood over a frog about to give birth in order to provide it shade from the scorching sun.

The most important temple here is dedicated to Sharada, the wife of Mandana Mishra. The original dedication built by Shankara to Sri Sharada was simply a yantra (or tantric design) carved on a rock in the middle of the Tunga with a sandalwood image installed on it, covered by a thatched roof. The temple now is grand, built in polished granite with a statue in gold of Sharada, a large hall outside the sanctum sanctorum, and a wide-pillared corridor for the *pradakshina* or circumambulation of the deity.

What caught my interest was the Sri Chakra, or tanric geometric design, on which the Devi is seated, and the line inscribed at the entrance of the temple: *Aham brahm asmi*: I am Brahman.

There are two other temples of note. One is dedicated to Shri Vidya Shankar, the twelfth Shankaracharya of the Sringeri Matha (1380–1386). He was a reputed scholar of Advaitic thought, but was also the sage, whose connection with the Vijayanagar kingdom, through his disciple Vidyaranya, helped to completely transform Sringeri from a modest religious encampment to a monastery of great wealth and influence. Vidyaranya was the counselor to Harihara and Bukka, the brothers who founded the famous Vijayanagar kingdom at Hampi. The rulers of Vijayanagar, in turn, honoured their advisor, by making lavish endowments for the running of the Sringeri Matha. They also helped to finance the temple in the memory of Vidya Shankar, the guru of their advisor. The temple is noteworthy not only for its grand structure, but for a large dome resting on twelve pillars on which are carved the twelve signs of the zodiac. Shankara could hardly have imagined that five centuries after he had passed away, Sringeri would see such a munificent resurrection.

The temple in which Adi Shankaracharya's statue is installed is a more modest affair. It is in the quadrangle of the old matha building, with an idol of Shiva next to it. It is said that Shankara brought a radiant Shivalinga of crystal, called the sphatika Chandramoulishwaralinga, to Sringeri, and this remains in the personal possession of the pontiffs.

To meet with the current Shankaracharya of the matha, Bharati Tirtha Mahaswamiji, I had to wear an angavastram, a single, unstitched cloth on my upper body. The pontiff was in audience in one of the main halls of the matha, but was gracious in giving his blessings. On his insistence, I had lunch in the dining hall of the matha, a delicious meal of rice, sambar, vegetables, rasam and a delectable dessert. The matha serves up to 15,000 free meals a day, and also provides mid-day meals to 9,500 children, an activity that would certainly have been approved by Shankara. It also runs colleges and schools for education, with a special emphasis on Sanskrit. I am told that a thirty-two feet tall statue of Shankara is shortly to be inaugurated at a place some two kms from the matha.

The setting and locale of the matha established by Shankara at Dwaraka on the western coast, overlooking the Arabian Sea, is totally different. The topography—consisting of flat land—the language, the food, the dress and the cultural milieu are in striking contrast to that of Sringeri. As against the verdant mountains and forests of the Western Ghats, we have here fields of groundnut, corn and cotton. In my mind I could imagine what it must have been like 1,200 years ago, as Shankara, with his band of dedicated disciples would have walked all the way to this western extremity, with shepherds in tight white pyjamas, short white coats and a coiled pugdi on their heads, herding their lambs, as his guide. The vegetarian Gujarati cuisine, tasty, but with a pronounced flavour of sweet in almost every dish, (of which I had a most delectable lunch in the form of the Gujarati thali at Khambaliya, a town midway between Jamnagar and Dwaraka) would have been quite alien to him.

Neither the food, nor the traditional attire of the shepherds, has changed today. But what has is the remarkable level of industrialisation in an otherwise predominantly agrarian region. Reliance, the giant Indian corporate conglomerate, has built the largest refinery in the world on the road from Jamnagar to Dwaraka. Essar, another private sector giant, has a huge fertiliser plant. And, the Indian Air Force has a large base at Jamnagar, which is also the nearest commercial airport to Dwaraka.

The Dwarakadheesh temple, which is consecrated to Krishna, and the matha are in the same compound. An ornate archway in sandstone, followed by a four-lane road, leads to the complex. Next to the idol of Dwarakadheesh, which overlooks a large mandapam, is one of Shankara, seated in the padmasana posture and holding a book in one hand, with the four Vedas—*Rig*, *Atharva*, *Yajur* and *Sama*—replicated in front of him. A mural depicting his shastrartha with Mandana Mishra provides the background.

The matha is adjacent to the temple. I meet Swami Svarupananda, the current Shankaracharya, as he comes out to give audience. Given his advanced years, he is seated on a wheelchair. His speech is not very clear, but later I have a more detailed discussion with one of his prominent disciples on the philosophical aspects of Vedanta. Interestingly, Dwaraka city has a temple where the deity is Rukmini, not Radha. It also has the Bhadrakali temple, where a large Sri Chakra, almost three by three feet, is installed, both on the wall behind the Devi, and on her two sides. Shankara, it is believed, had installed these Sri Chakras himself. When the current pontiff enters Dwaraka, he first comes to this Shakti Peeth, to take permission to enter the town, another evidence of the great veneration given to the shakti doctrine in Shankara's scheme of things.

The matha at Puri, on the eastern edge of India in Orissa, is also on the seafront, a gateway to the Bay of Bengal. Puri, the seat of the Jagannath temple, is one of the most revered pilgrimage centres in India. Not surprisingly, a modern highway has been built to the holy city from Bhubaneswar, the capital of the state, where the nearest airport is located. As I drove from Bhubaneswar to Puri, across lush green rice fields interspersed by an abundance of coconut trees, my thoughts were with Shankara, and his reactions to this new part of India, far away from Kaladi, but in some ways, in terms of is topography, not dissimilar to it.

We cross Kalinga, where the famous battle fought by Emperor Ashok took place in the third century BCE, after which, deeply anguished by the death and violence, the monarch embraced non-violence, and adopted Buddhism, thereby changing the course of history. Half way to Puri is also the town of Pipli, renowned for its applique work, but now struggling to compete with the synthetic mediocrity of manufactured arts. Enroute is also the village of Raghavpura, the home of Kelucharan Mahapatra, the legend of the Odiya dance form, and the Gotipua school of dance that he presided over.

This is a deeply Vaishnava country, where Krishna is the ruling deity. The Jagannath temple has the Blue God's idol, flanked by his elder brother, Balarama, and his younger sister, Subhadra. The matha is outside the temple premises, on a narrow lane, that must have at one point been on the sea. It is a rather unassuming building, in some neglect, with four important temples on the premises. The most important of these, is not unexpectedly, that of Bimla Devi, representative of Shakti, which, located at a higher level, literally towers over the other buildings. There is also a temple to Krishna—the name of the peeth is Govardhan Matha—and one to the androgynous deity, Ardhanarishwara. In the room dedicated to Shankara there is, I am informed, a bed made of *shaligrama* (compressed shell stone) on which the great sage used to sleep.

I met the current Shankaracharya, Swami Nischalananda

Saraswati, who as per the matha's records, is the 145th pontiff of this peeth. Swami Saraswati had strong views on the dates ascribed to Shankara's life. According to him, he was born more than 2,500 years ago, and not in the eighth century CE, as 'foreign' scholars had conspired to make us believe. Even as he expounded in categorical terms on this matter, and on many other issues far removed from Vedanta, a large picture of Shankara behind him, in his usual serene sitting posture, smilingly looked on.

The matha at Kanchipuram, in modern Tamil Nadu, is a matter of some controversy. Most scholars are convinced that Shankara established only four mathas—at Sringeri in the south, Dwaraka in the west, Puri in the east and Joshimatha in the north. However, those who run the Kanchi matha claim that it was set up by Shankara, and anyone who visits it, is left in no doubt about the deep faith that invests this claim.

When I entered the main mandapam of the matha, the aarti was on to the loud accompaniment of the mridangam and nadaswaram. The hall was packed with devotees seated on the red-tiled floor, the men bare-bodied above the waist, in only a veshti. The aarti was being performed for the sphatika Chandramoulishwaralinga in the sanctum sanctorum. A large portrait of Shankara, in a seated posture wearing a red cloth over his shoulders and a rudraksh necklace, a red tilak above his bright and piercing eyes, adorned the worship pedestal. In one corner of the hall were a series of paintings depicting the key episodes of Shankara's life. The current pontiff, Jayendra Saraswathi, who is now very old, and his chosen successor, Vijayendra Saraswathi, were gracious enough to spend considerable time with me.

The Shankaracharyas of Kanchi believe that Shankara passed away, or as it is put, attained Sarvajna Pitha, ascending the final Throne of Omniscience, here in this ancient temple town. Shankara, they maintain, established the four other mathas for the propagation of Vedanta and the protection and projection of Hinduism, but the Kanchi matha was a project he undertook 'for himself', and as the matha that would oversee the functioning of the other four.

There are several reasons they give for this belief. Kanchi, is, and was, among the most famous temple cities of the South, housing over a thousand temples. Kalidasa, the great poet, called it 'the city among cities', renowned for its learned scholars in both Tamil and Sanskrit. In ancient treatises, its location is referred to as 'the navel of the earth'. Kanchi was also the capital of the Pallava and Chola dynasties. The most celebrated Kamakshi temple in the city is dedicated to Parvati, where she is depicted as the Goddess of love. Given Shankara's belief in the shakti cult, and the fact that all his other mathas are known as Shakti Peeths, would it be possible that he would not have come to Kanchi, and set up a matha in this ancient city of temples and learning dedicated to Parvati?

In Kanchi, Vijayendra Saraswathi tells me that Shankara is near ubiquitous, and every temple has a statue or some form of dedication to him. In the beautiful Kamakshi temple, newly renovated by the Kanchi Matha (located next door), there is indeed, a resplendent statue of Shankara with a gold canopy, and it is placed in the temple compound, on a pedestal that is higher than that of Kamakshi.

According to the Kanchi Matha, it was Shankara who personally installed the Sri Chakra at the feet of Kamakshi. He came to Kanchi towards the end of his life, travelling through Rameshwaram, Sri Sailam and Tirupati, and this is where he died, or obtained samadhi, which, the Kanchi Matha claims, is within the precincts of the Kamakshi temple. Before samadhi, he entrusted the running of the matha to his principal disciple, Sureshvara, better known by his earlier name, Mandana Mishra. In fact, so Vijayendra Saraswathi informed me, there is a street in Kanchi called Mandana Mishra Agraha. Some of Mishra's descendants, originally hailing from Bihar, settled in Kanchi, although now, he said smilingly, they all speak Tamil. Within the matha's precincts, the most ancient structure is a temple with a statue of Sureshvara, and this is also thc spot where he was, the matha claims, cremated.

There is little doubt that Kanchi is essentially a temple town. In the little over an hour drive from Chennai to Kanchi, one sees large stretches of factories and private university campuses, but the moment one enters Kanchi, there are only temples in every direction. It is also true that Kanchi, along with Kashi, Ujjain, Dwaraka, Ayodhya and Haridwar, is recognised as a 'mokshapuri', the place where a Hindu upon death, is ensured salvation. It is, therefore, possible that Shankara, the peripatetic teacher, would have visited Kanchi as part of his travels. It is entirely possible too that he could have installed the Sri Chakra at the Kamakshi temple, because he had done the same for other temples dedicated to the Devi, and Kamakshi was always recognised as one of the most important Shakti Peeths.

However, not everyone—and least of all the pontiffs of the four principal mathas—supports the theory that Kanchi was the fifth matha set up by Shankara. The general belief is that the Kanchi Matha was originally a part of the Sringeri Matha. The Sringeri Matha had established a branch in Kumbakonam, a city in the Thanjavur district of Tamil Nadu state, in 1821 CE with the help of the Tanjore king, Pratap Singh Tuljaji. This Kumbakonam branch proclaimed independence from Sringeri and shifted to Kanchi somewhere around 1842 CE, the year it was appointed sole trustee of the Kamakshi temple by the English collector of the East India Company.

There is also strong disagreement on the claim that Kanchi is where Shankara attained samadhi. It is believed by most that Shankara left his mortal body at Kedarnath. The assumption that Sureshvara was appointed by Shankara to head the Kanchi Matha is also strongly contested. The most accepted belief is that Shankara put Sureshvara in-charge of his first matha at Sringeri.

The Kanchi Matha however does not accept any of these contestations. In fact the pontiffs here have scoured the extant biographies of Shankara to find as much evidence in support of their claims as they can, tracing their independent lineage back to 2,500 years. Even with regard to the place where Shankara died, they have with them a letter, dated 6 July 1958, written by Dr Sampoornanand, the then Chief Minister of the state of UP, to the Joint Director of the Department of Archaeology in New Delhi.

Dr Sampoornanand was instrumental in installing a memorial for Shankara at Kedarnath in association with the then head of the Dwaraka Matha. However, this notwithstanding, Dr Sampoornanand wrote a letter as follows:

> Recently I had occasion to discuss the matter with the Shankaracharya of Dwaraka Pitha also. In the first place, the word 'samadhi', (at Kedarnath), is a misnomer in this connection. There is nothing to prove that Shri Shankaracharya died at this spot.[4]

The Kanchi Matha, therefore, believes that Shankara only took a 'sankalpa samadhi', or a resolve to transcend the world at Kedarnath, while the place where he actually died, is Kanchipuram.

Such differences of opinion being as they may, the fact is that the Kanchi Matha appears to be well established, and well endowed. Devotees throng it; it conducts several charitable programmes in the areas of education and health across India; the pontiff receives great veneration and exercises considerable influence, especially in the region. The manner in which the matha has recently renovated the Kamakshi temple would have done Shankara proud.

I was witness to the evening aarti at the temple, and it is a most evocative experience, the Goddess resplendent in gold, her glittering eyes moving with the flame of the aarti, the Sri Chakra

---

4 Quoted in *Sri Shankaracharya and His Connection with Kanchipuram*, A. Kuppuswamy, Sri Kanchi Matha, 2003, p. 44.

glistening in front of her, the temple lit tastefully, the moon reflected in the *sarovar* (sacred tank or pool) built in the courtyard of the temple, a cool breeze teasing the fragrant bushes, and from the corner of the courtyard, Shankara's statue, seated in repose, silently contemplating the proceedings.

Shankara set up the Jyotir Matha in the Himalayas as his northern bastion. Joshimatha, as the town is called now, is a crowded hill station, most famous as the launching pad for the journey to the Badrinath shrine, some thirty kilometres beyond. The matha hugs a hillside whose base is encrusted with narrow and crowded streets and the ugly concrete that characterises the unaesthetic cacophony of all Indian cities. In order to reach the matha, one has to travel up one of these alleyways. The ramshackle 'Bharat Guest House'—one among many such shabbily built structures—greets you at the walkway going up to the monastery, hardly the best approach to a building of this prominence.

Although a large concrete gateway announces the matha, the premises appear to be singularly deserted. There is a reason for this. This is the only monastery set up by Shankara that has no resident Shankaracharya. The last 'legitimate' pontiff was Swami Brahmananda Saraswati, who was appointed in 1941. After his death in 1953, the succession has remained mired in multiple legal cases, and the current pontiff at Dwaraka now holds concurrent charge of this matha as well. I am told that the Allahabad High Court has recently pronounced that the matter of a duly designated pontiff should be decided soon, but there is no guarantee that the choice of whoever is chosen will not be legally challenged again, a sad commentary indeed, on the unseemly politics that is often part of religious power.

Brahmachari Shravanand, originally from Madhya Pradesh,

but who has lived here for three decades, seems to be the man in-charge and shows us around. For all its current neglect, this matha bears clear testimony to the presence of Shankara. There is a cave in the name of Shankara's disciple, Totakacharya, who was made the first pontiff of this matha by the Master himself. Totakacharya's original name was Giri. He joined Shankara during his stay at Sringeri, and became one of his four principal disciples. Giri was known less for his learning and erudition, and more for his unfettered devotion to his teacher.

One day, so the story goes, Giri was late for Shankara's daily class. The other disciples were restless, and wanted the class to begin, but Shankara urged them to wait. Giri then entered the classroom, and surprised everybody by singing a hymn composed by him in the metre called *totaka.* The short hymn, *Totakashtam,* was beautifully composed, a tribute to his teacher, and the role of the guru in attaining salvation. From then on, Shankara named Giri, Totakacharya. In fact, the Jyotir Matha gives great prominence to its first Acharya, Totaka.

The cave, in the name of Totakacharya, exists even today in a form not very different from what it must have in Shankara's time, simply because it has not been tampered with. A huge rock overhangs the cave, and Shravanand shows us what appears to be the form of an Om on the outside top of the rock. A lovely statue of Shankara, sitting in the meditative posture, is in the cave, as also a small sphatika linga installed by him. This is where, Shravanand says, Shankara meditated, as did Totakacharya.

There is another cave too in the premises, which Shankara used for meditation. As in all his mathas, there is a temple dedicated to Shakti. At Jyotir Matha she is represented as Rajrajeshwari Tripur Sundari. What struck me at the temple was the beautiful Sri Chakra at the entrance, where the geometric design is carved in white marble.

Within the matha's premises is also the *kalpa vriksha,* which some claim is the oldest tree in India. It does look ancient, with a heavily gnarled trunk and branches spread along all directions. Shankara is said to have meditated here too, and had installed a Shivalinga under the tree, which exists even today in a small temple. To my mind, the matha must have, in the time of Shankara, been a small settlement around a few natural caves suitable for meditation and shelter, amidst a forest, on a quiet hillside. Some traces of that original serenity remain, but the urban aggression all around is so strong that it requires a very strong imagination to resurrect what the original must have been like.

Not far from the matha is the Narasimha temple believed to have been established by Shankara. Narasimha is considered to be an incarnation of Vishnu in the form of part-man, part-lion, who was sent to earth to destroy evil and religious persecution. The temple's architecture is of the hills, a combination of wood and stone, the wooden panels brightly painted in red and blue. Within the precincts of the temple is a smaller shrine of Mahalakshmi, the invariable shakti peeth that always accompanies any religious establishment associated with Shankara.

The temple is on the ground floor. Above it is a hall, not very large but capable of small gatherings, which is known as 'Shankaracharya's Gaddi'. At the far end of the hall is a statue of Shankara. It would appear that this could well be the place where Shankara met with his disciples and held discourses on different facets of the Advaita doctrine. The fact that it is part of a temple established by Shankara adds credence to such a postulate. The actual matha, quite close by, could have been where he stayed, the place for him to be alone, or in meditation, whereas the Gaddi at the Narasimha temple may have been his place for public interaction.

Shankara established the mathas with the specific aim of creating institutions that would develop and project the Advaita doctrine.

His aim must also have been to give Hinduism, as a whole, an organisational structure, in a manner similar to what Buddhism had done through its monasteries. Until the mathas were set up, Hinduism was a pervasive way of life—which it continues to be—but without a nodal core that could preserve both its doctrine and practice.

It must be remembered that Shankara, while uncompromisingly an advocate of the non-dual Vedantic doctrine, in which rituals, prayer, bhakti and temples were not of fundamental importance at the level of *para vidya* (ultimate knowledge), simultaneously sanctioned these religious practices as preparatory steps within the rubric of *apara vidya,* practical knowledge. In this sense, he became the guardian not only of the Vedantic doctrine, but of Sanatana Dharma, Hinduism in its entirety, both in practice and philosophy. It is also significant that he established his mathas in what constitutes, broadly, India today.

This puts paid to the colonial theory, unfortunately endorsed by many ignorant Indians, that the idea of India was a British creation, and prior to their advent, India was just a geographical expression with no binding unity. Perhaps the British did create a nation-wide administrative structure, but India, as a definable civilisational entity, with an underlying cultural unity, far predates British conquest.

Today the mathas continue to be magnets for Hindu believers, and have fulfilled, in large measure, what Shankara set them up to achieve. However, there is little co-ordination between them, and often more than a semblance of competition that sees one underplaying the contribution of the other, or privileging one matha's Shankaracharya as superior to another. This is not unexpected, because loyalties and personal preferences will always exist in situations where human beings operate, and there is no overall framework of disciplined interaction or planned consultation. One also senses that the rituals of worship, including the pageantry and paraphernalia associated with each of the current pontiffs, have, in some measure, overwhelmed Shankara's original idea to make these mathas vigorous centres of Hindu philosophy and Sanskrit studies, particularly with regard to the Advaita doctrine.

Credit must, however, be given to Shankara that more than a millennium ago he sensed the need to set up such mathas, and displayed the organisational energy to achieve his aim. During his own lifetime, he appointed each of his four principal disciples as the head of the mathas, and completed other organisational details relating to their functioning. The chart below gives the organisational structure of the mathas, including the disciple who was initially made in-charge of each.

	East	South	West	North
Name of the Peeth	Govardhana Matha	Sringeri Matha	Kalika Matha	Jyotir Matha
Place of location	Puri (Orissa)	Sringeri (Karnataka)	Dwaraka (Gujarat)	Badrikashrama (Uttarakhand)
Divinities	Jagannath, Purushottama. Shakti—Vrsala, Vimala	Malahanikara Linga, Varah; Shakti—Sharada	Siddheshwara; Shakti—Bhadra Kali	Narayana; Shakti—Purnagiri
Tirtha	Mahodadhi (Bay of Bengal)	River Tungabhadra	River Gomati	River Alakananda
Veda	*Rig Veda*	*Yajur Veda*	*Sama Veda*	*Atharva Veda*
Sampradaya	Bhogavala	Bhurivala	Kitavala	Nandavala
Mahavakya	*Prajnanam Brahma*	*Aham brahm asmi*	*Tat tvam asi*	*Ayam atma brahm*
Titles to the pontificial seat	Aranya, Vana	All the titles, particularly, Saraswathi, Puri, Bharati, Aranya, Tirtha, Giri, Ashrama	Tirtha, Ashrama	Giri, Parvata, Sagara
First Acharya of the peeth	Sri Hastamalakacharya	Sri Sureshvaracharya	Sri Padmapadacharya	Sri Totakacharya

The great Himalayan pilgrimage sites of Badrinath and Kedarnath are within the purview of the Jyotir Matha. Badrinath, by road, is some thirty kilometres away, and is at a height of over 10,000 feet (3,133 metres). The shrine is open only for six months, from April to November, and closed during the winter because it is snowbound. From all accounts, Badrinath was much loved by Shankara. It is believed that the idol of Vishnu, to whom the temple is dedicated, was found by Shankara in the river Alakananda that flows next to the temple. Shankara retrieved it and had it installed in the sanctum sanctorum.

Interestingly, but not coincidentally, the shrine has no conventional features. One theory is that before the time of Shankara, during an attack by Buddhists from nearby Tibet, the keepers of the temple sought to preserve the idol by throwing it into the Narada Kund (a hot spring pool) that is a part of the river Alakananda. There it lay until Shankara retrieved it, but by then its basic features were eroded. The philosophical interpretation is that the significance of the idol, without a discernible face, mouth, or ears and eyes, is left to the imagination of the devotee. The temple is certainly Vaishnava, but its deity is transcendent in terms of appearance, much like Hinduism is above the differences among its many sects. Expectedly, Badrinath also has a shrine dedicated to Lakshmi, Vishnu's consort, and representative of Shakti. There is also a Sri Chakra in one of the rooms around the principal shrine.

The appearance of Badrinath is different from normal temples. The wide-pillared facade, and the pagoda style structure at the top, is, indeed, reminiscent of a Buddhist vihara. Perhaps, therefore, there is some credence to the belief that it was earlier a Buddhist structure, and was subsequently converted to a Hindu temple, after the arrival of Shankara.

In one corner of the temple's parikrama is a statue of Shankara, seated on a pedestal, with his four principal disciples sitting at his feet. In this statue, Shankara's face is depicted with startling clarity, and with features quite different to his standard portrayal. His face, outlined with a saffron cloak around his shaven head, has well delineated eyes, a prominent nose and clearly outlined lips with the suggestion of a beatific smile that simultaneously conveys realism and a deep sense of spirituality and *vairagya* or detachment.

The sheer scenic beauty of Badrinath, far above the din of the world, nestled among the towering snow-clad peaks of the Himalayas, with the roar of the youthful Alakananda bursting forth straight from the nearby glaciers, providing the only sound to break the perennial silence, must be why Shankara was so fond of this spot, and visited it often and for long periods to think, write and meditate. Some of his biographers believe that he visited Badri most frequently between 814 to 820 CE, staying for the summer months, and then retiring to Jyotir Matha when the temple was closed in winter.

If Badrinath is scenic, the location of Kedarnath at around 12,000 feet (3,583 metres) is just spectacular. The snow-bound Himalayan peaks create a feeling that the temple is situated in their lap, a small plateau at the edge of awe-inspiring valleys plummeting below. To reach Kedarnath by foot must have been a feat.

I did the journey in forty minutes by helicopter from Dehradun. Below me were mountains and valleys in seemingly unending sequence, forests that stretched as far as the eye could see, pellucid lakes, rivers cascading down from unknown sources high up in the mountains wrapped in clouds that appeared like interconnected pools of cotton fluff. Every now and then a hamlet would glisten in the sun, and I wondered whether any of them were old enough to have been places where Shankara would have rested and found food and shelter as he persevered with his herculean pilgrimage.

The Kedarnath temple is a traditional structure built in its present form (although renovations and modifications would have taken place later) by Shankara. It is dedicated to Shiva, and is one of the twelve holy jyotirlingas. The amazing part is that the linga is just a large rock protrusion, unchiselled, without the conventional shape.

To my mind, this veneration of the undefined is precisely because the linga, in conformity with the Advaita doctrine, is a symbol of the attribute-less nature of Brahman. The linga exists, but in empirical terms only as indefinite form, representing a higher reality that is beyond definition. It is an emanation, emerging from its eternal sub-stratum, earth, but is in unity with what it emerges from with no human embellishments, in much the same manner as the Atman, left to itself, is identical with Brahman.

In the face of that reality, all human divisibility ceases. The essential unity of things is illustrated by the demolition of geographical barriers. The aarti at the temple is in Kannada, a language from the state of Karnataka in the south. The idol of Vishnu at Badrinath has no distinguishing features. The head priest there is a Shaiva ascetic from the Nambudiri community of Kerala. At Kedarnath, the shrine is that of Shiva, but the deity itself is so remarkably devoid of explicit identification that it could represent any deity, or even the entire cosmos.

Shankara must have been spellbound by Kedarnath, where it is said, he came alone from Badrinath, asking his disciples to stay back. The Himalayan peaks here, even more than Badrinath, seem to be close enough to touch. Apart from the river Mandakini that flows next to the temple, there are at least four other rivulets cascading down from nearby glaciers to merge with each other and the Mandakini. The sheer picturesque serenity brings you effortlessly closer to the almighty. One has only to imagine Shankara, having trekked by foot to this remote site, so arduously inaccessible but steeped in lore going back to the Mahabharata, meditating at the temple, or along the banks of the Mandakini, in solitude, in complete communion with the majesty of nature and the silence.

The 2013 floods devastated the site of the Kedarnath temple.

In a flash, an unstoppable avalanche of water, rock and stone came down from the mountains above and swept away everything along its path, causing unprecedented destruction and loss of lives. The temple, however, survived. A giant piece of rock, rectangular in shape, carried by the raging flood, got wedged just behind the temple, causing the waters to part before they hit the temple directly. While everything else around was destroyed, the temple withstood the wrath of nature. Those who took shelter within it were saved, while those who didn't were swept away.

However, nothing now remains of the structures that stood at the back of the temple. These included, some thirty feet behind, a gate in marble that led to Shankara's Dandi Sthal, the place where he placed his traditional flagstaff. Further back, on the banks of the Mandakini, was a platform where he meditated. There was also a small temple nearby with a sphatika linga installed by him. And beyond, were the unchartered heights of the Himalayas, where, as per belief, he went into a cave to meditate, and took final samadhi, becoming one with Brahman.

By any touchstone, Shankara's was a remarkable life. In the space of the thirty-two years that he was given in the form of a mortal body, he plumbed the depths of the great legacy of Hindu philosophy, systematised and developed the Advaita doctrine into an imperishable school of thought, revived and reformed Hinduism, toured the length and breadth of India, from Kaladi in Kerala to Kedarnath in the Himalayas, and set up the four mathas to ensure Hinduism's preservation and propagation. Hinduism has not seen a thinker of his calibre, or witnessed, before or since, the indefatigable energy he displayed in pursuing the goals he set out to achieve.

The great seers who wrote the Upanishads could scarcely have thought that centuries after their remarkable insights, there would appear an individual who would give their ideas such widespread traction and appeal.

In his perennially peripatetic, eventful, yet much too short a life,

Shankara became a shining beacon in the evolution of Hinduism and the thought structure that has underpinned it. In this sense, he was a legatee of a larger legacy, that commenced millennia before, of profound intellectual spirituality, contemplation, debate, enquiry, discussion and ideas about the cosmos and our place in it. His seminal philosophical contribution can only be fully understood if we are aware, however briefly, of this legacy, and we shall provide an overview of it in the next chapter, before going on to examine his philosophy, and its amazing relevance to what science is telling us about the cosmos and our world today.

THE CANVAS BEFORE

The *Rig Veda*, written sometime between 1200 and 900 BCE, has this remarkable hymn (*Nasadiya Sukta*) on creation:

> There was neither non-existence nor existence then; there was neither the realm of space nor the sky which is beyond. What stirred? Where? In whose protection? Was there water, bottomlessly deep?
>
> There was neither death nor immortality then. There was no distinguishing sign of night or day. That one breathed, windless, by its own impulse. Other than that there was nothing beyond.
>
> Who really knows? Who will here proclaim it? Whence was it produced? Whence is this creation? The gods came afterwards with the creation of this universe? Who then knows whence it has arisen?
>
> Whence this creation has arisen—perhaps it formed itself, or perhaps it did not—the one who looks down on it, in the highest heaven, only he knows—or perhaps he does not know.[1]

1 Translation by Wendy Doniger, *The Rig Veda*, Penguin, 1981, pp. 25-26.

This hymn, perhaps the first recorded rumination in Hindu philosophy on the origins of the universe, is remarkable for its eclectic tone and tenor. There are no certitudes; no injunctions for obeisance; no religious commands, or call to ritual. There is awe, wonderment, but, above all, there is query, an emphasis on the need to probe, to go beyond conventional categories of thought to the realm of speculation, and an invitation to ideation.

The questions signify an impassioned yearning for truth, but this yearning is willing to accept that the answers may need to embrace negation even as they seek to find the right assertion, and that, in this process, the path to truth can be many things but not simplistic or dogmatic.

This wonderfully contemplative passage in the *Rig Veda* must have been written some two millennia before the birth of Shankara, but it indicates the foundational beginnings of a philosophical legacy that he would ultimately inherit.

The etymological meaning of Veda is sacred knowledge or wisdom. There are four Vedas: *Rig*, *Yajur*, *Sama*, and *Atharva*. Together they constitute the *samhitas* that are the textual basis of the Hindu religious system. To these samhitas were attached three other kinds of texts. These are, firstly, the *Brahmanas*, which is essentially a detailed description of rituals, a kind of manual for the priestly class, the Brahmins. The second are the *Aranyakas*; *aranya* means forest, and these 'forest manuals' move away from rituals, incantations and magic spells to the larger speculations of spirituality, a kind of compendium of contemplations of those who have renounced the world.

The third, leading from the *Aranyakas*, are the Upanishads, which, for their sheer loftiness of thought are the foundational texts of Hindu philosophy and metaphysics. Because they come at the very end of the corpus of the Vedas, they are also collectively called Vedanta, or the end of the Vedas, expounding the uncompromisingly non-dual nature of the cosmos—Advaita.

The word Upanishad literally means 'to sit down near' at the feet of a master or teacher who shares with his pupils spiritual truths or wisdom. One has to imagine a setting in a forest along the Ganga sometime as far back as 1500 BCE or earlier, where a sage, who has spent decades perhaps in the search for truth and wisdom, shares his thoughts, most often elliptically, with a group of students eager to begin their own journey in unravelling the mysteries of life. The conversation is not in the form of a formal dialogue, but through parable and suggestion, story and allusion, or statements of deep penetrative insight into what constitutes the transcendent reality underlying our lives and this universe.

The authors of the Upanishads are not known, nor do we have their exact chronology or date. It is certain that initially they were, like all Hindu texts, orally transmitted from generation to generation, and only reduced to text in classical Sanskrit sometime around 600 to 400 BCE. The Upanishads do not constitute a single volume; in fact, the exact number is not known either, but by common consensus, there are about twelve principal Upanishads attached to the *Sama*, *Yajur* and *Atharva* Vedas. Shankara wrote commentaries on ten of the *principal* Upanishads: *Isha, Kena, Katha, Prashna, Mundaka, Mandukya, Taittiriya, Aitareya, Chandogya,* and *Brihadaranyaka*.

An important point needs to be noted here. From the very beginning, Hindu religion had two distinct strands. The first was preoccupied with ritual and prayer and gods and goddesses, and at a baser level with superstition. This strand dwelt on the power and potency of a pantheon of gods, and the ritualistic actions by which they could be accessed and worshipped through the intervention of the Brahmins.

Very early on in the Vedic age we come upon an endless array of deities or quasi-deities, many of them representing, quite understandably, the dramatic forces of nature that were looked upon by early humans with wonderment and reverence. Hence we had gods like Indra, who controlled the elements, or Agni (fire), or

Aditi, who is an early version of the Mother Goddess, symbolising the mysterious powers of procreation.

But, as the *Aranyakas* and Upanishads show, as does the hymn on creation from the *Rig Veda* referred to earlier, there was, also from the very beginning, an equally strong strand that sought to understand the origins, meanings and purpose of life, and to explore what could be the one unifying force underlying the bewildering multiplicity of the universe. This strand was less taken up with ritual and divinities and the *practice* of religion and more with the philosophical substratum underlying the practice of religion. These two strands crystallised in time into two distinct schools: that of karmakanda, which privileged the paraphernalia necessary for the practice of religion, including all the rites and rituals, and *jnanakanda* which gave primacy to the pursuit of knowledge as the path to moksha.

In comparison with the other great religions of the world, Hinduism was probably not unique in nurturing two such divergent approaches, but it is almost certain that no other religious tradition so far back in time had such a pronounced emphasis on the pursuit of knowledge as an end in itself. Shankara believed in the jnana marga, the path of knowledge, as the sole means to salvation. *Satyam jnanam, anantam Brahma*: Knowledge is truth and Brahman is eternal, was what he proclaimed, and the Upanishads were the source of his jnana.

The Upanishads are metaphysical poems. They resonate with a wisdom that is a product of the deepest meditative insight, unhindered by structured presentation but robust, with a certitude of vision that is borne of unquestioned personal experience or *anubhav*. There is a self, Atman, beyond definition and name and form or attribute because any attribute would only circumscribe its limitlessness. This self is the highest reality. It encompasses all of creation: we are both part of it and its manifestation—*Tat tvam asi*—That thou art. The self is the same as Brahman—*Ayam atma brahma*—the self is Brahman. These utterances are two of the four *mahavakyas* or great sentences of the Upanishads. The Upanishads use self and Brahman interchangeably. The apparent multiplicity of the world is an illusion. Once the ego and the senses are stilled through deep meditation, we realise our true self, beyond all sorrow and pain, and realise that our true reality is 'that'. All human differentiation then becomes false, a product of the illusion or maya. In that non-dual, or Advaita identification with Brahman, we partake of a bliss that is beyond mortal comprehension.

Shankara looked upon the Upanishads as revealed texts, shruti, beyond human questioning, and took them as the basis of his philosophical system. Some critics, therefore, accuse him of lack of originality: he was but a *shrutivadin,* someone who blindly accepted the Upanishads as gospel truth. However, as we shall discuss later, Shankara's real—and unparalleled—contribution was to cull out a rigorous system of philosophy that was based on the essential thrust of Upanishadic thought but without being constrained by its unstructured presentation and contradictory meanderings. This is where his genius lay, and since the Upanishads played such a key role in the structuring of his philosophy, it is essential to provide a few samples of what they posited.

The *Mundaka Upanishad* says: 'The universe comes forth from Brahman and will return to Brahman. Verily, all is Brahman.' The *Katha Upanishad* elaborates:

> Above the senses is the mind,
> Above the mind is the intellect,
> Above that is the ego, and above the ego
> Is the unmanifested Cause
> And beyond is Brahma, omnipresent,
> Attributeless. Realizing him one is released
> From the cycle of birth and death.[2]

---

2 There are many exemplary translations of the Upanishads, but for flow of language and composition, I have chosen the one by Eknath Easwaran,

The *Mundaka Upanishad* also categorically proclaims the supremacy of the Atman or the self:

The effulgent Self, who is beyond thought,
Shines in the greatest, shines in the smallest,
Shines in the farthest, shines in the nearest,
Shines in the secret chamber of the heart.

The flowing river is lost in the sea;
The illumined sage is lost in the Self
The flowing river has become the sea;
The illumined sage has become the Self

The *Mandukya Upanishad* unequivocally asserts the unity between the Atman, and the cosmic cause, Brahman. The assertion of this unity, and indeed the unity of all things existent, is a repeated refrain in the Upanishads.

The *Chandogya Upanishad* explicates this beautifully in the story of Shvetaketu who asks Uddalaka, his father: what is wisdom? And, Uddalaka says to Shvetaketu:

As by knowing one lump of clay, dear one,
We come to know all things made out of clay:
That they differ only in name and form,
While the stuff of which all are made is clay;
As by knowing one gold nugget, dear one,
We come to know all things made out of gold:
That they differ only in name and form,
While the stuff of which all are made is gold;
As by knowing one tool of iron, dear one,
We come to know all things made out of iron:

The Upanishads, first published by the Blue Mountain Center of Meditation, 1987.

That they differ only in name and form,
While the stuff of which all are made is iron—
So through that spiritual wisdom, dear one,
We come to know that all life is one.

Having explained the unity of all things, the *Chandogya* sublimely puts an end to all notions of duality by pronouncing the foundational concept: Tat tvam asi: That thou art:

In the beginning was only Being,
One without a second.
Out of himself he brought forth the cosmos
And entered into everything in it.
There is nothing that does not come from him.
Of everything he is the inmost Self.
He is the truth; he is the Self Supreme.
You are that, Shvetaketu; you are that.

But camouflaging this fundamental and indestructible unity of the universe is the apparent multiplicity of the world. How do we then reconcile the two? The *Shvetashvatara Upanishad* provides the answer:

From his divine power comes forth all this
Magical show of name and form, of you
And me, which casts the spell of pain and pleasure.
Only when we pierce through this magic veil
Do we see the One who appears as many.

The Lord, who is the supreme magician,
Brings forth out of himself all the scriptures,
Oblations, sacrifices, spiritual disciplines,
The past and the present, the whole universe.
Invisible through the magic of maya
He remains hidden in the hearts of all.

How can an ordinary mortal free herself from this world of sorrow and grief and apparent dualities? The *Katha* sums up the answer of the Upanishads:

> When the five senses are stilled, when the
> Mind
> Is stilled, when the intellect is stilled,
> That is called the highest state by the wise.
> They say yoga is this complete stillness
> In which one enters the unitive state,
> Never to become separate again.
>
> When all desires that surge in the heart
> Are renounced, the mortal becomes immortal.
> When all the knots that strangle at the heart
> Are loosened, the mortal becomes immortal.
> This sums up the teaching of the scriptures.

Realisation brings freedom and infinite joy. The Upanishads are categorical that once an individual understands the pervasive omniscience of Brahman, and overcomes the sense of separateness created by the ego and the senses, the consequence is supreme bliss. As the *Taittiriya Upanishad* says: 'Realising That from which all words turn back, and thoughts can never reach, they know the bliss of Brahman and fear no more.' There is then the feeling of unblemished plenitude that is actually the characteristic of our real self. This sense is breathtakingly captured by the first shloka of the *Isha Upanishad*, about which Mahatma Gandhi is believed to have said that he would happily forego every scripture in Hinduism if he could keep just this one shloka:

> All this is full. All that is full.
> From fullness, fullness comes.

When fullness is taken from fullness,
Fullness still remains.

It is nothing short of amazing that these sermons on what constitutes ontological reality were taking place in forest academies some 3,500 or 4,000 years ago when most religious explorations at that time were restricted to the deification of natural phenomenon or simplistic magical incantations. The period, around 600 to 400 BCE, when the Upanishads were committed to text, did coincide with the classical age of Greece, but it must not be forgotten that for a millennium or more before that, they were already part of oral tradition.

Interestingly, in spite of their antiquity, western philosophers became aware of the Upanishads only in the beginning of the nineteenth century. A Frenchman called Anquetil Duperron brought out a Latin translation of fifty Upanishads using the Persian translation commissioned by Prince Dara Shikoh in 1657–68 CE. This generated sufficient interest for translation into other European languages directly from Sanskrit. Deussen's Sechsig *Upanishads der Veda* was published in 1897, dedicated to another great German Indologist, Arthur Schopenhauer.

But while the west may have been unaware of the Upanishads, in India they became the pivot of the unfolding philosophical discourse. The most authoritative text as part of this process was the *Brahma Sutra* by Badarayana written around 450 BCE. In Indian tradition, Badarayana is identified with the legendary Vyasa who compiled the Vedas. The *Brahma Sutra* is known by many names: *Nyaya-prasthana*, because it puts the teachings of the Upanishads in a structured order; *Vedanta Sutra,* since it is a text on the Vedanta; *Sariraka Sutra*, since it deals with the nature and evolution of the embodied soul; and, *Uttara-mimansha Sutra*, since it deals with the final section of the Vedas, unlike the *Purva mimansha* which deals with the earlier sections. Shankara's fundamental work is a lengthy—and possibly the first extant—

commentary or *bhashya* on the *Brahma Sutra*, a commentary so seminal that it has remained unchallenged for its depth, detail, lucidity and logical exposition.

A sutra 'is a short sentence or aphorism, shorn of all verbiage and designed to convey the essence of a religious or philosophical idea in the smallest space.'[3] In terms of the brevity of expression, and the intensity of thought compressed within it, the *Brahma Sutra* probably has no parallel in literary or philosophical discourse. For instance, the first sutra simply says: *Athato brahma jigyasa* (Hence now a deliberation on Brahman).

Max Mueller quotes Patanjali (the great grammarian) in stressing that sutra writers derived greater joy in reducing an aphorism by a word or a syllable than in the birth of a son!

The *Brahma Sutra* has 550 sutras, each not more than a word or two, which cumulatively constitute a systematic investigation into the worldview of the Upanishads, but are near impossible to understand in isolation. On this chiselled but ruthlessly attenuated allusion of thought, pregnant with meaning, commentaries were written running into hundreds of pages and thousands of shlokas.

Along with the Upanishads and the *Bhagavad Gita* (to which we shall refer later), the *Brahma Sutra* makes up the triad of the three foundational texts of Hinduism. To understand the Hindu system of elaboration and explication of philosophical and metaphysical concepts, it is instructive to look at the structure of the *Brahma Sutra,* which is divided into four chapters (*adhyayas*); each chapter, in turn, has four parts (*padas*), and each part has several sections (*adhikaranas*).

More importantly, the four chapters follow a sequence that combines assertion and dissent, synthesis and anti-thesis, concluding with the positive promise of moksha or salvation in this very life.

The first chapter is on *samanvaya* or harmony. The purpose here is to take the many disparate statements in the Upanishads

---

3 Y. Kesava Menon, *The Mind of Adi Shankaracharya*, Jaico, 1976, p. 5.

and harmonise them to grasp their one indisputable message: Brahman is the only, pervasive, and supreme reality, characterised by *sat chid ananda* or being, awareness and bliss.

The second chapter illustrates the great scope of both dissent and dialogue in the Hindu methodology of discourse. It is titled *Avirodha* (or non-conflict), and takes on board objections to the Vedantic assertion of the non-dual supremacy of Brahman. These objections emanate from the other schools of Hindu philosophy as also from Buddhism and Jainism.

The third chapter deals with the means to salvation, *sadhana*. The principal means is jnana or knowledge of the identity with, and non-difference from, Brahman, and meditation on this reality. Such meditation must transcend the ephemeral multiplicity of the phenomenal world. 'Just as light which has no form appears to be endowed with different forms because of the object which it illumines,' says the sutra, 'Brahman which has no attributes appears as if endowed with attributes,'[4] on account of ignorance. Brahman is non-dual pure consciousness, unconditioned and unblemished. That is why it cannot be circumscribed by definition and the Upanishads adopt the negative mode of description: *neti, neti,* not this, not this. To understand this is the means for release.

The last chapter dwells on the fruits of salvation, *phala*. In sum, it is the possibility of salvation through knowledge and anubhav in this very life.

But if Brahman is the only reality, and jnana consists in understanding our total identity with it, how do we deal with the phenomenal world and the actions it makes incumbent on human beings? How do we reconcile the transitory and unreal nature of things with the concrete and unavoidable requirements of daily life, work and activity? The answer to this is provided in

4 *Brahma Sutra Bhashya of Shankaracharya,* translated by Swami Gambhirananda, published by Advaita Ashram, 1965, from the Foreword, p ix.

the *Bhagavad Gita*, on which too Shankara wrote an authoritative and insightful commentary.

The *Gita*, consisting of 700 shlokas in eighteen chapters is imbedded in the Mahabharata, a voluminous literary epic, eight times the length of the *Odyssey* and *Iliad* combined. The epic was probably written around 500 BCE, and since it makes no reference to Buddhism, most scholars consider it to have been composed before the advent of Buddha.

When the Great War—Mahabharata—was about to begin, Arjuna, the most accomplished warrior among the Pandavas, refused to fight. Arraigned opposite him were his own kinsmen—uncles, brothers, teachers, elders, companions, and his will faltered. 'I desire not victory, nor kingdom, nor pleasures,' he told the Blue God, Krishna, 'if these are to be won at the cost of so much bloodshed.' Krishna, who was his charioteer or *sarathi*, then counselled him; and, in the end, Arjuna, his mental equilibrium restored and his sense of confusion removed, picked up his bow and arrow and boldly entered the fight.

The *Gita*, whose text unfolds in the nature of a dialogue between Arjuna and Krishna, did not purport to outline a rigorous or inflexible philosophical system. The votaries of Advaita Vedanta, Bhagavata theism, Samkhya dualism and Yogic meditation have all found in it ideas and passages in support of their predilections. The greatness of the *Gita* lies not in its philosophical chastity to any one school of thought, but to the solace it provides to the existential dilemma that often confronts human beings: one is born, one lives and one dies, and in between there could be joy, but there is also sorrow and grief. There is no redemption from the starkness of this sterile, predictable charade, and all of a sudden the purport of ambition and achievement, of causes and goals, becomes opaque.

In this sense, Arjuna's weariness, was symbolic of 'generic man'. He could not comprehend an imperative for action in a phenomenal world that was stubbornly inexplicable. The greatness of the *Gita* is that it enabled Krishna, through his discourse, to give purpose and meaning to the predicament of men like Arjuna.

The most important concept that the *Gita* enunciated was that of *nishkama karma*, of action, without attachment or thought of reward, done without selfish desire in a spirit of surrender. Krishna says:

> Hear my truth about the surrender of works, Arjuna. Surrender, O best of men, is of three kinds.
>
> Works of sacrifice, gift, and self-harmony should not be abandoned, but should indeed be performed; for these are works of purification.
>
> But even these works, Arjuna, should be done in the freedom of a pure offering, and without expectation of a reward. This is my final word.
>
> It's not right to leave undone the holy work which ought to be done. Such a surrender of action would be a delusion of darkness.
>
> And he who abandons his duty because he has fear of pain his surrender is of Rajas, impure, and in truth he has no reward.
>
> But he who does holy work, Arjuna, because it ought to be done, and surrenders selfishness and thought of reward, his work is pure, and is peace.
>
> This man sees and has no doubts: he surrenders, he is pure and has peace. Work, pleasant or painful, is for him joy.

> For there is no man on earth who can fully renounce living work, but he who renounces the reward of his work, is in truth a man of renunciation.
>
> When work is done for a reward, the work brings pleasure, or pain, or both, in its time; but when a man does work in Eternity, then Eternity is his reward. [5]

Nishkama karma is thus the *Gita*'s practical formula for a person to maintain equipoise and equanimity in interfacing with the actions and choices the mundane world demands. The Upanishads asserted that we are that—Tat tvam asi—but they did not elaborate on how, given this reality, we negotiate life at the empirical level on a daily basis.

The *Gita* provides the answer to this dilemma by stating that no one in this world can live by completely renouncing action. However, we can rid ourselves from the negative emotions produced by action if we act without thought of reward, and with detachment and in the spirit of surrender. Such an attitude is entirely consistent with the *Gita*'s reiteration that Brahman is the transcendent reality permeating and sustaining the universe. In fact, says the *Gita*, it is precisely that individual who has understood what his essential reality is who can best practice nishkama karma:

> The man who sees Brahma abides in Brahma; his reason is steady, gone is his delusion. When pleasure comes he is not shaken, and when pain comes he trembles not.
>
> He is not bound by things without, and within he finds inner gladness. His soul is one in Brahma and he attains everlasting joy.

---

5 This rendering, and the following extracts from the *Gita* have been taken from the lyrical translation of Juan Mascaro, first published in 1962, and republished by Penguin Books India, 1994.

> For the pleasures that come from the world bear in them sorrows to come. They come and they go, they are transient: not in them do the wise find joy.
>
> But he on this earth, before his departure, can endure the storms of desire and wrath, this man is a Yogi, this man has joy.
>
> This man has inner joy, he has inner gladness, and he has found inner Light. This Yogi attains the Nirvana of Brahma: he is one with God and goes unto God.
>
> Holy men reach the Nirvana of Brahma: their sins are no more, their doubts are gone, their soul is in harmony, their joy is in the good of all.

Following the Upanishads, the *Gita* affirms that the inner spirit in each individual—Atman—is identical with the cosmic energy of Brahman. Your doubts and grief are misplaced, Krishna tells Arjuna, because as part of Brahman, your essential nature is beyond death. Only the physical body decays and dies, while you yourself are part of the unchanging eternal:

> He is never born, and he never dies. He is in Eternity: he is for evermore. Never born and eternal, beyond times gone or to come, he does not die when the body dies.

But, Arjuna, like any mortal, was not content with only metaphysical assertions. He wanted the assurance of a divinity that he could identify with, a personal god, far more accessible than the attribute-less Brahman. 'In thy mercy thou hast told me the secret supreme of thy Spirit, and thy words have dispelled my delusion,' he beseeches Krishna, 'but show me, O God of Yoga, the glory of thine own Supreme Being.' And, Krishna grants him his desire, revealing to Arjuna his celestial form in all its plenitude:

> And Arjuna saw in that form countless visions of wonder: eyes from innumerable faces, numerous celestial ornaments, numberless heavenly weapons.
>
> Celestial garlands and vestures, forms anointed with heavenly perfumes. The Infinite Divinity was facing all sides, all marvels in him containing.
>
> If the light of a thousand suns suddenly arose in the sky, that splendour might be compared to the radiance of the Supreme Spirit.
>
> And Arjuna saw in that radiance the whole universe in its variety, standing in a vast unity in the body of the God of gods.
>
> Trembling with awe and wonder, Arjuna bowed his head, and joining his hands in adoration he thus spoke to his God.
>
> I see in thee all the gods, O my God; and the infinity of the beings of thy creation. I see God Brahmana on his throne of lotus, and all the seers and serpents of light.

In this one act of divine revelation, the *Gita* executes a remarkable sleight-of-hand by transmuting the indefinable Brahman-Atman of the Upanishads into a personal god. This derogation of the attribute-less or nirguna Brahman into a devotional theism was a concession made to the human urge to see divinity in a personalised form. The concession was made, but typically of the harmonised contradictions of Hinduism, without denying the ultimate supremacy of Brahman. In counselling Arjuna, Krishna synthesised several paths to moksha, all sanctioned by Hindu tradition: jnana marga, the path of knowledge, karma marga, the path of selfless activity, and bhakti marga, the path of devotion to a personal god.

Shankara was deeply influenced by these three basic texts of Hindu philosophy, the Upanishads, the *Brahma Sutra*, and the *Bhagavad Gita*, and wrote extensive and definitive commentaries on each of them. But, in addition to his Vedantic or non-dualistic Advaita system of philosophy, there were at least five other major schools which had evolved over a period of time. Several minor schools, that were not part of the six systems of Hindu philosophy, but still exercised considerable influence, also existed. And, of course, there were the philosophical doctrines of the two major religions outside Hinduism, Buddhism and Jainism. All of these contributed in substantial ways to Shankara's thought process.

The depth and range of philosophical churning that marked the growth and evolution of Indic thought in its formative years must have few parallels anywhere else in the world, including Greece.

This was characterised by a remarkable intellectual curiosity that refused to take anything for granted or to be confined to simplistic theism or conventional categories of personal prosperity and wellbeing. The concerns here were larger, about causes and origins, the nature of things, the secrets of the universe, the exactitudes of logic and inference, and the relationship between mind, the senses and the body—a collective rumination that soared beyond the finitude of the known into the infinities beyond.

The sages who founded these systems grappled not so much with faith and godhood. In fact, most of the six systems, including Vedanta, were at the level of pure philosophy, atheistic in tone, seeking instead to carry out a corrosive enquiry into the ultimate nature of substance and spirit. In this process, the emphasis was not on what dogmatically is, or what emphatically must be, or what necessarily should be, but what *possibly could be.*

The felicity and energy with which these thinkers volitionally left familiar—and more comprehensible—shores to plumb the depths of the unknown is nothing short of amazing. It would be essential to provide a glimpse of these strands of thought in order to understand the abundance of the complex philosophical lineage that Shankaracharya inherited and responded to.

The five schools of philosophy that preceded Shankara's systemic exposition of Vedantic metaphysics were the Nyaya, Vaisheshika, Sankhya, Yoga, and Purva Mimamsha. All these were essentially guided by two fundamental tenets, investigation or mimamsha, and reflection or *vichara*—about the ultimate nature of the world, and the consequential purposes of life. They overlapped in their concepts and reasoning in some respects, but their differences were equally marked, and in this sense, provide definitive proof of the eclectic milieu of those times, and the independence and robustness of thought they nurtured.

The *Nyaya Sutra* dates back to the third century BCE and is attributed to the sage Gautama. This school's principal preoccupation is with logic and dialectics, analysis and reasoning. To this end, the Nyaya relied primarily on four sources of knowledge: perception (*pratyaksha*), inference (*anumana*), analogy (*upamana*) and verbal testimony (shabda). Such tools were essential, the *Nyaya* stressed, to establish whether that which is posited exists or not. In other words, the importance of Nyaya lies in the fact that it set out the analytical framework for enquiry, and refused to accept anything only on face value or assertion.

The Vaisheshika school of the sage Kanada (third century BCE) relied closely on the tools of reasoning expounded upon by Nyaya, but went beyond to formulate what must arguably be the first philosophical doctrine based on the recognition of the atom.

All material objects, it asserts, are ultimately the product of four basic atoms found in earth, water, fire or air. Amazingly, for its times, the doctrine concludes that all finite objects can be broken down into parts and finally reduced to that one infinitesimal, indestructible and indivisible atom. A combination of atoms produces different products, which could, in their final form, be different from their constituent parts. The doctrine admits that in the evolutionary process, from the atom to a finite whole, the end result could be based on a dominant characteristic or *vishesha*, but essentially the worldview of the Vaisheshika is pluralistic.

While foundationally realistic in its approach, the Vaisheshika recognises that not all substances are material. The non-material aspects of cosmology include space, time, ether *(akasha)*, mind and soul. At this point, somewhat reluctantly, Kanada accepts the possibility of a God or Ishwara who combined the four kinds of atoms and five non-material substances into an ordered universe. The essential tone of the philosophy, however, remains atheistic, since even while conceding the presence of god, it limits his role to the ordering of the universe, and not to the creation of the elements that constitute it.

The Sankhya school was essayed by Kapila in the seventh century BCE, and is one of the oldest systematised structures of thought in Hindu philosophy. In essence, the Sankhya posits a cosmic duality to the universe, consisting of Prakriti and Purusha. Prakriti, unlike the pluralistic atomistic view of the Vaisheshika, is a pervasive singularity, eternal and independent, from which the universe evolves. But this evolution happens only when Prakriti comes under the influence of Purusha, which stands for awareness or the sentient principle.

Until the influence of Purusha, Prakriti, representing the 'potentiality of nature'[6] lies latent, its three constituents, sattva, rajas and tamas, in equilibrium. Sattva stands for that which is pure; rajas signifies energy and activity; and tamas connotes inertia and stolidity.

This equilibrium is disturbed when Purusha interfaces with

6 K.M. Sen, *Hinduism*, Penguin Books, UK, 1961, p. 80.

Prakriti, and evolution commences with all its manifest diversities. The emergence of the five cognitive organs—taste, touch, sight, sound and smell—and the five motor organs of movement are part of this evolution, as is the emergence of intellect (buddhi) and the ego (*ahamkara*). According to the Sankhya, this evolution is cyclical, with creation *shrishti* followed by dissolution (*pralaya*), and pralaya again followed by shrishti. For a human being, liberation consists in understanding the distinction between the material Prakriti and the sentient Purusha. This understanding comes by lifting the veil of ignorance through the pursuit of jnana.

For sheer conceptualisation, there is an awe-inspiring grandeur to the cosmic architecture profiled by the Sankhya. What is especially interesting is that in the self-evolving cosmic drama that it structures, there is no place for god. As we shall see later, there are many aspects of this school that influenced Shankara, including, in particular, the emphasis on knowledge as the way to salvation, although he remained resolutely opposed to the duality of the system.

The Yoga school broadly accepts the worldview of the Sankhya, but fleshes out the physical discipline and meditational regimen required by an individual to realise the separation (*kaivalya*) of Purusha, pure consciousness, from the non-sentient Prakriti. The *Yoga Sutra* is attributed to Patanjali and is dated to sometime before 400 CE. Several scholars believe it to be of much greater antiquity, and it is very likely that even if composed later, the sutra codifies a tradition and practice from several centuries earlier.

The *Yoga Sutra* begins with this aphorism: *Yogah chitta vrittih nirodha*: Yoga is restraining the mind from discursive thought. This restraint, it believes, can be brought about by discipline, both physical and mental. In the sutra, discipline is outlined as an eightfold path, starting from *yama* (self-restraint), *niyama* (virtuous observances), asana (posture), pranayama (consciously controlling breath), *pratyahara* (withdrawal of the senses), *dharana* (concentrating the mind), dhyana (meditation), and samadhi (a trance-like state in which there is complete union with the subject of meditation).

Yoga literally translates to 'union', and the purpose of the entire regimen of the eightfold path is to prepare the disciple for this union with Purusha. Unlike the Vedantic system, which believes that enlightenment, based on jnana, can come to anybody at any time through direct anubhav or communion, Yoga provides to Sankhya a carefully structured complementary system of mental and physical exercises that it believes is a necessary pre-condition to moksha. On one essential point, however, Yoga differs from Sankhya, and that is in its acceptance of a personal god, who directs the cyclical evolutionary process from creation to dissolution.

The practice of dharma, through ritual action sanctified by the Vedas, is the principal focus of the Purva Mimamsha. Jaimini (circa 400 BCE), was its chief theoretician. This doctrine believes in karma or action, and not jnana as the path to salvation. Its preoccupation is with the practice and interpretation of Vedic rites and rituals, which are to be performed out of a sense of duty, and in the manner prescribed by the orthodox texts associated with the Vedas such as the *Brahmanas*.

The school believes that performing the obligatory rituals, and abstaining from those that are proscribed, will lead by itself to the elimination of evil and the attainment, through the purification of the soul, of moksha.

In the seventh century CE, Kumarila Bhatta wrote an extensive commentary on the original treatise of Jaimini. Shankara, who believed that jnana not karma is the path to salvation, met with Kumarila Bhatta, and had, as has been described earlier, a definitive shastrartha or argumentation on this issue with Mandana Mishra.

In addition to the six major systems of philosophy described above, there were other significant elements in the landscape of Hindu thought, which had their own committed followers, and could not but have been taken note of by Shankara. For instance, the Charvaka Lokayatika school which provides a fascinating insight into the intellectual eclecticism of these times, and the degree of 'deviation' from conventional thinking that was tolerated. While it is true that several of the major schools of Hindu philosophy were less preoccupied with a personal god, and built their ideological structures on an atheistic template, the Charvakas openly denied the existence of god or of any supernatural forces, and argued a well thought-out materialism. The external world, they asserted, exists objectively, and is governed by verifiable laws and not by any supra-natural force.

The only valid source of inference is pratyaksha or perception, and what cannot be perceived does not exist, they asserted. The material substances that we can infer through direct perception are earth, water, fire and air. The world consists of varying combinations of these four fundamental elements (*mahabhuta*). Consciousness, they said, is not anything transcendental, but a combination of these elements in a specific form and under definitive conditions. There is no soul that survives death; the body returns to the four basic elements that constituted it. Nothing remains to transmigrate or be reborn. The Vedas are bereft of all sanctity since they suffer from the three errors of internal contradiction, untruth, and meaningless repetition.

It is said that Brihaspati, who founded the Charvaka school around the seventh century BCE, was a proponent of materialist hedonism. Since there was nothing before, and there will be nothing beyond the life that we have, it must be enjoyed to the full without inhibition or thought of extraneous forces:

> While life is yours, live joyously
> None can escape death's searching eye;
> When once this frame of ours they burn
> How shall it e'er again return?[7]

---

7 S. Radhakrishnan, *Indian Philosophy*, Vol 1, George Allen & Unwin Ltd, London, 1977, p. 281.

However, it can equally be argued that the real purpose of the Charvakas was to make an individual responsible for his own life without the crutches of an external deity or agency. Essentially, Brihaspati was a rebel. He was against superstition, ritualism, caste, scriptural authority, and Brahminical hegemony. Religion, he said, is an instrument in the hands of the priests to exploit the common person, and god is only the invention of the rich. It is this injustice and oppression that we need to fight in our present lives, instead of condoning matters by believing—as the priests would want us to do—that our miseries are due to deeds done in past lives. In this sense, Brihaspati and the Charvaka school predated Marx—who famously said that religion is the opium of the masses—by over a millennium and a half.

Another interesting strand of philosophy related to the sanctity of sound, is concretised through the word (shabda). Sometime between the sixth and fourth century BCE, the great grammarian Panini wrote the *Ashthadhyayi*, the foundational treatise on Sanskrit grammar. In the second century BCE, Patanjali wrote his *Mahabhashya* or 'Great Commentary' on the *Ashthadhyayi.* It is a matter of speculation whether this Patanjali was the same as the Patanjali who wrote the *Yoga Sutra*. This being as it may, the *Mahabhashya* which dwells extensively on *shiksha* (accent), *vyakarana* (morphology) and *nirukta* (etymology), is the earliest work on the philosophy underlying Hindu grammar.

Bhartrihari, in the fifth century CE, wrote the *Vakyapadiya,* elaborating further on this linguistic philosophy. The cumulative impact of such penetrative speculations by grammarians saw the emergence, before the time of Shankara, of a specific philosophy—Shabda Advaita—that believed in 'universal' sound or *dhvani* as an eternal, omnipresent and indivisible principle, *vaka shakti,* uniting the cosmos.

In the midst of these structured schools of philosophy, replete with complex concepts and clinical analyses, there was an undercurrent of simplistic devotional fervour, which had no inhibitions in looking for succour towards a personal god. This cult of bhakti, which believed in the manifestation of god, had adherents not only among the Shaivite and Vaishnavites, but also a host of other sects, many of whom worshipped local deities. Relatively aloof from the rarefied argumentations of metaphysics, bhakti drew inspiration from epics and the Puranas. Its followers composed devotional hymns of great emotional power, as can be seen in the compositions of Shaivite Nayanar, and Vaishnavite Alwar saints.

This human yearning for a more accessible deity in human form was something that Shankara could not ignore. That is why, as we shall see later, he sanctioned, for purposes of invoking the mood of surrender, personal theism without diluting his unflinching philosophical fidelity to the Advaita concept of a non-dual, omnipresent, but indefinable Brahman.

Among the bhakti schools, one branch which is of special interest is that of shakti, which involved the worship of the feminine principle, as embodied in Durga, the consort of Shiva. The practitioners of this form of devotion, who believed that Shiva's real power was sourced in, or incomplete without, his feminine consort, developed a complex system of secretive and mystical rites and mantras.

This gradually evolved into the esoteric tantric philosophy, which is codified and elaborated upon in the samhita or *agama* texts. In general, the cult of the Devi had great popularity, and was practiced on a pan-Indian scale. It's certain that Shankara was greatly influenced both by Devi worship and tantra, as is witnessed in the *Saundarya Lahari*, the passionate devotional hymn he wrote in homage to the Mother Goddess.

Apart from these various schools of thought and practices in Hinduism, there were two major religions, Buddhism and Jainism, which emerged around the same time, and in some manner posed a challenge to the entire spectrum of Hindu philosophy.

Buddha was born in Lumbini in 563 BCE in the royal kingdom of Kapilavastu, and lived to the age of eighty. As a young prince, he was deeply influenced by the human suffering he saw around him. This suffering, he was convinced, was inevitable in a life that was both transient and unfulfilling, and meaningless beyond the superficial cycle of happiness followed by sorrow, joy followed by grief. He decided then to renounce life, and search for the truth that would lead to nirvana or liberation from the cycle of birth and death.

Buddha's enduring concern was with *dukkha,* or suffering, inherent in incarnate life. On receiving enlightenment while meditating under the Bodhi tree in Bodhgaya (Bihar), he enunciated the four noble truths and the eightfold path to liberation. The four truths, simply put, were that there is suffering, there is a cause of suffering, there can be cessation of suffering, and the eightfold path is the way to the cessation of suffering. The eight steps, or the middle way, which he enunciated were right view, right intention, right speech, right action, right livelihood, right effort, right mindfulness, and right concentration.

Up to this point there was nothing in what the Buddha preached that was either entirely original or in conflict either with Hinduism as a whole or with the Advaita philosophy of the Upanishads and Shankara's elaboration of it. However, the metaphysical reasoning underpinning Buddha's preoccupation with sorrow, and the way out of it, was, in many respects, directly at variance with the Upanishadic doctrine. There is nothing like an enduring self, Brahman or Atman, said the Buddha; in this state of non-self (*anatta*) what exists is only the body (*rupa*) and the mind (*nama*). Everything that we see is an aggregate (*samghata*); all is inherently unsubstantial (*nairatmaya*). Moreover, even the self, at the level of body and mind, is eternally transient and impermanent (*anityatva*).

He further said that the reality that we see around us has no transcendental substratum (*svabhava*); it is in constant flux (*samtana*), and all experience is a series of impressions, conceived and extinguished in the same instance (*kshana bhanga vada*), so that no one can ever step into the same river twice. Nirvana, and in this context meaning liberation from sorrow, is literally the realisation of the emptiness of the notion of self, a process of blowing out and extinguishing oneself from the binding shackles of the web of life, *samsara*.

This kernel of Buddha's philosophy was taken to new extremes by later Buddhist thinkers. The Yogachara school of Mahayana Buddhism asserted that only thought, in its ever-changing flux, is real, and there is no external reality whatsoever. This exclusive emphasis on the ephemeral mind as the only identifiable reality to the exclusion of all else took subjectivism to another level, and was called vijnanavada.

Another school, whose chief proponent was Nagarjuna (circa 150 CE), founded the Madhaymika school of Mahayana Buddhism. Nagarjuna postulated the theory of *shunyata* or emptiness, in which he denied not only the existence of external objects but also the perceiving self. Since there is nothing like a self, and all things are transient and a product of dependent origination (*pratityasamputapada*), the entire world, mind and matter, is illusory. Nirvana is the outcome of the understanding of this nihilistic void.

Quite obviously, there was much in the metaphysics of Buddhism that militated directly against Advaita and the thought structure (which we shall discuss in greater detail later) of Shankara. The denial of the self, or of the ontological reality of Brahman, was a negation of the grand cosmic design of the Upanishads. Equally, the later evolution of Buddhist thought, that either completely denied external reality or even the mind, signified a subjectivism and skepticism not countenanced by Shankara. In more ways than one, Buddha also registered his protest against the ritualistic aspects of Hinduism and this he did by consciously repudiating the philosophical underpinnings of Upanishadic thought.

Perhaps the most significant difference between Buddhist thought and Vedanta was on the emphasis each placed on dukkha, *suffering*, and ananda, joy. Shankara, in conformity with the Upanishads, defined the ultimate realisation of Brahman as indescribable bliss. Buddha defined nirvana as the cessation of sorrow, not the benediction of bliss. Nirvana, in the Buddhist sense, is negative, an emptiness where all cravings and aversions have ceased.

Vedanta is positive, where, after one has transcended the limitations of body and mind, what is left is the union with Brahman and the rekindling of the flame of unalloyed joy. Nagarjuna's shunyata was nihilistic; it essayed an exhilarating emptiness that stilled the normal turbulence and agitations of the mind. But Nagarjuna would not make the quantum leap to describe shunyata in positive terms as bliss.

But, this notwithstanding, there were similarities also between Buddhism and Vedanta. The devaluation of the external world was common to both. The need to find a way out of sorrow was an imperative for both. Ways to still the sterile agitations of the mind was something they agreed upon. Shankara endorsed many of the injunctions of Buddha's eightfold path. And, both Buddhism and Vedanta were convinced about the end goal of philosophy, liberation, moksha or nirvana.

However, the basic dichotomy between dukkha and ananda continued to distinguish the two. In Buddhism, bliss could be an end product of the elimination of sorrow, but it was not considered to be the animating impulse of the cosmic order, as Vedanta, in its contemplation of Brahman asserted. In one of the Buddhist texts, *Milinda*, the Indo-Greek king of North-western India around 150 BCE, asks the revered Buddhist sage, Nagasena about the nature of Buddha's nirvana.

> 'What would your majesty say—if a great fire were blazing, would it be possible to point to a flame which had gone out and say that it was here or there?'

> 'No, Your Reverence, the flame is extinguished, it can't be detected.'
>
> 'In just the same way, Your Majesty, the Lord has passed away in Nirvana.....'[8]

In Buddhism, nirvana was an act of negation, as in a flame ceasing to exist; in Advaita, the knowledge and revelation of Brahman was an act of affirmation, where the flame burnt even more brightly, having burnt the dross of conventional cravings the Buddha too sought to extinguish. It was a difference of emphasis, but that difference changed the centrality of the narrative, and created a sub-structure of opposing philosophical assumptions.

There was one aspect of Buddhism, though, that greatly influenced Shankara. The three 'jewels of Buddhism', the Buddha, the dharma, and the sangha—the last being the order of monks especially created by the Buddha for the preservation and propagation of his teachings. Shankara realised the immense value of the sangha, and sought to emulate this by creating his own order of monks through the mathas he set up at Sringeri, Puri, Dwaraka and Joshimatha.

Between the certainties of Advaita, which asserted the pervasive presence of Brahman signifying sat chid ananda, and the certainties of Buddhism, which denied the existence of anything permanent amidst an ocean of impermanence and sorrow, was the deliberate ambivalence of Jainism. Although twenty-four Tirthankars or spiritual teachers had preceded him, Mahavira is accepted as the principal icon of the Jaina faith.

Like the Buddha, he was born in a royal family, in the Muzzafarpur district of Bihar in 599 BCE, and died at Pawapuri in 527 BCE. Around the age of thirty, he too, like the young prince of Kapilavastu, left home to search for truth. After twelve years

---

8 Quoted in *A Treasury of Indian Wisdom*, Karan Singh, Penguin India, 2010, pp. 64-65.

of intense penance and meditation, he acquired *kevala jnana* or infinite knowledge.

As against the assertions of absolute truth, Jainism consciously postulates a doctrine of uncertainty. The significant point is that it does so not by simplistic rejection, but in keeping with the intellectual rigour of those times, through a considered theoretical structure of thought. Reality, Jainism says, is complex and admits a plurality and multiplicity of viewpoints, *anekantvada*. The search for truth must eschew absolutisms and accept the validity of partial standpoints, *nayavada*. No postulate can be made in such a manner that it denies the possibility of conditional predications, *syadavada*.

In support of such a deliberate doctrine of relativity, Jainism cites the parable of seven blind men examining an elephant, and depending on what part they are in touch with, arriving at a different conclusion of what it is. More formally, Jainism sought to debunk the proponents of 'one-sidedness' by its *saptabhangi* or seven-step theory, whose purpose is to establish that knowledge of reality is relative. The seven possibilities that the saptabhangi doctrine outlines are: maybe, it is; maybe, it is not; maybe, it is and is not; maybe, it is inexpressible; maybe, it is and is inexpressible; maybe, it is not and is inexpressible; maybe it is and is not and is inexpressible.

The one word that is common to all seven viewpoints is 'maybe'. In Jainism, 'maybe' is the antidote to dogmatism, and, in particular that of Hindu and Buddhist metaphysics.

But, Jainism was not without its own absolutes. The jiva or soul is contaminated it believes, by the infiltration of karmic matter, ajiva, and becomes, as a consequence, heavy in bondage (*bandha*). The purpose of the spiritual quest is to rid the jiva of this ajiva, by first stemming the influx of new karmic matter, and second, by destroying the accumulated karma from the past. To achieve this end, Jainism advocates a path of extreme asceticism, and an equally rigorous emphasis on non-violence.

On the moral front, it has its own three jewels or *triratna* — right faith, right knowledge, and right conduct. Through the practice of severe penance, absolute non-violence, and the adoption of the three jewels, a person can restore the soul to its original state of purity, and obtain nirvana. Jainism is ambivalent on the question of god, but believes that divinity lies in the obtaining of infinite knowledge or kevala jnana.

There is, thus, a contradiction in the Jaina theory of the relativity of knowledge, and the Jaina practice that postulates its own certainties. Jainism must also answer to the query, that if all knowledge is relative, why should its negation of absolutisms also not be so? Shankara critiques Jainism for its reluctance to take the leap of faith towards affirmation. Purely on epistemological grounds, he also disagrees with the assertion that something can both be, and not be. Commenting on the Jaina emphasis on the 'many-sidedness' to reality, he argues that two directly contradictory states cannot be attributed to the same thing at the same time.

And yet, Jainism brings to the ideological debate a freshness of view that is invigorating for its sheer audacity to question the propensity of other systems of philosophy to believe that they alone are right. And, in many ways, the relativism that it outlines does deeply influence the future evolution of Indic thought, including, for instance, in Shankara's definition of maya as something that is, and is not, and is inexpressible.

In the millennia that preceded Shankaracharya, empires rose and fell, armies won and lost, kings came and went, and cities flourished and dwindled, but the philosophical academies of the mind never ebbed. The preoccupation about who we are, what the universe is about, and what are the end goals of human existence, remained a vibrant continuum.

Systems of thought, once articulated, never died out. Some, like Buddhism, in particular, received extensive royal patronage, and reached out to shores far beyond India. Others, even without being adopted by emperors, had a band of dedicated followers who continued to codify, discuss and elaborate upon the original teachings of their founders. The Indic system of explicatory commentaries or bhashyas ensured that thought structures did not fade away. At the same time, the tradition of argumentation and debate, often even a trifle acrimonious, preserved the activism of both critics and defenders.

The important thing was that all these argumentations were not confined to hermitages or monasteries or to a handful of disciples, but acquired a larger momentum and popularity that permeated to people at large who, even if not involved in the finer metaphysical nuances, were more than aware of the broad contours. The depth, robustness of argument, courage of conviction, and sanction to dissent and, where necessary, synthesise, is what made the philosophical canvas leading up to Shankara different. It was this amazing mosaic of philosophical enquiry, spiritual quest, religious practice and metaphysical analysis that he inherited. He was, thus, ideologically heir to much more than merely a formal education normally available to a child born in a small hamlet on the banks of the Purna in Kerala. The meticulous structure of thought that he built on the basis of this legacy is what we shall discuss in the next chapter.

THE AUDACITY OF THOUGHT

Shankara's contribution to global metaphysics is the creation of a structure of thought that is rigorously consistent, internally cohesive and groundbreaking in projecting the non-dual reality of the cosmic play. On the basis of the enigmatic utterances of the Upanishads on Brahman and Atman, the cryptic aphorisms of the *Vedanta Sutras,* and a deep study of the other schools of philosophy that preceded him, he built a vision that sought to explicate both the bewildering plurality in our lives, and the eternal substratum of unity underlying it.

What is noteworthy in his project is the sheer quantum of application of mind, analysis and observation.

As mentioned earlier, there are some critics who cast a doubt on the originality of his contribution. Their view is that essentially he was a shrutivadin—someone who took the Upanishads to be revealed text, and only elaborated upon the insights they had already provided. This critique is understandable, but not correct.

It is true that Shankara looked upon the Upanishads as irrefutable. However, the Upanishads themselves did not constitute a self-sustaining or logically elucidated body of thought. They were a compilation of pronouncements based in parts on profound intuition, but also a compendium of several other views, a great deal of *obiter dicta*, including conventional theism. Beyond the breathtaking glimpses they provided of the absolute, there was no attempt towards the structuring of a coherent philosophy.

Shankara's genius lay in building a complete and original philosophical edifice upon the foundational wisdom of the Upanishads. This philosophy validated what the Upanishads alluded to, but going far beyond, provided an entire system of intellectual enquiry and analysis. In this pursuit, he was the quintessential *paramarthachintakah*, one who wished to search for the ultimate truths behind the mysteries of the universe, and not just a *srishtichintakah*, one whose concerns are restricted to explicating the empirical world.

Thus, Shankara's was not an act of reiteration only. His originality lay less in his unflinching belief in the truths of the Upanishads, but in the system of thought he devised to support his belief. 'With great ingenuity, remorseless logic, obvious sincerity, profound conviction and deep learning.....Shankara unfolded the teachings of (the Upanishads) and the *Vedanta Sutras* as he understood them.' In doing so, he developed 'independently a really remarkable "system" of idealistic philosophy and an unflinching monistic metaphysics, both of which are characteristically Shankara's own.'[1]

The most audacious part—and the lynchpin—of his philosophy was the conceptualisation of Brahman as the all-pervasive and only absolute force permeating the universe. For Shankara, Brahman is *urja* or infinite energy, pure consciousness, and unsullied awareness. It is intelligence personified—as can be inferred by the verifiable order in the universe, both at the micro and macro level. In fact, Shankara says that intelligence is Brahman's exclusive nature as saltiness is the unmistakable characteristic of a lump of salt.

The embodiment of perfect knowledge, Brahman is beyond knowledge, the knower or the known. It has no beginning, for

1 P.D. Devanandan, *The Concept of Maya*, Y.M.C.A Publishing House, 1954, p. 91.

it is eternal; it has no cause, for it is beyond the categories of time, space and causality; it has no end, for it always was and will always be. Its powers are unlimited; it is omnipotent and omniscient, a singular, indivisible fullness — *purna*—and universal force—*ekam eka sarvavyapi.*

A key aspect of Brahman is that it's completely transcendent. Does an intelligent force have to have a purpose? And, if so, does that purpose have to conform to conventional human comprehension? Can its purpose be judged by a goal that we believe is right, even if we accept that there is a notion of right in an absolute sense that has universal acceptance in our everyday, human life?

Everything in the cosmos is an emanation of Brahman, but it is beyond all activity and purpose as per our finite ways of thinking. Unchanging, it has no need to evolve or develop, grow or diminish. In its passivity, it's potentiality itself; in its aloofness, it's omnipotent; in its apparent purposelessness, it's infinite intelligence; and, in its indefinability, it's definitiveness itself. It is. Nothing without it is. And yet, in its undifferentiated fullness, it's path is supremely overarching, beyond all compulsions of choice or will. Like the sun, it continues to shine even if there were no object to be illumined. Its uniformity (*ekarasa*) has no parts; its identity is division-less (*akhanda*). In this sense, it is self-luminous, without the need of predication, conditionality or qualification. In Shankara's words, Brahman is 'eternally pure, intelligent and free, never changing, one only, not in contact with anything, and devoid of form.'[2]

Shankara endorses the Upanishadic injunction that Brahman is inexpressible. Any attempt to define it would circumscribe its infinitude. Neti, neti—not this, not this, is the best way to approach it, because, in this very negation is the assertion of its unlimited positivity. Shankara explains that it is,

> not a thing in the empirical sense which we may indicate by words; nor is it an object like a cow which can be known by

2 *Shankara Bhashya* on the *Brahman Sutra.*

> the ordinary means of knowledge. It cannot even be described by its generic properties or specific marks; we cannot say that it acts in this or that manner, since it is always known to be actionless. It cannot, therefore, be positively described.[3]

But while Brahman is nirguna or attribute-less, it is not a void, or an indeterminate diffusion. This is where Shankara veers away definitively from the *shunyavada* of Buddhism which concludes that the ultimate truth is a void. Neti, neti, or not this, not this, implies not that Brahman is to be perceived negatively, but indicates a reluctance to dilute the infinity of Brahman through definitions conceived by the human mind. In fact, Shankara is quite sharply critical of those who would want to interpret Brahman in negative terms. In his bhashya on the *Vedanta Sutras,* he says: 'Brahman, transcending space, attributes, motion, fruition and difference, which is Being in the highest sense, without a second, appears to the slow of mind no more than non-being.'

He reiterates this in his commentary on the *Mandukya Upanishad*:

> No, Brahman is not a void, never a non-entity. Brahman always underlies the changes and sustains them. All manifestations come out from that underlying sustaining ground. The ground that gives support to these changes and constantly sustains them cannot prove to be a mere void or non-entity. If the sustaining ground is held to be a non-entity—nothing—then, can mere 'nothing' give birth to the positive things of the world?[4]

---

3 ibid. Quoted by S. Radhakrishnan, *Indian Philosophy,* Vol 2, OUP, 1923, p. 450.

4 See Kokileshwar Shastri, *An Introduction to Adwaita Philsophy*, University of Calcutta, 1926, pp. 15-16.

Quite to the contrary, therefore, Shankara's Brahman is positivity itself, pure being, characterised by existence (sat), consciousness *chitta* and bliss (ananda): satchittananda. To some this may appear contradictory. If, on the one hand, you say that Brahman is inexpressible and indefinable, how can you then ascribe to it such expressly defined features? Shankara gives a twofold answer. Firstly, these features are *inferred* from what Brahman is not. It is not non-existent, so it is sat, existence par excellence, unchanging through all the *kalas* (periods of time); it is not devoid of consciousness, so it is chitta, pure consciousness, the nature of absolute knowledge; and, it is not of the nature of distress, so it is ananda, bliss supreme, the nature of absolute happiness. Secondly, the being of Brahman is experiential, not intellectual. The cognitive process, where the mind intervenes, can teach us intellectually about Brahman, but cannot provide the sublime experiential moment, where thought ceases and intuition takes over. We shall discuss this process in greater detail later, but suffice it to say at this stage that for Shankara, Brahman was absolute plenitude, a fullness that, once experienced, leaves an individual in no doubt about the certainty of its being.

Having posited the absolute immanence of Brahman as the only real in the universe, Shankara asserted that Brahman and Atman are the same. Human beings, who have the faculty of reflection and will, are more than the sum of their body and mind. There is in each of us an observer—*sakshin*—who stands apart from the incessant but transient preoccupations of the mind. This witnessing consciousness is above the sensory perceptions that govern our body. It may become dormant, or even ignored, in the perennial agitations of everyday life, but it exists in each of us as a focus of awareness (chitta shakti), only waiting to be discovered.

Matter and consciousness, says Shankara, are two separate realities. The first is the object, the second the subject. A subject and an object can never be the same. This subject in all of us is the Atman. The mind is in flux, our senses are volatile, and our body mutates, but the Atman is the changeless, all-knowing consciousness—*sarvapratyayadarshin*.

While the entire universe is an emanation of Brahman, Atman and Brahman are identical. Both are the substance of pure consciousness. One exists at the individual level, the other at the cosmic, but they are of each other, two sides of the same coin. When we peel away the empirically manifest—mind, body and senses—what is left is *nirvisheshachinmatram*—undifferentiated consciousness that is the characteristic of both Brahman and Atman. The objective and the subjective then become the same. *Atma cha brahm*—Atman is Brahman—says the Upanishads. We, at the level of consciousness are that, in conformity with the Upanishadic injunction—Tat tvam asi—That thou art. The same thought is mirrored in another mahavakya or 'great sentence' of the Upanishads: Aham brahm asmi—I am Brahman.

But, if there is one, unchanging, eternal and all-pervasive consciousness and nothing else, both at the cosmic level and hidden away in our individual selves, what is this visible, pulsating plurality of the universe? If the real admits of no other to it, and permeates everything that exists, why do we have a derogation of that consciousness in our lives, and in the myriad aspects of the universe around us? Why do infinitude and finitude co-exist? Does the former dilute itself in creating the latter, or does the latter irrevocably change the former? If Brahman is indivisible, and beyond all mutation, how do we account for so many manifestations of that indivisibility? If the cause is beyond activity and completely self-sufficient, needing nothing beyond it, how do we see it giving rise to so many effects? If Brahman is all that exists, admitting of no duality, how do we explain the multiplicity of the universe? Is Brahman then but a notion, merely an intellectual construct, and the world the reality we cannot escape? Or, is the world an illusion, a cosmic sleight-of-hand, and Brahman and Atman the only reality?

Shankara's answer to this conundrum is to audaciously assert that this phenomenal world is real at one level, but Brahman is the only reality at the ontological level. In the midst of this bewildering plurality, Brahman continues to remain unchanging and eternal, immanent in everything, a witness to the empirical multiplicity, but completely untouched or modified by it. Brahman, as the cause of all that is, ever was and ever will be, is present in the effect. But, in the dialectic between cause and effect, the latter is completely subsumed by the former, while the cause remains unaffected by the effect. The one remains the one, while the many proliferate as its reflection, as it were, without changing the essential nature of that one.

He explicates this by his theory of causation. The essential feature (svabhava) of the universal cause remains unchanged; the effect is only a transient condition (*avastha* or vishesha). Between cause and effect, there are two possible kinds of transactions. The first is called *parinamvada,* where the cause changes in order to produce the effect. The second is called *vivartavada,* where the effect is produced while the cause itself remains untransformed. Shankara explains the phenomenal world as vivartavada. The effect is neither latent in the cause, nor is its manifestation inevitable, and nor is it distinct from the cause. If inherently latent, it would have a substantive autonomy independent from the cause. If manifestation is inevitable, then it would in no way be dependent on the cause. And, if distinct, then it would create a duality that was completely unacceptable to the monism of Shankara.

For Shankara, Brahman is the cosmic cause from which the transient pluralities of name and form (nama-rupa) emerge, and, into which they lapse. The names and forms can be endless, but the cause is one and unchanging. When a cause creates an effect without effort or volition, and without transforming itself, the causal process is called *nimitta karana*. The relationship between cause and effect has certain features, argues Shankara. Firstly, it is non-reciprocal: the substratum of the phenomenal world is Brahman, while Brahman itself is transcendent of the phenomenal world. Secondly, it is non-dependent: the empirical world visible to our sensory perceptions is dependent on Brahman, while Brahman is independent of them. Thirdly, cause and effect are non-different (*ananya*) and non-separate (*avyatirikta*).

Shankara's essential point is that the distinction between cause and effect is erroneous. Nothing can originate on its own; and so, if the effect has to have a cause, that can only be the cosmic ground or essence represented by Brahman. 'Cause alone is real and change is only phenomenal. The cause only appears to change into effect; what actually changes is the name and form. The clay and the pot have clay for their essence; but there is a change of name and form when the pot is made. Similarly, the space enclosed in the pot may appear to be an effect of infinite space, but it is manifestly one with the cause.'[5] A cloth and the threads woven to make it may appear to be different, but on deeper scrutiny, the cloth is only a different form of the threads. Devdatta (the equivalent of John Smith) remains Devdatta, says Shankara, even if his form changes when he sits or stands. 'A child in the womb is not reckoned as distinct in essence from the child that is born. We should not be misled by the manifestation of that which is latent. We cannot see the pattern of a cloth until it is unrolled. The plant is concealed within the seed....'[6]

The primal cause of all the diversity we see is, thus, Brahman. The phenomenal world is an emanation of it, and together the eternally whole and the infinitely divisible constitute a benevolent identity-in-difference, *tadatmaya*. The difference of the effect

5 Y. Kesava Menon, ibid, p. 57.

6 ibid, p. 59.

with the cause is apparent, but the end product is not entirely illusory like a barren woman's son, or a square circle. The effects, consisting of the vast animate and inanimate forms inhabiting the universe, exist, but only relatively so. Shankara recognises three forms of reality: the extra-empirical (*paramarthik*); the empirical (*vyavaharik*); and, the illusory (*pratibhasika*). From the viewpoint of higher knowledge para vidya, the empirical has no authenticity or ultimate reality. However from the plane of a lower level of knowledge (apara vidya), the empirical cannot be denied. Shankara, therefore, did not dismiss the ordinary world of name and form as entirely illusory, as some of his critics misinterpreted his philosophy to mean. He merely made the fundamental difference between the real and the unreal from an ontological point of view.

Brahman, as the unchanging, indivisible pure consciousness and energy pervading the cosmos, is eternal, and, therefore, the only real; the world of our ordinary cognition, divided into false binaries of subject and object, is transient, and, therefore, even if existent, cannot be real. It is subject to change, decline and decay. It exists but only ephemerally. It originates, subsists, and disintegrates. In a universe that has existed, as modern science now indicates, for close to fourteen billion years, entire galaxies are born and die. Against the canvas of eternal time, their existence is as fragile as bubbles on water or a spark alight but briefly in the dark. Anything as transient cannot be real in an absolute sense. Beneath the near unlimited array of names and form, there has to be another reality, which is subject to neither origination nor eclipse. Nothing that is by definition volatile, or so vulnerable to mutation, or so inherently impermanent, can be the absolute. What is in incorrigible flux, coming into existence only to be extinguished, cannot be eternal. A foundation that is itself perennially unstable cannot uphold the ordered super structure of the universe. Shankara's purpose, thus, is not so much to deny the relative reality of the world in empirical terms as to assert its lack of substance in absolute terms. In his commentary on the *Taittiriya Upanishad*, Shankara succinctly sums it up: 'What is eternal cannot have a beginning and whatever has a beginning is not eternal.'

If the difference between the finite and the infinite is so stark, so unmistakable and crystal clear, why do we mistake one for the other? Shankara's answer is that it is due to *avidya* or nescience. Avidya creates an error of perception that blurs the distinction between the real and the unreal, the eternal and the transient. And to do so, it has, in each of us as human beings, the most responsive ground. To understand why, it is essential to follow Shankara's clinical analysis of what constitutes the individual human being, jiva, and how, by the very nature of our own limitations, *upadhis*, we become so readily the victims of the powers of avidya.

The finite world consists of five basic elements or mahabhutas: akasha or space, air, fire, water and earth. Akasha arises first, and from it, in ascending order, come air, fire, water and earth. Each of these elements has a primary quality associated with it. From akasha arises sound, from air, heat, from water, taste, and from earth, smell. All matter is a combination in varying form of these five elements and the qualities associated with them. Inert or inorganic matter is non-intelligent (*achetana*), serving a secondary purpose (*parartha*). Human beings are different. They have the power to think, reflect, reason and analyse. As compared to gross matter that is non-intelligent and lacks cognitive capacities, or other species that are guided primarily by instinct or biology, human beings have the power of discrimination and understanding, and the capacity to make choices. It is for this reason that the jiva or individual human being is the focus of Shankara's special observation.

In conformity with the findings of many other schools of Indic thought, the jiva is a complex compound. It too is constituted of the five basic elements that account for all animate and inanimate matter. In addition, it has five organs of perception, five of motion, five of breath and, most importantly, mind and intellect. Sight, sound, touch, taste and smell constitute its perceptional apparatus. Their corresponding organs are eyes, ears, skin, tongue and nose. The five organs of motion are those that create speech, plus the hands, the legs, the anus and the genitals. Prana or the act of breathing is a vital function, and consists of five sub-classifications (*prana, apana, udana, samana* and *vyana*).

But, the fundamental distinguishing human feature is mind and intellect, collectively called the *manas*, which interprets and structures what is received through the senses. The manas is located in an internal organ called the *antahkarana*, which has four identifiable segments. When merely an indeterminate cognitive faculty, it is called mind or manas; when that cognitive ability leads to understanding, it is called buddhi or intellect; when, as a consequence of such understanding, it creates self-consciousness, it is ego or ahamkara; and when, beyond the ego, it is in a state of higher concentration or awareness, it is chitta.

Each of the elements that constitute the jiva endow it with powers, many of which are unique; but, equally, each of them act as limitations to its ability to recognise the fundamental principle underlying the plurality of the universe. For instance, our sensory faculties, *indriyas*, are highly advanced, but they cognise objects only as per the categories of perception ordinarily comprehensible to the brain. We see objects when actually modern science reveals that shape and form are delusions of our mind, since all objects in their essence are nothing but a combination of empty space and waves of energy. The confusion with regard to the difference between the transcendental and the empirical is due, in part, to the limitations of our cognitive apparatus. As Dr S. Radhakrishnan says: 'As we perceive by our senses sound and colour, while the reality is mere vibrations, even so we see the variegated universe for the reality of Brahman.'[7]

However, the greatest barrier to our knowing our true self is the mind and the ego. Shankara treats the mind as *sukshma* or subtle matter. Observation shows that it is highly agile, perpetually unstable, constantly transient and congenitally volatile. Like a monkey forever jumping from one branch of a tree to another, it is never still. Like litmus paper, it takes on the colour of a ceaseless series of thoughts and impressions (*vrittis*). Its mode is reactive, completely in the grip of the external, whether objects or happenings. Rarely reflective and always mobile, it is forever a prisoner of memories, wants, and emotions, so prone to modification that thoughts often take birth and die in the same moment. It either lives in the past, or in an imagined future, but almost never at rest in the present. In short, the mind, and under its perennial shadow, the intellect, are powerful cognitive tools but, by their very nature, impulsive, fickle, capricious and unsteady, and thus, easy prey for the powers of avidya.

The ego is the second great obstacle. What is it that makes the ego so completely the central focus of our lives, making us almost oblivious to any other concern? The ego creates in each jiva a false sense of 'I-ness' that forms a near impenetrable barrier to the understanding of the unitary supremacy of Brahman-Atman. The cosmos, as science is revealing now, is in essence an undivided whole. Every part in it is inter-connected and inter-dependent within the unitary, pervasive energy of Brahman. And yet, the ego gives to each of us a sense of separateness. The universe then shrinks to a delusionary subjectivity, whose principal consequence is to foster the absurd notion that we, at our individual levels, are the prime movers of the world (karta), when actually we are only the agents of existence (*bhokta*). Existence then splits up into the artificial binary of a permanent subject and object. The limitless

7 S. Radhakrishnan, ibid, p. 536.

objective is reduced to the limited subject. With this I-ness comes the baggage of an entire range of emotions: want, desires, pride, ambition, joy, grief, envy, anger, pain, joy and hate. These emotions when added to our belief in a separate 'I' then become the limits of our make-believe world.

The manner in which we acquire this I-ness is worth observation. A newborn child has no sense of ego. But soon enough, he acquires a name or identity, a context of family and address, and the original innocence is lost. We become prisoners of our own simulated construct. This stubborn insularity obliterates all sense of reason or objectivity. Everything is seen from the prism of our notion of self. We forget that an inherent fragility beyond our capacities underlies our puny lives at the finite level. After all, a person, who is completely defined by his ego, can die tomorrow, given the fragility and uncertainty that governs our finite lives. Like a frog in the mouth of a serpent trying to catch an insect, we act as though we shall always be. The ego creates the illusion of self-centred permanence that, in reality, is inherently ephemeral. Moreover, when juxtaposed to the infinite canvas of time and space, how can an individual believe that he or she is the karta, or the prime mover, when his own existence is more fleeting than the blinking of an eyelid?

The limitations of our sensory perceptions, the instability of our mind, and the false sense of ego that becomes a permanent adjunct to our lives, cumulatively create a jiva that revels in its own finitude oblivious to its real nature. The power of avidya becomes entrenched in direct proportion to the vulnerabilities of the jiva. It is for this reason that Shankara calls avidya natural (*naisargika*), eternal (*anant*) and beginning-less (*anadi*). Avidya is able to effortlessly make us devalue the real, while giving the unreal primacy. This error of perception (*dosha*), in which value is mistakenly attributed to something that is devoid of it, is called *adhyasha*, and it operates in a two-fold manner. Firstly, avidya has the ability to mask the truth of things (*avarana*), and secondly to misrepresent them (*vikshepa*). In this way, a veil of distortion hides the true nature of reality (*vastusvarupam*).

Avarana hides the pervasive reality of Brahman; vikshepa misrepresents it by making us believe that only the passing phenomenon of the world is real. As a result, the silent sakshin or observer within each of us becomes dormant, and the presence of the Atman is marginalised. It is important to remember that the finite jiva and the infinite Atman are not two separate entities. Atman-Brahman permeates all, but through the operation of avidya, the jiva becomes a reflection of the Atman in the shackles of finitude. Like the sword in a scabbard, the pure consciousness of the Atman is, to use Shankara's analogy, sheathed in ignorance. The self-limiting adjuncts or upadhis of our psychic apparatus hide the absolute from our reflective consciousness (*upadhi parichinna*). We are overwhelmed by the transient effects, and lose sight of the unchanging cause. We mistake chaitanya or pure consciousness for the transient plurality of the world. While Brahman is the original and permanent point (*bimba*), and the world only its reflection (*pratibimba*), we begin to see the reflection as the reality that defines our lives. As Shankara writes: 'The whole empirical reality, with its names and forms, which can be defined neither as being nor as non-being, rests upon avidya; while in the sense of highest reality, Being persists, without change or transformation.' [8]

Shankara's assertion that the world appearance (*jagat prapancha*) is neither being nor non-being makes a significant point. From the standpoint of Brahman, it is not, and can never be (*asat*); but from the distortion created by avidya, it is, and must always appear to be (*sat*). How do we explain this conundrum where both sat and asat have different validities? Shankara gives several analogies to do so. The most famous of these is that of the rope and the snake: the rope is the reality, but we mistake it to be a snake. Similarly, a piece of shell is mistaken to be silver; a crystal appears to be red

8 *Shankara Bhashya*, cited in S. Radhakrishnan, ibid. p. 540.

in colour due to a red flower near it; a straight stick appears to be bent in water; a mirage in the desert appears to be real; and the sky, although colourless, appears to be blue. All of these are due to an error of perception creating false knowledge (*mithyasvarupah*).

The significant point, though, is that while the error lasts, the snake does exist in the mind of the perceiver, as does the silver, the red crystal, the bent stick, the mirage, and the blue sky. The distortion is manifest, but the perception until corrected is not non-existent. It is precisely in this way that the empirical world of our daily experience exists, and is assumed to be the only reality, but the moment it is tested against the higher reality represented by Brahman, the error in perception ends. Thus Shankara's intention is not to assert that avidya creates an entirely non-existent world. Such a world does exist, but only for so long as we do not remove the veil of avidya. His purpose is not so much to negate the world of sense-experience as to reinterpret it. 'What is actual has certainly no independent existence, yet it has existence: it is unreal only if we mistakenly attribute independence to it. The world is unreal but not illusory.' [9]

Given the omnipotence of Brahman, it must require a force of considerable power to mask its manifest reality. Avidya, at the individual level, is maya at the cosmic level, and both together, do, indeed, possess this kind of power. Since Brahman is the only reality, and has no second, maya and avidya cannot but be a part of it. In fact, Shankara regards maya—that mysterious but cosmic veil of illusion—as the *bija* shakti—the seed power—of Brahman. It is Brahman that empowers this creative power, much like a spider weaves a web from its own body. The ground for the distortion created by maya remains Brahman. 'Even when a snake, a silver, a mirage appears to arise, all these appearances are invariably found to be supported, in each case, by a sustaining ground on which they appear, viz., a rope, a shell, and the surface

9 P.D. Devanandan, ibid, p. 110.

of a desert, unsupported by which these appearances cannot for a moment stand.' [10]

If Brahman and Atman, and maya and avidya, are essentially the same, and represent no duality, how do we explain the need for the empirical world, where the real and the unreal are seemingly coterminous? Shankara's candid answer is that it is inexplicable and indefinable: *anirvachaniya*. Ignorance exists. So does perfect knowledge. The eternal exists. But so does the transient. The one is never changing. Yet, it countenances ceaseless flux. That which is beyond all time and cause and beyond purpose, co-exists with causal time, and finitude. What then is the mysterious relationship between Brahman and maya, the progenitor of avidya?

The relationship is inexplicable precisely because it cannot be explained logically. Shankara analyses the different possibilities that could explain this phenomena but finds them untenable:

> To say that the infinite Brahman is the cause of the finite world and creates it, is to admit that the infinite is subject to the limitation of time. The relation of cause and effect cannot be applied to the relation of Brahman and the world, since cause has meaning only in relation to the finite modes of being where there is succession. We cannot say that Brahman is the cause and the world is the effect, for this would be to distinguish Brahman from the world and make it into a thing related to another thing. Again, the world is finite and conditioned, and how can the infinite unconditioned be its cause? If the finite is the limited and the transitory, then the infinite, as the limit of the finite, is

10 *Shankara Bhashya,* quoted in Kokileshwar Shastri, p. 16, ibid.

> itself finite and not infinite. It is difficult to conceive how the infinite comes out of itself into the finite. Does the infinite come out a particular instant of time under the necessity to become finite?[11]

Shankara admits that he has no clear-cut answer. On one basic point, however, he remains inflexible. Maya and avidya may exist, but their existence does not in any way change the unchanging Brahman-Atman. He explains it further as follows:

> All our experiences are various, successive and they change their aspect always. But underlying these changing experiences and unaffected by them, there is our true Self which experiences them as they arise. This Self is the sustaining ground of all our experiences, in the absence of which the latter cannot stand and operate. The experiences are successive, multiple in their nature and transitory. But the underlying Self which lives in them and sustains them is a unity and maintains its identity unaffected by these changing experiences. Our Self is in touch with the transcendental Brahman, which is our real Self....Brahman is regarded in the Vedanta as perpetually present and operative, as an inexhaustible source, behind the changes or transformations evolving from it. It is thus intimately related to the nama-rupas, the vikaras or changes, as their ever present ground and controller.[12]

Thus, the unchanging Brahman produces the world or *vyapara* of Maya, just as in Shankara's analogy, a conjuror creates an illusion while remaining himself unaffected by that illusion. Or, as a magnet, changes the properties of iron with which it comes into contact

---

11 S. Radhakrishnan, ibid., pp. 528-529.
12 Kokileshwar Shastri, ibid., pp. 16-17.

while remaining immutable itself. Maya, and the relative reality it projects, are an overflow of the boundless energy of Brahman. It is Brahman at play (leela), without cause and without purpose. There is no reason for the magician to enact a trick; and yet, he does so, in a spontaneous duet with maya. Such apparent contradictions abound—and not without purpose—in Hindu mythology.

We see this most spectacularly in the persona of Krishna, the ever-alluring Blue God. In the dance of the rasa, Krishna frolics with uninhibited abandon with the gopis in Vrindavana, and is said to have 16,000 wives, while simultaneously being eternally celibate! He is omnipotent, and yet, as a child, he steals butter and is punished for it by his mother. The universe is at his command, and still he accepts the subordinate role in the Mahabharata of being Arjuna's charioteer. In reality, Krishna does nothing at all, being completely above the fray, only indulging in sport. The sublime and the ridiculous, the sacred and the profane, coexist in Hindu imagination precisely to emphasise their difference, and where necessary, to stress their identity. Without diluting fundamental tenets, other categories are never impervious to creative categorisations.

There is also the theory that Shankara was influenced by the tantric notion of female primacy, embodied in the force of Shakti, and as we have noted (and will discuss further), all the mathas he set up are called 'Shakti Peeths'. Maya, although inseparable from Brahman, symbolises shakti, the creative energy represented by the goddess. For instance, in the *Ananda Lahiri*:

> Shankara addresses Maya as the supreme queen (first among many) of the Para-Brahman (*tvamai para Brahman mahishi*). She is also called Lakshmi. She says of herself: "That which exists in Brahman as the 'I', the ancient 'I-ness', that am I. He who is the inner soul of all beings becoming 'I' is remembered as the Hari. I am, therefore, that ancient 'I-ness' of all beings……God Narayana exists and

> I, Lakshmi, and His highest Idea, and the meaning of 'I' becomes accomplished when it is united with I-ness. That which takes rise from the idea of 'I' is known as I-ness. I do not exist without Him, nor He without me. We both exist together, depending upon each other. Know, therefore, that the relation between me and the Lord is that of substance and quality. Without I-ness, the 'I' deprived of its expression becomes meaningless; and without the idea of the 'I' the I-ness, losing its support becomes meaningless."[13]

The powers Shankara invested in maya also gave him the reason to accept, at the vyavaharik or practical level, a personal theism embodied in the form of Ishwara. For a person, who so inflexibly believed in the non-duality of Brahman-Atman, this was metaphysically a remarkable sleight-of-hand. But Shankara could do so in a manner consistent with his own reasoning, and without deviating from his essential and uncompromising fidelity to Brahman.

As has been mentioned, Shankara recognised two kinds of knowledge: para vidya or higher knowledge, and apara vidya or knowledge of a lower order. These two levels coincided with his dual levels of reality, one paramarthik or transcendental, and the other vyavaharik or practical. Now, if the indefinable maya had the powers to create the relative reality of the empirical world, it also could, create, at the vyavaharik level, an Ishwara or God as its efficient cause. Shankara's own concern was not with godhood but with the difference between the real and the unreal. However, once he conceded that Brahman, the only real, could, through the cosmic illusionary powers of maya, create the impression of a world that appeared real, there was no contradiction in accepting, within the parameters of apara vidya, a personal God, Ishwara, who is Brahman at the level of the phenomenal universe, and

13 P.D. Devanandan, ibid., p. 107.

presiding deity in the transient world of name and form created by maya. If Brahman is without attributes, nirguna, Ishwara is saguna, with all the attributes that allow for personal worship. The jiva or individual becomes the worshipper and the doer (karta), while Ishwara is the worshipped. However both Ishwara and maya are not non-different from Brahman, but operating through maya; Brahman creates Ishwara, and while operating through avidya, Brahman creates the individual jiva.

There are scholars (Hermann Jacobi, V.S. Sukhtankar) who felt that Shankara's somewhat convoluted attempt to assert the one and only reality of Brahman while accommodating the relative reality of the phenomenal world is unconvincing. Their view is that *mayavada*, where maya accounts for the world at the phenomenal level, is but an adaptation of the Buddhist concepts of vijnanavada or shunyavada, wherein the external world did not exist, or was nothing but an empty void. It is true that Shankara learnt at the feet of Govindapada, whose father, Gaudapada, wrote the *Karikas*, a seminal commentary on the *Mandukya Upanishad*. Quite obviously, Gaudapada, influenced by the predominant Buddhist scholars, Ashvaghosha, Nagarjuna, Asanga and Vasubandhu, came perilously close to endorsing the view that the world was entirely an illusion. Brahman is the only reality, argued Gaudapada—unseen (*adrishta*), unrelated (*avyavaharyam*), ungraspable (*agrahyam*), unthinkable (*achintyam*) and unspeakable (*avyapadesya*). The rest is all illusion. In fact, going further, and in a vein similar to the shunyavadins, he even seemed to negate individual consciousness:

> Therefore the idea (chitta) does not originate, nor does the object of the idea originate; those who pretend to recognise the originating of ideas may as well recognize the trace (of birds) in the air. [14]

It is more than probable that Shankara internalised at least some of

14 Gaudapada, *Karikas* (verse iv, 28), see, P.D. Devanandan, ibid., p. 88.

this extreme monism. That alone can account for his famous lines:

> *Shlokardhena pravakshyami yad uktham granthkotibhi*
> *Brahma satyam jagan mithya jivo Brahmaiva naparah*
>
> (In half a stanza, I will explain the meaning of a crore of texts; Brahman is real, the universe an illusion, Brahman and jiva are inseparable.)

Even so, it is equally true that Shankara had reservations in dismissing the world as completely illusory. He needed to rescue his interpretation of Advaita from the nihilism of Buddhist scholasticism, and, indeed, from Gaudapada himself. Hence his theory of mayavada, while Brahman is the only reality. The genius of Shankaracharya was that he was willing to assert certitude where he felt he could; but, he was also carefully ambivalent about matters to which he felt there can be no definitive answer. His certitude about Brahman is coterminous with his deliberate ambivalence with regard to the relation of Brahman to Maya. That relation he grants is indefinable: anirvachaniya.

He can explain why the vulnerabilities of the individual, especially with regard to the limitations of sensory faculties and the illusions created by the mind and ego, allow for the operation of avidya. But he admits that why this should happen in the first place when Brahman is omnipotent, is inexplicable. In other words, he was not willing to weaken his principal argument by being dogmatic about the total non-existence of the phenomenon we see around us. In fact, this strategic ambivalence is precisely the reason why his principal certitude about Brahman remains logically consistent even today.

However powerful maya may be, can we, as individuals, pierce through its veil of illusion, and realise the difference between the real and the unreal? Shankara's categorical answer is: yes. Brahma jnana, or abiding knowledge of Brahman, is possible, but it requires, firstly, a sincere effort to acquire it. Knowledge is the corrosive that melts the veil, removes the error of perception, and dissolves the avidya engulfing us. This knowledge can be gained by a deep study of the foundational texts, including above all the Upanishads, the *Brahma Sutra*, and the commentaries on them (*sravana*), followed by reflection (*manana*) and meditation (*nididhyasana*). In this process, the presence of an enlightened teacher or guru is of pivotal importance because it is he who helps the pupil to successfully navigate the path towards right knowledge. In his evocative stotra, in tribute to the guru, Shankara says:

> Though the lore of the Vedas take up its dwelling on your tongue,
>
> Though you be learned in scripture, gifted in writing prose and verse,
>
> Yet if the mind be not absorbed in the Guru's lotus feet
> What will it all avail you? What, indeed, will it all avail?

The right guru gives soul and depth to knowledge, for mechanical knowledge is not enough; knowledge must lead to understanding, understanding to contemplation, and contemplation to the wisdom to differentiate between the eternal and the ephemeral—*nitya-anitya viveka*. One of Shankara's most quoted aphorisms is: *Satyam jnanam, anantam brahma*: Knowledge is truth, Brahman is eternal.

And yet, knowledge has its limitations. The intellect is finite even when it seeks to know the infinite. The acquisition of knowledge equips the individual but within the boundaries of the intellect. As Dr Radhakrishnan quips, 'the highest intelligence consists in the knowledge that intelligence is not enough.'[15] Logical learning or *paroksha jnana* needs the catapult to put us in the orbit of the actual experience of what is learnt, *aparoksha jnana*. A quantum leap has to be made, beyond knowledge to insight. Shankara calls that insight *brahmanubhava*, the experience of Brahman. This is that explosive moment when knowledge is instantly transformed into intuitional consciousness. Shankara described intuition as that one infallible step which lies beyond reason.

> There exists a function of our faculty of knowing which we feel is more penetrating, less mediated, more satisfactory than the ordinary operations of the mind. We call this intuition, insight, and at times experience.[16]

He believed that a glimpse of the real beyond the veil of maya can happen in that split second of intuitive insight, when suddenly that which we conventionally take to be real is seen as false, and the real, which may have receded from our consciousness, abruptly embraces us in a certitude that is incapable of contradiction—*abadha*. This intuitive moment, according to Shankara,

> is not capable of production like a jug from clay, nor is it brought about through mortification, like curds from milk; nor is it capable of being reached, like a home by a traveller; nor is it to be attained through mere internal purification, like the cleaning of a soiled mirror. It is an indefinable, inexpressible intuition that one is Brahma.[17]

Thus, brahmanubhava happens when intelligence pole-vaults beyond its own horizons. This can happen to anyone at any time.

---

15 S. Radhakrisnan, ibid., p. 584.

16 Richard De Smet, (Edited by Ivo Coelho), *Understanding Shankara*, Motilal Banarsidass, Delhi, 2013, pp. 211-212.

17 Y. Keshava Menon, ibid., p. 131.

It requires merely a turn of the antenna within us to vibrate to the cosmic energy that is Brahman. Shankara is clear that knowledge is not a precondition for this cataclysmic moment. However, the acquisition of knowledge can help, as can several other preparatory steps. As we have discussed earlier, the ceaseless volatility of the mind, and the illusions of I-ness created by the ego, are major stumbling blocks to a realisation of our true selves. Any activity, therefore, that helps to still the mind and dilute the ego is beneficial. In this context, Shankara accepts the utility of Yoga, both for its physical exercises, and for the training of the mind. Apart from asana or postures and breathing or pranayama, the self-restraining disciplines of yama and niyama, and the mind-control steps—pratyahara or withdrawing the mind from the senses, dharana or steadying the mind, dhyana or focussed contemplation, and samadhi or deep meditation—have his approval.

The well known author, Eckhart Tolle and philosopher-writer J. Krishnamurti have also spoken of ceaselessly observing the mind in a non-judgemental manner, and believe that this process helps in equanimity. The mind, and its incessant noise, must be first observed and devalued, before it is elevated. Only when we remove the mind from its conventional rut of routine emotions, like want, fear, insecurity, anger, envy, gratification and pain, that it acquires the pellucid stillness to be able to get a fleeting glimpse of the bliss associated with Brahman. This is what Shankara calls the *lakshanas*, which only a still mind has the ability to perceive.

Equally important is to adopt those behavioural practices that are conducive to mental serenity. Shankara recommends overcoming emotions like hatred, envy, want and greed, and commends those that foster tranquility (*sama*), restraint (*dama*), renunciation (*uparati*) and resignation (*titiksha*), precisely because the latter lead to more stable mental equilibrium.

The uncontrolled mind works to reinforce the ego. In fact, the mind and the ego are inextricably linked, both feeding off each other. If the inherent restlessness of the mind is difficult to control, loosening the hold of the ego is an even more intractable challenge. When the sense of I-ness is strong, the Atman becomes dormant. As Shankara writes in the *Upadeshasahasri*:

> When and to whomsoever the notion of the personal ego conveyed by "I" (aham) and the notion of personal possession conveyed by "mine" (*mamah*) cease to be real, then he is the knower of Atman.[18]

Thus, an important preparatory step to internalise Brahman jnana is to marginalise the ego, and reduce the self-centeredness and separateness it nurtures. Nishkama karma, or action without obsession about the reward, is one way to reduce the ego, and Shankara's commentary on the *Bhagavad Gita* clearly brings this out. The moment this is practiced, we become free of the sterile obsession with the ego, and floating lightly, acquire a state of mind that is open to a glimpse of that oneness where all human divisions disappear leaving us at one with the one.

Another antidote to the ego, says Shankara, is the inculcation of surrender or *atma samarpana*. When a person dissolves his conviction that he is the prime mover or karta of the universe, and surrenders his personal will to the intelligence and benevolence of a higher power, the stranglehold of the ego loosens. Ideally, this surrender should be at the altar of Brahman, the all-powerful repository of intelligence. But since Brahman, in its attribute-less form as pure energy, is difficult to identify with, especially for those who are but beginning the spiritual quest, Shankara has no objection to the mood of devotion engendered by personal theism.

Shankara effortlessly lived this dichotomy. His belief in the formless Brahman was unflinching; but his acceptance, at the vyavaharik or practical level, of devotion to a personal deity was

18 From the *Upadeshasahasri*, quoted by S. Radhakrishnan, ibid., p. 584.

deeply evocative. In fact, he has penned some of the most moving stotras in Hinduism. In praise of Vishnu, he writes:

> Save me from pride, O Vishnu! Curb my restless mind
> Still my thirst for the waters of this world's mirage
> Be gracious, Lord! To this thy humble creature
> And rescue him from the ocean of the world.

His bhakti for Shiva is unstinting:

> Him do I worship, the Param Atman,
> One and without second
> Who is the Cause of the Universe
> The Primal, Spirit formless and actionless
> Who is attained through the syllable Om
> Him do I worship
> Shiv, of whom the universe is born
> By whom it is sustained
> In whom it merges!

Several of his devotional stotras are for Devi, the Mother Goddess, the embodiment of power or shakti:

> No father have I, no mother, no comrade
> No son, no daughter, no wife, and no grandchild
> No servant or master, no wisdom, no calling:
> In thee is my only haven of refuge
> In thee, my help and my refuge, O Bhavani!

His devotional canvas includes a beautiful stotra in tribute to the river Ganga or Bhagwati, as Shankara addresses her:

> Banish O Bhagwati! All my illness;
> Take away my troubles, my sins and my grief;

Utterly crush my wanton cravings,
Goddess, supreme in all the worlds!
Thou, Mother Earth's most precious necklace!
Thou are my refuge here in this world!

If Shankara's depiction of Brahman is austerely majestic, his devotional outpouring is extravagantly lyrical. It almost appears that for delineating Brahman, he has used to the maximum the resources of intellectual rigour, while for his devotional stotras, he has allowed his heart to sing in abandon. The common thread in each of his hymns is the need for total surrender to Ishwara as embodied in a particular deity. In this surrender lies redemption. When a person has discarded his sense of self-importance in the presence of a higher force, and overcome the agitations of the mind in the bathos of devotional fervour, he is porous to divine grace. In such a state, intellectual learning (*panditYam*) gives way to a childlike simplicity *(balyam*), and there occurs a purification of the heart (*chittashuddi*). This is precisely the state when one is most open to the possibility of the intuitional cognisance of Brahman.

Shankara's primary concern however was brahmanubhava, where the individual realises his true self, and sees through the transient seductions of the ephemeral world. Knowledge, Yoga, meditation, bhakti, surrender, and an intense desire for salvation (*mumuksutva*) are, for him, efficacious tools in this endeavour. They create, as Shankara says in the *Atmabodha*, the polished surface within the individual which best enables the reflection of the Atman. He is not convinced, though, about action or karma as an end in itself. It was on this point that he disagreed with the mimamshakas, who gave disproportionate importance to Vedic ritualism.

Actions, in accordance with prescribed practice, may not be lacking in piety, and could, if carried out with detachment and a sense of duty, create a conducive mood for higher spiritual insight; but mostly, their primary aim is to obtain some object or goal within the actual world of samsara—*abhyudaya*—and not *nihshreyasa* or salvation. Action without thought of reward—nishkama karma—is the ideal way to negotiate the daily requirements of life. But action with the sole purpose of advancement, he believes, leads to greater attachment to reward, and ultimately ensnares the practitioner even more in the many-ness (*nanatvam*) of the material world.

As he writes in his commentary on the *Taittiriya Upanishad*, actions as rituals—even when sanctified by the Vedas—seek either 'production of a new thing (*utpatti*), change of state (*vikara*), consecration (*samskara*) and acquisition (*apti*); moksha is none of these.'[19]

When, through the acquisition of brahmanubhava moksha is achieved, it is of the nature of infinite peace and pure bliss. Nothing changes on the surface, neither the individual nor the material world around him. But everything is transformed within the individual and in his way of interfacing with the world. Moksha does not connote a physical transformation, a reaching somewhere, a heaven apart, or the completion of a certain form of sadhana. It merely and emphatically consists of a revolutionary transformation in our way of looking at things, and in that transformation, the priorities of realities change: what we thought was real is revealed to be unreal, and what we took as non-existent is revealed in all splendour as the only real. The world and its flux continue unabated; only we realise their impermanence secure in our oneness with the eternal.

Grace and joy embrace us when we realise that our true self is one with Brahman. Subsumed in that energy, we see the

19 From Shankara's commentary on the *Taittiriya Upanishad*, ii, 11, quoted in S. Radhakrishnan, ibid., p. 587.

inter-connectedness of the universe. Those who identify with this energy, by discarding what is ephemeral, transient and unreal, feel a sense of joy, of serenity and bliss, of being at rest with the cosmic reality that Shankara defines as Brahman. Those who *resist* it, by mistaking the unreal for the real, and consider their puny worlds as the limit of their horizons, remain vulnerable to the emotions of pain, envy, grief, and anger interspersed with moments of fragile happiness.

This bliss is in congruence with the rhythm of the universe, not in illusory and unproductive opposition to it. In its embrace, our sense of separateness evaporates. The barriers between subject and object collapse. The agitations of the mind cease. We live in this world but without being affected by its ups and downs, aware that our true self is transcendent of the transient pluralities created by avidya. The dosha or error in our perception is replaced by a profound insight into the real nature of things. No longer do illusions beguile us—the rope is seen for what it is, and is not mistaken for a snake; the shell may appear as silver, but it no longer fools us; the crystal is seen as white, even though a flower gives it a red tint; the stick is known to be straight, even if the eye sees it bent; and the sky is seen as colourless, even if it appears to be blue. The Atman, ever-present but dormant within us, awakens in a joyous reunion with Brahman.

An important distinction needs to be kept in mind. Brahman is not a promise of joy, like heaven is portrayed as the reward in conventional religions. Brahman *is* joy. Shankara distinguishes between three kinds of ananda or joy. The first is the consequence of the fulfillment of some desire that yields worldly enjoyment, *laukika ananda*. The second is the joy that comes to the one who has acquired the knowledge of Brahman. That is *brahmananda*. And, the third is the bliss of the non-dual nature of Brahman itself. This joy is the highest, beyond all mortal conceptions of joy. When the person seeking moksha goes beyond knowledge to the experience of Brahman,

> he enjoys all desires, all delights procured by desirable

> objects, without exceptions. Does he enjoy sons, heavens, etc, alternately as we do? No, he enjoys all desirable things simultaneously, as amassed together in a single moment, through a single perception, which is eternal like the light of the sun, which is non-different from the essence of Brahman and which we have described as Reality, Knowledge, Infinity....He enjoys all things by that Brahman whose nature is omniscience.[20]

Shankara wanted to portray the immortal peace and fulfillment that descend, like a shower of grace, on he who once experiences Brahman. That experience is liberation or moksha and it is of the essence of Brahman.

> That which is real in the absolute sense, immutable, eternal, all-penetrating like akasha, exempt from change, all satisfying, undivided, whose nature is its own light, in which neither good nor evil, nor effect, nor past nor present nor future has any place, this incorporeal is called liberation.[21]

Shankara indicates a parallel between the experience of Brahman and our cognitive states. Our cognition has three levels of consciousness: the waking state, the dreaming mind, and the stage of deep sleep. When awake, we are aware of the world around us. Our knowledge then is outward knowing (*bahish prajnya*), gross (*sthula*) and universal (*vaishvnara*). The dreaming mind is inward looking (*antah prajnya*) and reflects our subtle body. In deep sleep, our underlying consciousness is undistracted, and we are in touch with the Lord of all (*sarveshvara*), the knower of all

---

20 *Shankara Bhashya* on the *Taittiriya Upanishad*, quoted in Richard De Smet, ibid., p. 344.

21 *Shankara Bhashya*, quoted in S. Radhakrishnan, ibid., p. 593-94.

(*sarvajanya*), the inner controller (*antar-yami*), and the source of all (*yoni sarvasya*). In the waking state, the sense of 'I' is dominant; in the dreaming mind, it is diluted; and, in deep sleep, the mind is closest to the experience of transcendence.

There is a fourth stage, *turiya,* which is even beyond deep sleep. The *Mandukya Upanishad* (verse vii) describes this evocatively:

> Not inwardly cognitive, not outwardly cognitive
> Not a cognition mass, not cognitive, not non-cognitive
> Unseen, with which there can be no dealing
> Ungraspable, having no distinctive mark
> Non-thinkable, that cannot be designated
> The essence of assurance
> Is the state of being one with the Self
> The cessation of development, tranquil, benign
> Without a second
> Such they think is the fourth
> He is the Self (Atman); He should be discerned.[22]

In the state of turiya, insight becomes *amatra*—immeasurable or measureless, equivalent to that which is achieved in samadhi in the Yoga system, and the bliss it confers is same as that of brahmanubhava.

There are, and have been, countless individuals who have described the ecstasy and bliss of being one with the higher energy that is Brahman, and their experience shows how that sudden, intuitional consciousness can awaken in any of us.

Eckhart Tolle is a world-renowned contemporary spiritual thinker living in Canada not aligned with any particular religion or tradition. In his best-selling book, *The Power of Now,* he describes the moment. At that time, Tolle was going through a period of

22 Robert Ernest Hume (trans.), *The 13 Principal Upanishads*, OUP, 1921, pp. 391-393.

deep anxiety bordering on suicidal depression. Everything seemed meaningless to him, and one night he felt a 'deep longing for annihilation, for non-existence.'

> I cannot live with myself any longer. This was the thought that kept repeating itself in my mind. Then suddenly I became aware of what a peculiar thought it was. "Am I one or two? If I cannot live with myself, there must be two of me: the 'I' and the 'self' that 'I' cannot live with.". "Maybe", I thought, "only one of them is real."
>
> I was so stunned by this strange realization that my mind stopped. I was fully conscious, but there were no more thoughts. Then I felt drawn into what seemed like a vortex of energy. It was a slow movement at first and then accelerated. I was gripped by an intense fear, and my body started to shake. I heard the words "resist nothing", as if spoken inside my chest. I could feel myself being sucked into a void. I have no recollection of what happened after that.
>
> I was awakened by the chirping of a bird outside the window. I had never heard such a sound before. My eyes were still closed, and I saw the image of a precious diamond. Yes, if a diamond could make a sound, this is what it would be like. I opened my eyes. The first light of dawn was filtering through the curtains. Without any thought, I felt, I knew, that there is infinitely more to light than we realize. That soft luminosity filtering through the curtains was love itself. Tears came into my eyes. I got up and walked around the room, and yet I knew that I had never truly seen it before. Everything was fresh and pristine, as if it had just come into existence. I picked up things, a pencil, an empty bottle, marveling at the beauty and aliveness of it all.
>
> For the next five months, I lived in a state of uninterrupted

> deep peace and bliss....I understood that the intense pressure of suffering that night must have forced my consciousness to withdraw from its identification with the unhappy and fearful self, which is ultimately a fiction of the mind. This withdrawal must have been so complete that this false, suffering self immediately collapsed, just as if a plug had been pulled out of an inflatable toy. What was left then was my true nature as the ever present *I am:* consciousness in its pure state prior to identification with form. Later I also learned to go into that inner timeless and deathless realm that I had originally perceived as a void and remain fully conscious. I dwelt in states of such indescribable bliss and sacredness that even the original I just described pales into insignificance.[23]

Eckhart Tolle's description of that apocalyptic moment of revelation, and the distinctions he draws between the false 'I' and the self, and between an empty void and the sheer bliss and joy he experienced, is completely Vedantic in tone. Its deeply personal and authentic quality cannot be doubted. The 'indescribable bliss and sacredness' that Tolle experienced, and which remained with him, came suddenly, but transformed his life.

Quite amazingly, Sadhguru Jaggi Vasudev, one of contemporary India's leading spiritual masters, has an almost identical story to tell. As a young man, Sadhguru, who had just fallen out of love, sat on his motorcycle and drove to Chamundi Hills, close to Mysore where he lived. About two-thirds of the way uphill, he took a break and sat on a rock, his 'contemplation rock' as he describes it, and looked down on the city below.

> Until that moment, in my experience, my body and mind

23 Eckhart Tolle, *The Power of Now*, Yogi Impressions, Mumbai, 2001, pp. 1-3.

was "me" and the world was "out there". But suddenly I did not know what was me and what was not me. My eyes were still open. But the air that I was breathing, the rock on which I was sitting, the very atmosphere around, everything had become me. I was everything that was. I was conscious, but I had lost my senses. The discriminatory nature of the senses simply did not exist anymore. The more I say the crazier it will sound because what was happening was indescribable. What was me was literally *everywhere*. Everything was exploding beyond defined boundaries; everything was exploding into everything else. It was a dimensionless unity of absolute perfection.

My life is just that moment, gracefully enduring.

When I returned to my normal senses, it felt as if just ten minutes had elapsed. But a glance at my watch told me that it was seven thirty in the evening! Four and a half hours had passed. My eyes were open, the sun had set, and it was dark. I was fully aware but what I had considered to be myself until that moment had completely disappeared.

I have never been the teary kind. And yet, here I was, at the age of twenty-five, on a rock on Chamundi Hill, so ecstatically crazy that the tears were flowing and my entire shirt was wet!

Being peaceful and happy had never been an issue for me....But here I was exploding into a completely different dimension of existence of which I knew nothing, drenched in a completely new feeling—and exuberance, a blissfulness—that I had never known or imagined possible.[24]

---

24 *Sadhguru, Inner Engineering—A Yogi's Guide to Joy*, Penguin Random House, India, 2016, pp. 8-9.

There are striking commonalities between the separate experiences of Tolle and Sadhguru. To both of them the experience came suddenly, corresponding with Shankara's theory of a sudden intuitional consciousness, beyond the horizons of the intellect. Both of them say that the experience was 'indescribable', again in consonance with Shankara's view that words are not adequate to describe that transformative moment. Both of them talk of a transcendence in which all is perceived to be one and the sense of 'I' is extinguished, in the interconnected pervasiveness of Brahman. And, both speak of a feeling of unsurpassable bliss and ecstasy, which, as Shakara says, is the very essence of Brahman.

Such experiences, perhaps not so well documented, have happened to individuals and sages and mystics, since time immemorial. The well-known saint from Bengal, Swami Ramakrishna Paramahamsa (1836–1886), experienced such blissful trances as a young child. As described by him, his first such experience happened as a young child of six. He was walking along the paddy fields in rural Bengal when he saw a flock of white cranes against the backdrop of dark thunder clouds. Watching this, he suddenly lost outward consciousness and was subsumed by an indescribable joy.

This feeling came to him several times again while still a child, when he was praying, as he has recalled, to the Goddess Vishalakshi, or portraying Shiva in a play on Shivaratri. Such trances of pure bliss became common from his tenth year onwards, and in his later years they occurred almost daily. It is significant that Swami Ramakrishna was a Vedantin, and was taught the basics of Advaita Vedanta by an itinerant monk, Totapuri. Ramakrishna himself acknowledged that the trances he experienced were in the nature of nirvikalpa samadhi, that state of complete oneness with Brahman that Shankara speaks of.

Many more such examples can be given from across religions—Christianity, Buddhism, Islam, Judaism—even Sufism, of individuals who have had blissfully transformative experiences identical to brahmanubhava. What is startling, though, is that accounts of Near-Death Experiences (NDEs), speak of exactly the same sense of joy and bliss.

Anita Moorjani in her bestselling book, *Dying to be Me*, speaks of her near-death due to advanced cancer, and her recollection of that experience. She writes that as she went into a deep coma, akin to death because all her organs had failed, and the doctors had given her but a few hours to live, she felt 'free, liberated and magnificent. Every pain, ache, sadness and sorrow was gone.'

> As my emotions were being drawn away from my surroundings, I started to notice how I was continuing to expand to fill every space, until there was no separation between me and everything else. I encompassed—no *became*—everything and everyone....It was as though I was no longer restricted by the confines of space and time, and continued to spread myself to occupy a greater expanse of consciousness. I felt a sense of freedom and liberation that I'd never experienced in my life before. I can only describe this as the combination of a sense of joy mixed with a generous sprinkling of jubilation and happiness....I felt all my emotional attachments to my loved ones and my surroundings slowly fall away....Love, joy, ecstasy, and awe poured into me, through me, and engulfed me. Although I was no longer using my five physical senses, I had unlimited perception. Time felt different in that realm, too, and I felt all moments at once....And then I was overwhelmed by the realization that God isn't a *being*, but a *state of being..... and I was now that state of being!*....I was transformed in unimaginable clarity as I realized that this expanded, magnificent essence was really me....Nothing interfered with the flow, glory, and amazing beauty of what was taking place....I became aware that we're all connected....I

> realized that the entire universe is alive and infused with consciousness....[25]

After her near-death experience, Anita Moorjani's condition had improved substantially. She was soon released from hospital, and miraculously without a trace of cancer. Her experience of being in a state of pure bliss and luminosity compares with the accounts we have seen of people who experienced it when alive and well. The link between the two sets of experiences—one, without a fatal disease, and the other literally on the other side of life—is that both were of a life-changing intensity, and vividly remembered for the feeling of bliss and wellbeing they conferred. In fact, Anita gives a very apt analogy to describe what she experienced. It seemed as though until she almost died, she had tried to negotiate a huge, dark warehouse with just a flashlight, whereas what she experienced on her deathbed was as if someone had flicked on a switch and there was a sudden burst of brilliance and sound.

The question then arises: what is the relationship with the empirical world for someone who has realised the oneness with Brahman, and experienced the indescribable bliss that comes with this realisation? Is she bound anymore by the norms of society? Do the rules made by human beings, as part of the paraphernalia of conventional life apply at all to the liberated? Can the experience of the transcendent be subjected to censure by the customs and rituals of the transient? Are those who have gone beyond the veil of maya, subject to the worldly regulations it dictates? Once the impermanent world created by nescience is demolished in that one

25 Anita Moorjani, *Dying to be Me*, Hay House Publishers, India, 2012, pp. 62-70.

burst of blissful knowledge, is a person obligated to follow the regulations of that very world that is seen to be unreal?

These questions arise in order to understand Shankara's approach to ethics. There is no doubt that if his own reasoning is taken to its logical conclusion, a person who has understood the sole reality of Brahman, has gone beyond societal norms of conventional rectitude. For such a person, there is, as he himself says so evocatively in the *Nirvana Shatakam* stotra, no *punyam* (virtue) or *papam* (sin), nor is there any more the relevance of the four purusharthas, dharma, artha, kama and moksha. Neither mantra (incantations), nor *tirtham* (pilgrimage), nor the Vedas nor yagnas (rituals) are of any consequence to him. Not even the guru is indispensable then. All that matters is the knowledge and experience of chid, awareness, and ananda, bliss.

Such an approach has attracted criticism from those who believe that Shankara, in his absolutism about the sole reality of Brahman, is indifferent to a definitive moral code of conduct, and unconcerned with the differences between good and evil, right and wrong. Purely from a theoretical interpretation of his philosophy, this inference is not misplaced.

If all that exists is Brahman, then the moral distinctions of the phenomenal world cannot have ultimate sanctity. They are merely the outcome of the human mind, a variable construct of contingent societal beliefs, different for different sets of people, an adjunct of the world of avidya. A moral code of conduct is of little consequence when the empirical world that creates it is itself devalued. Since, for Shankara, the visible empirical world itself exists only transiently under the influence of maya, how can the mores it dictates be binding?

The truth is that, in consonance with the structure of his

philosophy, Shankara's preoccupation was more with spiritual salvation than conventional ethics. However, it would be wrong to assume that he was in some manner a moral anarchist. It is true that he believed that for a person who has achieved moksha by understanding the non-dual reality of Brahman, the ordinary laws of the world are not applicable. But, in so believing, he was not as much decrying the relevance of basic ethical behaviour as he was asserting the transcendence of the liberated state. In many of his writings he emphasises the importance of cultivating such conduct that prepares one for the experience of brahmanubhava. This would include shunning violence, anger, greed, envy, hatred, dishonesty, deceit and other such vices that lead to mental agitation. In contrast, he recommended virtues such as ahimsa, forgiveness, compassion, love, honesty, charity and detachment that lead to the creation of mental equipoise.

For him moral goodness, as normally understood, was not an end in itself, but a means to prepare one for the higher understanding of Brahman. Morality, pursued for rewards in this world, or only to further prescribed ritual or prescriptive behaviour, was not favoured by him since it only reinforced the sense of I-ness that is one of the biggest obstacles to Brahman jnana.

Shankara believed in the path of knowledge as a means of liberation. Knowledge was the launching pad for the moment of intuitional consciousness, brahmanubhava. In such a framework, action, considered morally correct had relevance only to the extent that it furthered the primary goal of the realisation of Brahman. It follows, therefore, that he did not give much importance even to the so-called obligatory duties of varnas (estates) or ashramas (stations) assigned to lay persons by society. But, nor did he consider them irrelevant if pursued, as the *Bhagavad Gita* says, without thought of reward, in a spirit of renunciation, and selflessly.

Additionally, Shankara had another theoretical tool to sanction generally accepted moral practice. As we have discussed, he made the distinction between paramarthik and vyavaharik levels of knowledge. At the practical or vyavaharik level, where the seeker of moksha has still some way to go in acquiring in full measure the knowledge of Brahman, conventional morality in the right spirit of renunciation has a place. But once a person has reached the transcendental or paramarthik level, and has overcome the limitations of the empirical world, he must, naturally, also transcend the compulsions of morality imposed by this empirical world. For one who has achieved moksha, there is no difference between action and non-action. Such a person has surpassed the binaries of right and wrong in the transcendent bliss of liberation. 'The liberated person does not so much become wholly good; he transcends good and evil. He is not under any moral compulsion. Ethical values have ceased to apply to him.'[26]

In short, Shankara was not dogmatic about the rites of morality for the liberated, but he was clear that certain moral practices had an undeniable utilitarian value in the goal of Brahman realisation. For him, this was the only relevant aspect of ethics. As the well-known historian, Dr G.C. Pande says:

> It must not be supposed that the knowledge of Brahma requires the performance of Dharma or that is itself an obligation enjoined by the Veda. Shankara here distinguishes sharply between the life of spiritual freedom or philosophical wisdom, on the one hand, and the practical life of morality and religion on the other.[27]

For those who have achieved this freedom and wisdom, conventional ethics have little meaning; for those who wish to achieve such freedom and wisdom, selfless moral action is a valuable means to that end.

---

26 Y. Keshava Menon, ibid., p. 126.

27 G.C. Pande, *Life and Thought of Shankaracharya*, Motilal Banarsidass, Delhi, 1994, p. 219.

In this sense, Shankara both overarched man-made morality, and gave it due importance. He supported *pravrittilakshana* dharma, or a code of moral behaviour pursued with renunciation, for those on the path to Brahman realisation. He privileged *nivrittilakshana* dharma, the conduct of wisdom and contemplative transcendence for those who had achieved Brahman realisation.

One thing is clear, though. Even for those who have achieved Brahman jnana, Shankara is not against constructive action for the good of society. His own commitment to the setting up of mathas at Sringeri, Dwaraka, Puri, and Joshimatha is proof of this. As one, who had experienced oneness with Brahman, and lived the bliss that it entailed, he could have opted out of the endeavours of the samsaric world, and retired to a life of actionless solitude. But, he chose to work and created institutions for the propagation and preservation of Vedantic philosophy. He made his four principal pupils their heads, and involved himself personally in the organisational structure and curriculum.

While Shankara was committed to the setting up of mathas, he did not consider mendicancy to be compulsory for the spiritual aspirant, nor was he against those who chose to adopt it. In keeping with his metaphysical theory, Brahman jnana could grace anybody at any time in a quantum leap from intellect to intuition. Thus, it was not necessary for a person to renounce life to achieve the knowledge of Brahman. In *Life and Thought of Shankaracharya*, Dr G.C. Pande elaborates on this premise and says:

> For Shankara the essence of sanyasa or parivajya consists in the knowledge of non-duality....The real sanyasin is none other than the really enlightened person who has attained to jnana and naishkarmya...It follows that since even a householder may attain such a knowledge he too would qualify for sanyasa.[28]

28 ibid., p. 247.

Merely the acquisition of the staff or water gourd, considered the conventional symbols of mendicancy, did not make a person a mendicant, or qualify him to become one.

> For Shankara it is only the person with the Vedantic knowledge of unity who may rightly renounce works for mendicancy....In disparaging the obvious insignia of the sanyasin in terms of the staff or water gourd, he actually seeks to identify the sanyasin not with a formally recognized group of persons but with those who have actually attained wisdom or jnana.[29]

However, when it came to his personal choice, Shankara chose mendicancy. He renounced life at a very early age, and against the wishes of his mother, who acquiesced in his decision only once she realised that his mind was entirely made up. The sheer freedom he experienced in a life without material possessions, devoted entirely to knowledge, transcendent of all attachments, and suffused with the bliss of Brahman jnana, comes out beautifully in a short stotra he wrote on the *kaupina* or loin-cloth worn by a mendicant:

> Sitting at the foot of a tree for shelter
> Eating from his hands his meager portion,
> Spurning wealth like a patched up garment
> Blest indeed is the wearer of the loin-cloth.
>
> Chanting Brahma, the word of redemption,
> Meditating only on 'I am Brahma'
> Living on alms and wandering freely
> Blest indeed is the wearer of the loin-cloth.

---

29 ibid., p. 247.

Since Shankara believed that jnana was the most efficacious tool to Brahman realisation, it follows that he did not set much store to the oppressive stranglehold of the caste system. While the caste system judged people on the accident of their birth, the jnana marga judged them on the quality of their knowledge. Both viewpoints were directly antagonistic.

The traditional societal structure sought to restrict access to spiritual knowledge only to the upper castes. Shankara, on the contrary, believed that anybody could attain this knowledge, and in fact, was willing to accept anybody who had this knowledge, as his guru. As we have seen, this was vividly demonstrated in his meeting with a chandala, a person of the lowest caste, in Banaras. The sheer disjoint between his belief that Brahman pervades all, and, the discriminatory social practices of the day, must have struck Shankara, motivating him to unreservedly embrace the chandala, and declare emphatically in his *Manishapanchakam*: 'He who has learnt to look on phenomenon in this non-dual light is my true guru, be he a chandala or a twice-born man. This is my conviction.'

This conviction is reiterated in several of Shankara's writings. The *Nirvana Shatakam* has the line: *Na me mrityu shanka, na me jati bheda.* (I doubt not what death is, nor do I believe in caste discriminations.) In the *Upadeshasahasri,* he explicitly instructs his disciples to give up all connections with caste, and meditate only on the self. Similarly, in his commentary on the *Brihadaranyaka Upanishad*, he bluntly says that a person who identifies himself only with varna or even ashrama or the stages of life, is ignorant, not unlike an animal! Again, in his bhashya on the *Gita*, he ridicules those who believe that the omnipresent Brahman becomes contaminated by dwelling in a chandala. Shankara's essential point is twofold: one, that Brahman makes no distinction between such man-made distinctions, and two, that for the knower of Brahman, such distinctions have no consequence. In the *Shankara Bhashya*, he profiles one who has attained Brahman jnana:

> Who is neither high nor lowly born
> Or is considered erudite, or non-erudite,
> Or is credited with good deeds, or of evil deeds,
> He is veritably a true Brahmin.[30]

The fact that Shankara could adopt such a radical stand in times when caste discriminations were deeply entrenched, should not be underestimated. Most Hindu spiritual thinkers of his time would have sought to seek some intellectual accommodation with the prevailing sentiments relating to the hierarchical structure of Hindu society, if for no other reason than to gain greater acceptance in the more influential segments of that society. That Shankara was willing to risk alienating large sections of conservative Hindu opinion is a tribute to his courage of conviction.

There is a view, however, that, whatever Shankara's thinking may have been at the level of paramarthik satya (ultimate reality), at the vyavaharik level, he 'fought shy of putting his non-dualism in practice because it would have brought about a social revolution and shaken the foundations of the caste system.'[31] Other scholars aver that while Shankara believed that Shudras were equal to others under the indivisible embrace of Brahman, he did not contest the then discriminatory practice of debarring them from studying the Vedas, and only concurred in their acquiring knowledge from the Puranas.

At the philosophical level, Shankara was categorical that social inequality was unacceptable. Indeed, there could be no other inference given the structure of his philosophy, which considered

30 *Yam na santam na casantam, nashrutam na bahushratam, na suvrittam na durvrittam veda kashchit sa Brahmanah.*

31 Kuldeep Kumar, article in *The Hindu*, 11 June 2016.

the empirical world, and all its man-made customs and rituals as but a trick played by maya to hide the non-dual and sole reality of Brahman. If such a world itself was ephemeral, and Brahman recognised no distinctions in its indivisible plenitude, how could humanly ordained inequality have sanctity?

At the same time, the weight of prevalent social thinking could have initially had an influence on Shankara, and, in the beginning of his philosophical journey he may have hesitated to make a frontal attack on the fundamentals of the existing social system. After all, as a child, brought up in a conservative milieu, he would have, initially at least, internalised the inequities of the given social system, especially since, as a Brahmin, he was a beneficiary of that system.

A human being is a product of his times, and cannot be judged in hindsight in absolute terms. Even so, there is no doubt, that Shankara's views, in time, evolved beyond the limitations of his personal experience, and later he was emphatic in his rejection of the caste system. This is clearly brought out in his *Manishapanchakam*, and other writings. The story about his meeting with a chandala in Banaras has to be seen in this context. As Professor G.C. Pande argues, even if historical proof cannot be advanced in support of this incident, 'if the anecdote were unhistorical it would be difficult to explain its fabrication in later times. The very fact that it was accepted even as part of the Shankara legend is not without significance.'[32] In fact, S. Radhakrishnan is clear that, 'Shankara ignored caste distinctions in the monastic order he founded.'[33]

If Shankara's actions were influenced by his ideology, what

32 G.C. Pande, ibid., p. 250.

33 S. Radhakrishnan, ibid., p. 577.

explains his acceptance of tantric beliefs? Many scholars believe that as a Vedantin, he could not have endorsed the ritualistic devotion that tantric practice sanctioned. Others are in no doubt that even as a practitioner of Advaita, he had not only studied tantric thought but was also a deeply committed devotee of shakti, personified as Devi or the cult of the goddess, that is at the heart of most forms of tantric practice.

Certainly, a reading of *Saundarya Lahari*, his emotional ode to the Mother Goddess, leaves one in little doubt about his worship of the female deity, generically described as shakti, but known by many other names, such as Durga, Lakshmi, Saraswati, Kali, Uma, Amba, Gauri and Bhavani.

The *Saundarya Lahari* is not simply a prayer to shakti. It is a passionate outpouring of deep obeisance, with decidedly erotic overtones in the physical description of the goddess. The erotic aspect has led some to question whether Shankara actually authored this work, but the balance of opinion is that he did. How do we reconcile such a work, so transparently physical in its adoration, with the reclusive philosopher who was, in terms of his delineation of Brahman, against both theism and ritualised worship?

The answer probably lies in the philosophical overlap between Advaita and aspects of tantra. Brahman, as we have discussed, is omnipresent formless energy; but, if for human purposes (which Shankara accepts as valid at the vyavaharik level), it is given form, Shiva is chitta, the pure, attribute-less consciousness within all of us, and Shakti is chittarupini, the power inherent in that consciousness. Shakti is nought without Shiva, but equally, Shiva is powerless without Shakti. The two are complementary to the point that they are indistinguishable. They are equal in every respect, be it abode (*adhishtana*), occupation (*anushtana*), condition (*avastha*), form (rupa) and name (nama). Neither can exist without the other, but together they actualise this universe and transcend it. In the very first stanza of the *Saundarya Lahari*, Shankara bows to this union:

> O Bhagwati,
> Only if Shiva is conjoined with You can He create
> Without You, O Shakti, He cannot even move
> O, Mother, Hari, Hara and Brahma worship You
> Only because of my virtuous deeds in the past
> Can I salute You!

In such a conceptualisation, Shiva is Brahman, the unmoving, changeless potentiality, and Shakti is the power latent within him. The analogy of one that is still in perfection and the other that can ruffle that stillness, as part of an integrated cosmic design, is part of the Shiva-Shakti construct. If Shiva is the still waters of the cosmic pool, Shakti is the ripple that emanates from it. That ripple, part of the cosmic unity signified by Brahman, but symbolising the energy within it, is personified for purposes of theism, in the form of the Devi.

As we have discussed, Shankara sanctioned personal theism, at the practical level, as a preparatory step for a sadhaka to inculcate the enabling mood of absolute surrender in the journey towards Brahman jnana. He wrote hymns in praise of many deities, but his personal preference appears to have been the *upasana* or worship of the Mother Goddess. It is significant that the four mathas he established are known as Shakti Peeths, or the abode of the power of the Devi. In Sringeri, the first matha he established, there is a temple dedicated to Devi in her form as Sharada.

> Sharada who represents the saguna form of the Supreme Absolute is the great Matrix of the Universe displaying in Her hands the symbol of the jar of nectar and immortality, a book signifying supreme knowledge, a rosary, the beads of which, signify the subtle aksharas of bijas from which the gross

> forms of the universe emanate, and the Chinmudra standing for the awareness of the Jiva with Brahma. She is the light of all Upanishadic knowledge and as such is Brahmvidya.[34]

The theistic worship of Sharada, as one form of Shakti, is thus not contradictory to the simultaneous assertion of the attribute-less Brahman. However, the tantric aspect of this philosophical co-relation becomes obvious by the fact that Devi Sharada is seated in the Sringeri temple on a replication of the Sri Chakra, which is an explicitly tantric symbol representative of the supreme goddess, Lalita.

The Sri Chakra is a complex geometrical design consisting of a circle with a point, bindu, at the centre, surrounded by nine triangles, four of them with the apex pointing upwards, and five pointing downwards. The multiple intersections of these nine triangles lead to the formation of forty-three further triangles, with the bindu considered the forty-fourth. The circle in which these nine triangles are interlocked is enclosed in two concentric circles, the first with eight lotus petals, and the other with sixteen petals. This entire figure is bounded by a quadrilateral in three parallel lines.

In tantric vidya, the Sri Chakra, which represents the deity in a geometrical design, is considered the highest form of compressed energy. The design is replete with symbolisms. The bindu stands for pure bliss and consciousness, representing the primordial divine being. When this pure consciousness seeks to manifest itself, there begins a process of contemplation or *vimarsha*. Shiva is the primordial undifferentiated consciousness, and Shakti the vimarsha that leads to creation. In the Sri Chakra, the triangles with apex upward represent Shiva and the triangles with apex downwards represent Shakti. A combination of the two depicts Brahman, both in its static and dynamic forms.

It is not the intention here to describe in further detail the

---

34 *The Greatness of Sringeri*, published by Sri Sri Jagadguru Mahasamsthanam Dakshinamnaya Sri Sharada Peetham, February 2012, p, 15.

elaborate ritual and theory of tantric practice relating to the Sri Chakra. Suffice is to say that no less a person than Sri Bharati Tirtha, the current Shankaracharya of the Sringeri Matha, testifies to Shankara's association with tantric worship:

> Worship of the Almighty has two aspects—Nirguna upasana and Saguna upasana. The former envisages the Supreme Being as formless and attribute-less, while at the other extreme is the attribution of various human forms. In between comes the Chakra, which is also for external worship, but more abstract than worship through images. The limitless One limits itself to a form, one could say. According to the Tantras, worship of the Chakra of a deity enables a concrete realisation of the deity. Adi Shankara has set forth worship of the Devi in Sri Chakra form in his *Saundarya Lahari* and *Prapanchasara*. This form of worship occupies a high place in all the mathas established by him.[35]

In stanza eleven of the *Saundarya Lahari*, Shankara explicitly pays homage to the Sri Chakra: 'Oh! Supreme Power, Your angles of abode become forty-four in number with four wheels of auspiciousness, five different wheels of power, nine basic roots of nature, and three encircling lines encasing eight and sixteen petals.' In his bhashya on the *Kenopanishad,* he emphasises the complete identity between the all-knowing Atman and its chitta, Shakti: *Sa atma sarva pratyaya darshi chitta Shakti svarupa matraha.*

It is not surprising, therefore, that he made Shakti upasana compulsory in all his mathas. In fact, many authorities on tantra recognise him as Sri Chakra Pratishtapana Acharya—the master who established the Sri Chakra. The tantric work, *Srividyarnava* regards Shankara as the founder of a line of tantric worship. It is said that he also authored the *Prapanchasara,* which is a

---

35 *Sri Chakra*, published by Sri Sharada Peetham, Sringeri, June 2016, p. 5.

compendium of tantric lore and practices, although authorities like G.C. Pande believe that he may have merely helped to edit it.

According to one tradition, Shankara was acquainted with tantrism in Kashmir. The fact that he visited Srinagar, and was deeply influenced by Kashmir Shaivism, has been discussed earlier in detail. Other accounts say that he mastered the esoteric practice in Bengal. This is what is believed in Omkareshwar, where, as referred to earlier, there is even today a hypnotic idol of Kali in the cave where Shankara met with his philosophical mentor, Govindapada. That idol, it is said, was installed when Shankara returned to Omkareshwar to master Kali siddhi after having been worsted in debates with tantrics in Bengal.

It must also be borne in mind that Shankara was extremely attached to his mother, who he left to become a sanyasin. She was then a widow with no other relatives, and although she finally agreed to let her only child go, Shankara's possible sense of personal guilt at her lonely plight may have been a contributing reason for his compensatory—yet philosophical—devotion to a Mother Goddess.

Tantra must have appealed to him also for its intuitional quotient. We must recall that he believed that brahmanubhava is, ultimately, a moment of supreme intuition, where the very certainty of the experience supersedes the conventional limitations of rationality. In the intensity of experience enabled by the tantric worship of the Mother Goddess, he may have found the most efficacious path to the mood of surrender so conducive to the experience of Brahman.

On the whole, Shankara displayed an intellectual adroitness that assimilated many existing traditions without diluting his unwavering and fundamental thesis on the primacy of Brahman. He had the courage to transcend the ritualism and devotional worship associated with conventional religion; but, simultaneously, he conceded that such theism, in as much as it negated the ego and nurtured the mood of surrender, was useful. He did not accept the dualism of Purusha and Prakriti of the Sankhya school, but many of the features of the quiescent and omnipresent Purusha are reflected in the grandeur of his concept of Brahman. He did not endorse the notion of a personal god in the Yoga school, but he accepted the physical and meditational aspects of the discipline of yogic training. He did not agree with the atomistic plurality of the Nyaya-Vaisheshika school, but he borrowed from its rigorous system of logic and reasoning. He decried the mechanical karmakanda or ritual exercises of the Purva Mimanshaks, but accepted that such rituals, if performed in a spirit of detachment, help to prepare the individual in the journey towards brahmanubhava. He may not have agreed with every aspect of tantric practice, but he saw merit in adopting those that, he believed, were conducive to the ultimate realisation of Brahman.

This assimilative approach was visible in his interface with non-Hindu religions as well. Positioning himself strongly against the nihilistic shunyavada and the extreme idealism of vijnanavada that later dominated Buddhist metaphysics, he incorporated elements of the Buddhist devaluation of the transient material world in his own theory of mayavada. Again, while differing from Jaina pluralism, he was influenced by its theory of syadavada, which accepts that absolute answers cannot be provided to every phenomenon. He uses this aspect, in particular, when he accepts that the relationship between the indivisible Brahman and the material manifestations that constitute the empirical world, are inexpressible, or anirvachaniya.

In other words, Shankaracharya was both the absolutist Vedantin, uncompromising in his belief in the non-dual Brahman, and, the great synthesiser, willing to assimilate within his theoretical canvas, several key elements of other schools of philosophy. While crystal clear, at the paramarthik or ontological level of the sole cosmic plenitude of Brahman, he was too much a pragmatist not to concede at the lower vyavaharik plane, many of the practices that make up the world of the ordinary aspirant to spirituality.

He understood that the attribute-less Brahman may appear to be far too abstract for mortals seeking more accessible forms of redemption or succour.

The challenge before him was, thus, how to retain his undiluted chastity to the supremacy of Brahman, while, at the same time, appealing to, and persuading the greatest number of Hindus to understand and appreciate the audacity of thought as articulated in the Upanishads, and elaborated upon by him. For his ideological opponents, his approach was not one of disdain or dismissal. He was willing to debate and discuss, and won most of his theoretical duels through the civilised modality of shastrartha or informed argumentation.

It is for this reason that Shankaracharya is called *Sanmatha Sthapanacharya*: the man who brought together under one grand intellectual awning the six systems of Hindu worship: Shaiva, Vaishnava, Shakta, Ganapatya, Saura and Kaumara (or Kapali), thereby reviving and restoring Hinduism both as a philosophy and a religion that appealed to its followers. In this endeavour, his great achievement was to strengthen the core intellectual foundations of Hindu philosophy, while accommodating long established traditions of religious practice within that philosophical framework. His austere and uncompromising metaphysics did not become a peripheral ivory tower reserved only for scholars, but was internalised in varying degrees even by ordinary Hindus, and that legacy continues even today.

THE REMARKABLE VALIDATION OF SCIENCE

Given the stupendous discoveries in science in recent times, scientists are, understandably perhaps, skeptical of philosophers and philosophy. In the face of hard, mind-boggling data about our universe that science is revealing on a daily basis, do human-centric theories about mind and matter, and the place and potential of a puny individual in the world, matter anymore?

Most western philosophers were quick to accept defeat in the face of the relentless scientific discoveries of the last few centuries that upturned the world, as it was known till but a few hundred years ago.

Galileo's discovery that the earth was not the centre of the universe, and that our solar system was but a part of a much larger universe—which, incidentally had been foretold by Indian astronomers and mathematicians much earlier—made many philosophies genuinely outdated. Charles Darwin's 'natural selection' theory about the evolution of the human species put a serious question on Biblical origins of the human race. As the universe of science expanded, that of philosophers and religious thinkers contracted.

In the nineteenth century, the German philosopher Freidrich Nietzsche pronounced that 'God is Dead'. In our own time,

Stephen Hawking grandiosely proclaimed that 'philosophy is dead.' According to him, 'philosophy has not kept up with modern developments in science, particularly physics.'[1]

However, it is most unlikely that either Nietzsche or Hawking had any real knowledge about the insights of the Upanishads, or about Shankaracharya's systematic structure of philosophical thought. If they had, they might have been surprised to discover how much of what modern science has revealed, particularly in the areas of cosmology, quantum physics and neurology, were anticipated by Shankara, and become explicable in the light of the philosophical theory he articulated more than a millennium ago.

A word of caution though, is necessary. This is not an attempt to mechanically glorify Shankara's thinking as part of an agenda to 'promote' either Hinduism or the achievements of ancient India. Hinduism itself has many strands of thought, not all of which so fully validate what science is telling us today. Equally, other eastern religions, including, in particular Buddhism and its offshoots, also presage at least some of the latest discoveries of science.

However, it is our attempt to show that Advaitic philosophy, as systemised and propounded by Shankaracharya, is capable of accommodating to the greatest extent possible, what science is revealing today. It is our proposition that this claim can be verified by juxtaposing what we know of the universe today and the laws that govern its functioning, with the philosophical tenets that Shankara laid down. If what he said in the eighth century CE can be coherently and convincingly correlated to the scientific knowledge of today, then our proposition would be valid.

Cosmology, which maps the evolution of the universe, tells us now

1 Stephen Hawking & Leonard Mlodinow, *The Grand Design*, Bantam Books, 2010, p. 13.

that the universe is near infinite. This has been proven beyond doubt by several remarkable telescopes, satellites and probes, peering into the vast universe beyond. The most important of these remarkable gadgets are the Hubble Space Telescope, the International Space Station, the Cosmic Background Explorer satellite (COBE), and the Wilkinson Microwave Anisotropy Probe (WMAP). Through these eyes in the skies, we now know that our solar system, in which the earth is a small planet orbiting the sun, is part of a much bigger galaxy that is called the Milky Way. Light travels at the speed of 186,282 miles or 299,792.5 kilometres per second. The Milky Way is some 150.000 light years across, so vast that it would take some 26,000 light years for the earth to reach its centre. Such distances already boggle the mind, but amazingly, there are, at the least, 125 billion such galaxies in the known universe, and each galaxy has about two hundred billion stars, most of them larger than the sun.

Most recently, a group of Indian scientists in Pune and Kerala have discovered a new 'supercluster' of galaxies, which they have named Saraswati. Identified as part of the Sloan Digital Sky Survey, Saraswati is 600 million light years across and 4,000 million light years away from earth!

The age of the universe has been estimated at around 13.7 billion years. The sun, which is the centre of our solar system, has been dated to be about 4.6 billion years old. The sun, and the planets that circle it, make one revolution of the Milky Way in 220 million years. The galaxy closest to ours is Andromeda, some 2.5 million light years away. The galaxy that we can observe as being the most distant from us is about 45 billion light years away. It would take some 13 billion years for light from this distant galaxy to reach us.

Amazingly, this already vast universe is not static, it's constantly expanding, and that too at speeds approaching the velocity of light. This was the great discovery made by astronomer

Edwin Hubble in 1929. He did so by analysing the colour spectrum of the galaxies he had discovered. The colour of radiant objects depends on whether they are moving towards or away from us: blue, if they are coming closer, and red if they are moving away. Hubble discovered that most of the galaxies were red in hue, thereby proving that they were moving away from us.

> Now, when we think of an expanding universe, we picture the galaxies flying across empty, static space like geese flying across a winter sky. But this is not what is happening. It is space itself that is expanding, and carrying the galaxies with it.[2]

The example that best illustrates what is happening is that of a balloon with dots painted on it. If we blow up the balloon, the dots will move away from each other. The universe is expanding in a similar way, and this assumes that there is space to expand into outside the universe. If not, the universe is creating space where there was none, or cloning space. In fact, scientists now do not rule out the possibility of multiverses, a cosmos where there are many universes.

> Hundreds of years ago people thought the earth was unique, and situated at the centre of the universe. Today we know that there are hundreds of billion of stars in our galaxy, a large percentage of them with planetary systems, and hundreds of billions of galaxies. The results…indicate that our universe itself is also one of many, and that its apparent laws are not uniquely determined.[3]

---

2 Dr Mani Bhaumik, *The Cosmic Detective*, Puffin Books India, 2008, p. 34.

3 Stephen Hawking & Leonard Mlodinow, *The Grand Design*, Bantam Books, UK, 2010, p. 183.

Therefore, if we now know that the universe could be infinite in scale, or certainly as close to infinity as can be imagined, then the notion of Brahman too is that of infinitude. Shankara's concept of the Vedantic absolute was ab initio conceived as a force that is beyond human categories of visualisation, all-pervasive, beyond boundaries, and cosmic in scale. It is for this reason that it was not limited to a deity as conjured by the human mind, or equated with a messiah as interpreted by human needs. Because of the sheer scale of this concept, Brahman had to be attribute-less, because any attribute given to an entity so vast and beyond human understanding would limit its cosmic magnitude, and reduce it to the level of human imagination.

Equally, the age ascribed to the universe, makes our human time horizons literally a child's play. We have been used to measuring time in multiples of thousands of years. The division between Before Christ, BC, and After Christ, Anno Domini (AD), may have been replaced by the more secular labels of Common Era (CE) or Before Common Era (BCE), but our imagination of time and antiquity is still in thousands.

The oldest signs of human presence on our planet could go as far back as ten thousand years ago. The evolutionary process from the amoeba to the homo sapien could take us back to some millions of years ago. But, now we have evidence that the universe is as old as around fourteen *billion* years. This does not rule out the fact that there could have been another universe before the Big Bang that supposedly brought forth our current universe, or that, following the Big Crunch when the universe will once again self-destruct, another universe will emerge. In other words, cosmology points to the fact that the creation and destruction of this vast universe is an eternal process, without, as per current scientific knowledge, a finite beginning or a finite end. This conforms exactly to the concept of Brahman, anant, something that always was and never will not be. In those times, so many centuries before the knowledge that the universe is so unimaginably vast or old, philosophical conjectures were limited in scale, confined to the belief that the earth is the centre of the universe, or at best limited to the sun and its orbiting planets, and that this definable universe evolved within a comprehensible and fixed time frame.

But in Advaita we have a philosophical construct that uncompromisingly refuses to reduce the absolute to familiar territory, in the nature of a personal god with attributes that we can identify with in physical and emotional terms. This, in itself, is nothing short of revolutionary, signifying a prescience of intellectual imagination that would stun scientists today. Shankara's absolute, in terms of a formless infinity, pulsating through the Brahmand —the universe Brahman created—is, in fact, in perfect consonance with what cosmology is telling us today.

Cosmology also tells us that this vast universe is underpinned by an intelligence that is verifiable. The universe, for all its unimaginable magnitude, works in perfect harmony. Planets orbit larger stars with a precision that can be calculated to the last second. Solar systems revolve at fixed speeds around their galactic centre. Galaxies remain where they are because the balance between cosmic gravitational forces is fine-tuned to the nth degree.

There is the Big Bang theory that is based on the question that if the universe continues to expand today, what is it expanding from? At some very distant time in the past, what is expanding today must have had a beginning, and if the expansion process could, like a film, be rewound, we could come to a precise moment when the expansion began. That moment is what scientists call the Big Bang, according to which, some 13.7 billion years ago, the universe we see today was incredibly condensed to just a few millimeters across.

When the Big Bang occurred, there was a huge physical expansion of space, which scientist Alan Guth in 1979 called the inflationary theory of universal expansion. If, following the Big Bang, such an inflation did in fact occur (and there are scientists that question both assumptions, although most of them support the theory), the rate of cosmic expansion would have to be to a precision of one part in ten to the fiftieth power, otherwise the fine balance between expansion and contraction would have been lost and the emerging universe would have collapsed on to itself, or expanded without symmetry or control. As Hawking says: 'If the rate of expansion one second after the Big Bang had been smaller by even one part in a hundred thousand million million, the universe would have recollapsed before it ever reached its present size.'[4]

In other words, the universe is governed, for the most part, by a supreme intelligence at work, and that is visible even at the limited scale of our personal lives, where, given the precision with which the earth orbits the sun, and the moon orbits the earth, we have the exact timings when the sun will rise and set, and when the moon will wax or wane, and when the seasons will change. There is in the universe an amazing consistency and uniformity of design that cannot but presuppose a remarkably intelligent directive power.

What is the nature of this intelligence? Shankara stated that Brahman, although without attributes as per human categories, was of the nature of intelligence itself. This intelligence is transcendental, and may appear to be without purpose to the human mind. Why was the universe born? Why are there so many galaxies with countless stars? Why are hundreds of super novae—the giant explosions caused by the collapse of dying stars—taking place every second somewhere in the universe? What, after all, is the purpose of this whole cosmic drama?

Shankara's answer, completely in consonance with latest science is, that the purpose of the universe may be incomprehensible to human minds, but all the cosmic fireworks are still part of an intelligent design emanating from an inexhaustible and identifiable

4 Stephen Hawking, *A Brief History of Time*, Bantam Books, 1988, p. 134.

source of energy, called Brahman. That energy (or consciousness, as we shall later discuss) is the source of all activity while remaining above it, immanent yet transcendent, and without purpose definable in human terms.

Hawking rightly notes that the universe does seem to have a set of laws in its functioning, but that higher power—god as per Hawking, or Brahman according to Shankara—'has since left the universe to evolve according to them and does not now intervene in it.'[5]

Brahman is the ground from which all things emanate and lapse into. It is the one constant eternal, intelligence personified, unchanging and transcendent. Cosmology is saying exactly that today. There is an energy that suffuses the universe, omnipresent, which remains unchanging even as that which emanates from it undergoes change and mutation, creation and destruction.

This is verifiable in the observable working of the universe. Entire galaxies die only to be reborn again over millions of years. Stars burn out and new stars are born from the debris of their explosive remnants, at a rate hundreds of times more often than babies born on earth. The Milky Way and our nearest galactic neighbour, Andromeda, are inching closer to each other and will, in a couple of billion years, collide to create a giant black hole that will obliterate everything that exists in its current form in both the galaxies.

Perhaps, even before that happens, in another five billion years or so, our sun will burn all its hydrogen and die, leaving a red giant in its place. The universe is in flux, but its ground is that unchanging energy which Shankara and the Upanishads called Brahman.

Mani Bhaumik, an American of Indian origin, who won fame for his work on lasers and whose contributions to science merited election as a fellow to the American Physical Society and

5 Stephen Hawking, ibid., p. 135.

the Institution of Electrical and Electronics Engineers, reiterated that the immanence and transcendence of a higher power bears resemblance to the concept of Brahman,

> which the great rishis of the Vedic tradition have seen and experienced in their greatest meditations, for modern science tells us that the whole of the universe is flooded by a sea of energy—a clear light if you like (the 'self-luminosity' of Shankara) that fills what is known as the quantum vacuum. It is a light so pervasive that we would, in truth, only be able to 'see it' if it were not there. The entity that created it, the Brahma of both science and spirit, is an even more wondrous and perplexing thing to contemplate, *for it is a single point and at all points.*[6] (Italics mine)

Do we have proof that anything can actually pervasively inhabit this unimaginably vast cosmos? If the universe, as we know it today, can be traced back to a Big Bang, wherein an incredibly dense speck expanded to create the billions of galaxies that constitute the cosmos, then that explosion must have been of an intensity that would leave, even so many billions of years after it occurred, an 'afterglow' throughout space. Scientist George Gamow in the 1940s first postulated this possibility. He argued that although the universe has considerably cooled down now, the incredible heat created by the Big Bang could still be found evenly suffusing the cosmos in the form of microwaves.

> In 1965, Arno Penzias and Robert Wilson, two young radio astronomers at Bell Labs, New Jersey, accidentally found Gamow's predicted microwave relic of the Big Bang using a big horn antenna that picked up radio waves from all

---

6 Mani Bhaumik, *Code Name God,* Crossroad Publishing Company, New York, 2005, p. 32.

> across the sky.....They kept hearing a hissing sound from the speakers, but had no idea at first that what they were hearing was the energy of creation itself, and that this energy was everywhere. Literally everywhere! Talk about evidence. This was the clincher.[7]

This evidence of the explosive birth of the universe is called Cosmic Microwave Background Radiation (CMBR). There is further evidence of a cosmos-wide commonality. The Cosmic Background Explorer satellite has discovered that across the universe, the background microwave radiation has minute variations in temperature. These variations are a continuation on a cosmic scale of the 'wrinkles' in primordial space-time at the time of the Big Bang, and their discovery confirms that, for all its vastness, the universe is interconnected, and represents a common field for an undifferentiated energy permeating its every nook and corner.

Modern science also validates Shankara's view of the empirical world. As we have discussed, he believed that the only reality was Brahman. The material world, if not an illusion, was far from being the enduring, static and predictable entity our senses (and mind) took it to be. Until 1687, when Sir Isaac Newton published his paper, *Philosophiae Naturalis Principia Mathematica,* which postulated a universal law of gravitation, scientists would have dismissed Shankara's view as nonsense. The Newtonian view visualised a world that was real as seen, verifiable, and explicable in its behaviour by the laws of gravitation.

However, in 1915, Albert Einstein, a clerk in the Swiss patent office, published a paper on the theory of relativity that upturned the neatly conceived world of Newtonian physics. Simply put, and without going into a great deal of scientific jargon, Einstein proved that there is no fixed frame of reference of the universe. Neither time nor space is absolute. Events that occur at the same

---

7 Mani Bhaumik, *The Cosmic Detective*, ibid., p. 70.

time for one observer could occur at different times for another. In a universe never at absolute rest, everything is moving relative to everything else. Space and time are not separate entities but are part of a single continuum called space-time. Mind and matter are not eternally separate, as per the Cartesian assertion of Descartes, but that matter is just a different manifestation of energy, as exemplified in the famous equation, E=mc2. Space is not statically stable, but can be bent by the gravitational pull of massive objects, as a trampoline would if a boulder is placed on it.

Even light, compared to which nothing travels faster, can be bent by the forces of gravitation. Indeed, space-time itself can be warped or curved. Given the vast distances of the universe, and the time taken by light to traverse them, what is happening today on earth, would be seen somewhere else in the cosmos hundreds or thousands or even millions of years later. Our past could thus be someone else's future, and vice-versa. Even the sun as we see it, is how it was eight minutes ago, because that is the time light from it takes to travel to us. The absolute distinctions between past, present and future also thus became obliterated.

Einstein's theory of relativity revolutionised modern physics and completely changed the traditional view of what constitutes the material world. Space and time are so central to the conventional description of reality that if they themselves are seen as relative, it transforms the nature of reality itself. In other words, Einstein made clear that the world that we see or believe in is not what actually exists. As he himself said, 'As far as the laws of mathematics refer to reality, they are not certain; and as far as they are certain, they do not refer to reality.' What we, as humans, considered to be immutable is mutable; what we took as granted is, in fact, ephemeral. The entire notion of reality, if judged only by how it appears to us, is a chimera.

If Einstein's work was subversive to conventional notions of the empirical world, the discovery of quantum mechanics took that process to another level. Quantum theory is the science of studying matter at its most microscopic level. This had been done in the past as well, but our knowledge then was basically restricted to the fact that the smallest unit was an atom with a positively charged nucleus orbited by negatively charged electrons.

But from the early twentieth century, as scientists probed deeper into the mysteries of the nanoscopic world, they discovered an entire universe of sub-atomic particles consisting of protons and neutrons, quarks and gluons, and bosons, baryon and photons, in fact as many as some two hundred sub-particles. New discoveries continue to keep scientists amazed. In July 2017, scientists at the Large Hadron Collider, located in a twenty-seven-kilometre tunnel beneath the Swiss-French border, discovered a never-before-seen baryon that has a pair of two quarks circling it, and a third one dancing around the pair.

This universe in its patterns of behaviour at the sub-atomic level is truly bewildering. In 1924, French physicist Louis de Brogile (1892–1987) showed that there is no distinction, in terms of behaviour or pattern, between energy and matter, since either may behave as if it was made of particles or waves. In the same year, German theoretical physicist, Werner Heisenberg (1901–1976) demonstrated his 'Uncertainty Principle' by which the precise and simultaneous measurement of the position and momentum of a sub-atomic particle is impossible. The more closely one establishes one coordinate, such as the position of a particle, the less accurate another measurement, such as its momentum, must become.

Going further, Danish scientist Niels Bohr (1885–1962), who won the Nobel Prize for physics in 1922, articulated the Copenhagen Interpretation of quantum theory, by which a particle has no absolute properties, but is whatever it is measured to be, and in this sense, it cannot even be assumed that it exists until it is measured. Many years later, in 1984, a 'string theory' was mooted according to which there were no particles at all, only waves that except for length have no other dimension, and can be identified only like sensations vibrating down a kite string.

What Bohr, and scientists after him, was saying is that *objective reality does not exist.* In accordance with a principle he postulated called superposition, while we do not know what the state of any object is, it is actually in all possible states simultaneously. The multiverse theory establishes that as soon as there is the potential for any object to be in a particular state, the universe of that object transmutes into a series of parallel universes equal to the number of possible states in which that object can exist. Essentially, therefore, all matter is probabilistic, its properties constantly mutating, and unverifiable in precise terms as would be possible in a static and fully knowable world.

Such is the degree of uncertainty, or lack of definitiveness, that Erwin Schrodinger (1887–1961), who won the Nobel Prize in physics in 1933, proposed in 1935 the 'cat hidden in a sealed box' experiment to his good friend, Einstein. According to this whether a cat would live or die in a sealed box, would depend on the state of a particular sub-atomic particle. Until the box would open, the cat would be, theoretically, both dead and alive, because the probability of a particle transmuting into a wave can be measured, as per the 'uncertainty principle', only at the time of measurement! Thus, a given reality, could, at any time be, as Shankara had said, an admixture of both sat (real) and asat (unreal).

Discoveries of this kind revealed a world very different from what our limited sensory faculties could see or grasp. Neurologists today confirm that what we perceive is what our brain thinks it perceives.

> Nothing enters consciousness whole. There is no direct, objective experience of reality. All the things the mind perceives—all thoughts, feelings, hunches, memories, insights, desires, and revelations—have been assembled piece by piece

> by the processing powers of the brain from the swirl of neural blips, sensory perceptions, and scattered cognitions dwelling in its structures and neural pathways.[8]

Our brain is fitted with an apparatus that gives a certain familiar concreteness to the material world. But it cannot grasp that even the familiar, or seemingly known, such as a table, is just light scattered by the table representing an electro-magnetic field seething with sub-atomic particles that are invisible but there. Reality, as comprehended by us, is thus very different from how it actually exists.

> Macroscopically, the material objects around us may seem passive and inert, but when we magnify such a "dead" piece of stone or metal, we see that it is full of activity. The closer we look at it, the more alive it appears. All the material objects in our environment are made of atoms which link up with each other in various ways to form an enormous variety of molecular structures which are not rigid and motionless, but oscillate according to their temperatures and in harmony with the thermal vibrations of their environment.[9]

But this reality is not what we either see or comprehend, and is thus, for all practical purposes, illusionary to our sensory faculties.

Einstein himself acknowledged that, 'Physical concepts are free creations of the human mind, and not, however it may seem, uniquely determined by the external world.'[10] Indeed, his discovery that mass is only a form of energy fundamentally changes the notion of matter itself. The world around us is not confined, as we

---

8 Andrew Newberg, Eugene D'Aquili & Vince Rause, *Why God Won't Go Away*, Ballantine Books, 2002, p. 36.

9 Fritjof Capra, *The Tao of Physics*, Flamingo, London, 1976, p. 215.

10 Quoted in Andrew Newberg, et. al., op. cit., p. 170.

believe, to definable physicality. On the contrary, it is just a flow of energy in constant state of flux. This flux can be identified by modern science, but it is inherently unpredictable. In the quantum universe, the same particle can occupy two places at the same time! Moreover, there is no distinction between time and space. In fact, as Hawking says, 'time is imaginary and is indistinguishable from directions in space.'

Most recently, physicists Mathew S. Leifer at Chapman University in California, and Mathew F. Pusey at the Perimeter Institute of Theoretical Sciences in Ontario, have come out with the idea of 'retrocausality', which proposes that the future can influence the past and the effect happens before the cause! Both these scientists found that the measurement of a particle can influence the properties of that particle in the past, even before experimenters had made their choice. Such a proposition takes the concept of time symmetry, according to which physical processes can run forward and backward in time while being subject to the same physical laws, a quantum leap forward. Leifer concludes that 'the only option seems to be to abandon realism or to break out of the standard realist framework.'[11] Interestingly, Huw Price, a professor in Philosophy at the University of Cambridge, who focuses on the physics of time, strongly supports the concept of 'retrocausality'. In this surreal world where material objects are in essence just wave-like patterns of probabilities, and the future can be the past and vice-versa, it could well be possible, as Hawking surmises, that the 'so called imaginary time is really the real time, and that what we call real time is just *a figment of our imagination* (and) *what we call real is just an idea that we invent to help us describe what we think the universe is like.*'[12] (*Emphasis* mine)

Stephen Hawking could well have been a disciple of

11 See bigthink.com, for full report.

12 Stephen Hawking, *A Brief History of Time,* ibid., p. 155.

Shankaracharya! But, other scientists are equally categorical on the unresolved and maddening paradoxes of the empirical world. There is, as quantum theory reveals, no such thing as empty space. It is filled with pairs of virtual particles and anti-particles, which have infinite energy. Magnets, even operating in a vacuum, have a gravitational pull. The universe may be vast beyond imagination, but its total energy is zero. As Hawking explains:

> The matter in the universe is made out of positive energy. However, the matter is all attracting itself by gravity. Two pieces of matter that are close to each other have less energy than the same pieces a long way apart, because you have to expend energy to separate them against the gravitational force that is pulling them together. Thus, in a sense, the gravitational field has negative energy. In the case of a universe that is approximately uniform in space, one can show that this negative gravitational energy exactly cancels the positive energy represented by the matter. So the total energy of the universe is zero.[13]

The amazing thing is that while the net energy of the universe is zero, there is still, as Mani Bhaumik points out, 'more energy in the vacuum of space than in all the stars.'[14] Even more interestingly, virtual particles can suddenly and on their own emerge out of empty space, and disappear into the void, without any other attracting particle being present, thereby obliterating the distinction between matter and empty space. Notwithstanding the discoveries of science, the remarkable fact is that ninety-six per cent of the quantum universe is dark matter and dark energy about which nothing as yet is known. And, 'if a theory called the holographic principle proves correct, we and our

13 ibid., p.143.

14 Mani Bhaumik, *Code Named God*, ibid., p. 11.

four-dimensional world may be shadows on the boundary of a larger, five-dimensional space-time.'[15]

In fact, faced with the sheer unpredictability and elusiveness of the quantum world, scientists like George Chew have now postulated a 'bootstrap philosophy' that,

> not only abandons the idea of fundamental building blocks of matter but accepts no fundamental entities whatsoever—no fundamental constants, laws or equations. The material world is seen as a dynamic web of interrelated events. None of the properties of any part of this web is fundamental; they all follow from the properties of the other parts, and the overall consistency of their inter-relations determines the structure of the entire web.[16]

Shankara's philosophical interpretation of the empirical world—that it may exist, but it is not what it appears to be—is now being definitively borne out by theories of relativity and quantum physics. Shankara stated his position not on the basis of mathematical equations but from a philosopher's perception that there cannot be two ultimate realities, and that even if this duality seems to exist, one of them is unreal, both as perceived, and for its transience. The quantum world demolishes the notions of conventional reality, while simultaneously establishing that all phenomena is inherently and constantly in flux, coming into existence in one nano second and being extinguished in another, an entire series of transient configurations.

15 Stephen Hawking & Leonard Mlodinow, *The Grand Design*, Bantam Books, UK, 2010, pp.59-60.

16 Fritjof Capra, op. cit., p. 365.

However, what Shankara asserted with calm certitude has exasperated modern scientists, unable, perhaps, to fully accept the fact that 'all their theories of natural phenomena, including the "laws" they describe, are creations of the human mind; properties of our conceptual map of reality, rather than of reality itself.'[17] Quantum physicist Richard Feynman exclaimed that quantum mechanics deals with 'nature as she is—absurd.' Einstein himself took some time to come to terms with the new world of modern science, famously remarking that 'God does not play dice.' But, ultimately, he had no other recourse than to endorse, albeit reluctantly, the findings of quantum physicists, which so closely resemble Shankara's concept of the material world. Centuries before the world of quarks and quantum packets, Shankara could say with equanimity that what is transient cannot be real and what is eternal cannot be transient, but this simple inference came as a shock to Einstein himself. As the great scientist wrote in his autobiography, 'it was as if the ground had been pulled out from under one, with no firm foundation to be seen anywhere upon which one could have built.'

Some prominent western philosophers echoed Shankara's Advaita vision. David Hume (1711–1776) argued that there is no rational ground for believing in an objective reality. George Berkeley (1685–1753), in a tone reminiscent of the subjective idealism of the Vijanavada Buddhist scholars, went further to state that nothing exists except the mind and its ideas. The amusing thing is that many quantum physicists, faced with the inferences of their own research, referred to these western philosophers, while being seemingly unaware of the Upanishad-based insights of Shankara's views, systematised into a rigorous structure of philosophy at least a millennium earlier!

While physicists in our time looked outward, both into the macro cosmos and the microscopic sub-atomic world, Shankara,

17 ibid., p. 317.

hundreds of years ago, looked inwards into the nature of the real itself. This inward journey, no less meticulous than mathematical equations, telescopes and microscopes, led him to infer that outward reality, as we think it exists, is maya. It exists, at a certain level (sat), coterminous with the limited comprehensive powers of our sensory faculties, but is illusionary at another level (asat). The mind is a gullible prey to the immediate seductions of what it sees. Thus, the real nature of the empirical eludes it, and it becomes a victim to maya's veil, which masks reality, avarana and distorts it, vikshepa. These self-limiting upadhis or limiting adjuncts of our mind-body apparatus allow the unreal and transient—the universe of nama-rupa, name and form—to appear as real and permanent. We dance to the Great Conjurer's illusions (maya), and lose our faculty of discrimination, nitya-anitya viveka. This error of perception, avidya, blurs the real nature of empirical reality, and can only be corrected by correct insight, either of the mind or—as we have now learnt—the microscope.

It is interesting that a renowned physicist like David Bohm (whose views we shall discuss in greater detail later), actually endorses the concept of maya, in terms of the specific analogy of a veil. He argues that,

> whereas to Western society, as it derives from the Greeks, measure, (which is related to an external standard), is the very essence of reality, or at least the key to this essence, in the East measure has now come to be regarded commonly as being in some way false and deceitful. In this view, the entire structure of order and forms, proportions and "ratios" that present themselves to ordinary perception and reason are regarded as a sort of veil, covering the true reality, which cannot be perceived by the senses and of which nothing can be said or thought.[18]

18 David Bohm, *Wholeness and the Implicate Order*, Routledge Classics, 1980, p. 31.

The Greek word metron, which means measure, and the word maya, come from the same root, which means illusion. This, Bohm says, is an extremely significant point. When juxtaposed to the immeasurable, all measure is an illusion created by the human mind. And if, as Shankara says, the primary reality is, indeed, immeasurable, then measure, as descriptive of the reality that we assume to be real, is also an illusion.

Danah Zohar, who studied physics and philosophy from MIT and completed three years of postgraduate study in Philosophy and Religion at Harvard University, puts her finger on the nail when she writes:

> The full nature of this quantum indeterminism goes straight to the heart of the central philosophical problem raised by quantum mechanics—the nature of reality itself. Some quantum theorists, foremost among them Niels Bohr and Heisenberg himself, argued that fundamental reality itself is essentially indeterminate, that there is no clear, fixed, underlying "something" to our daily existence that can ever be known. An electron *might* be a particle, it *might* be a wave, it *might* be in this orbit, it *might* be in that—indeed, *anything* might happen. We can only predict such things on the basis of what is most probable given the overall constraints of any given experimental situation. On this view, where the essential basis of reality, as we know it consists of just so many probabilities, we are left with the central unanswered problem of quantum theory being: How can anything in this world *ever* become actual or fixed? It's the very opposite of dilemma raised by Newton's clockwork universe, in which there is no scope for the new. Reading Newton, we have to ask: How can anything ever *happen?* With the Bohr-Heisenberg interpretation of quantum mechanics, the great

problem becomes: How can anything ever *be*?[19]

That is exactly the question that Shankara, in his appraisal of empirical reality, raised. He said that Brahman is indivisible. It cannot be broken into any constituent parts, simply because it is an all-pervasive whole, immanent in all that exists, and beyond any sub-categories or limiting divisions. If this is its nature, it must be reflected in the world that it gives rise to. The cosmos may indeed be unimaginably vast, and the sub-atomic world a bewildering multitude beyond human computation, but all that exists, emanating from Brahman, and reflecting its unified and overarching character, must also be inter-connected, part of a verifiable network, where no individual part is distinct or autonomous or separate from the larger whole. This inter-connected indivisibility is precisely what modern science has accepted today. 'In modern physics, the image of the universe as a machine has been replaced by that of an inter-connected dynamic whole whose parts are essentially interdependent and have to be understood as patterns of a cosmic process.'[20] David Bohm, puts this eloquently:

> One is led to a new notion of unbroken wholeness which denies the classical idea of analyzability of the world into separately and independently existing parts—-Rather we say that inseparable quantum interconnectedness of the whole universe is the fundamental reality, and that relatively independent behaving parts are merely particular and contingent forms within this whole.[21]

The mind-boggling degree to which the universe is interconnected

---

19 Danah Zohar, *The Quantum Self: Human Nature and Consciousness Defined By The New Physics*, William Morrow, USA, 1990, pp. 27-28.

20 ibid., p. 363.

21 D.Bohm & B.Hiley, 'On the Intuitive Understanding of Nonlocality as implied by Quantum Theory', Foundations of Physics, Vol. 5, 1975.

was proved by the Einstein-Podolsky-Rosen (EPR) experiment in 1935, and subsequently by John Bell's theorem derived from this experiment. The EPR experiment involved two spinning electrons. Quantum physics shows, the amount of spin of an electron is always the same, but its direction can be different—clockwise or counter-clockwise. The direction of spin of two electrons along a given axis will always be opposite to each other, up or down, but this can only be known at the time of measurement because until then they exist only as probabilities.

The crux of this experiment is that once the two electrons were separated in space, where one could theoretically be in New Delhi and the other in Seattle, or for that matter on the moon, and were made to spin along a given axis, they still retained a correlation that defies logical explanation. 'At the instant we perform our measurement on particle 1, particle 2, which may be thousands of miles away, will acquire a definite spin along the chosen axis. How does particle 2 know which axis we have chosen? There is no time for it to receive that information by any conventional signal,'[22] for not even light can travel at the speed at which the two electrons seem to be linked by instantaneous, non-local connections.

This interconnected nature of the world is in striking conformity with Shankara's vision. His assertion of Brahman as the sole cause and ground of the universe naturally eliminates divisibility. As individuals, we may believe that we are autonomous but 'just as there is no space or time between two separate laser beams (their wave patterns interfere across space and time), so there is no real division between space and time between selves. We are all individuals, but individuals within a greater unity, a unity that defines each of us in terms of others, and gives each of us a stake in eternity.'[23]

As mentioned elsewhere, the cause, as Brahman, is unchanging,

22 Fritjof Capra, op. cit., p. 345.
23 Danah Zohar, op. cit., p. 151.

indivisible and omnipresent, beyond the duality of whole or part, and is uniform in character (*ekarasa*). The cause can give rise to infinite pluralities, but remains unchanged itself, vivartavada. The seemingly plural manifestations we observe are not other (*anya*) from Brahman, but only an emanation of it. In conformity with such a view, the multiplicity that we witness has an underlying unity, an inseparability that is but a reflection of the nature of Brahman itself. In his stotra to Dakshinamurti (Shiva), Shankara pays obeisance to Him who 'perceives that the world is composed of multiple entities joined in relation to one another, as cause and effect, owner and owned, teacher and pupil, sire and son.'

This essential indivisibility is now being proven, not only by the inter-relatedness of the macro cosmos, but at the sub-atomic level too, where, as the EPR experiment shows, two electrons correspond with each other even when spatially separated by huge distances, and do so in a manner that has no scientific explanation except the philosophical acceptance—there is something in the working of the universe that demonstrates a remarkable and overarching unity, obliterating distinct or separate autonomies.

But, in spite of this underlying unity of the cosmos, reflecting the indivisibility of Brahman, why should the completely self-contained Brahman create a universe in the first place? Why does that which needs no manifestation, and is self-sufficiency itself, need to conjure up a transient world of nama-rupa? And, if such a world of name and form exists, even transiently, what is Brahman's relation to it?

The essential question is, unless explicable by a cause and determinate structure, why do we need this cosmic multiplicity? While Shankara was clear that Brahman is the only reality pervading the universe, he accepted that he has no clear answer to this question. Why this universe exists, and what is its relationship with Brahman, was, he said, anirvachaniya, indefinable and inexpressible.

Modern science too is saying the same. The more we probe

the world, at both its macro and micro level, the more we are stumped about how it came about, why it exists, how long it will last? Does it have a conventionally definable creator? And what is the relationship between the creator and the universe? Till a few centuries ago, scientists believed that they could—and indeed had—solved the riddle of the universe. The cosmos was explicable through verifiable causes, and the effects of such causes could be comprehensibly established. But this smug certitude has eroded in direct correspondence with the greater knowledge we have about the cosmos today. Scientists too are grappling with the larger questions of 'why' and 'what for', and looking for that one cause that can fully provide a unified theory of the universe. That search has not yet yielded a final answer, and so the relationship of the universe to a creator or first cause remains precisely what Shankara said, anirvachaniya, indefinable.

Scientists did not accept this easily. Einstein continued to believe—in spite of his own discoveries refuting absolute time and space—that there had to be some explanation to why the universe exists, some fundamental laws that make this cosmic magnitude, in terms of final answers, less opaque. 'The most incomprehensible fact about nature', he once said, 'is that it is comprehensible.'

A couple of decades later, Stephen Hawking was equally reluctant to accept defeat. 'Was it all just a lucky chance?', he asks with obvious incredulity. If the Big Bang was, indeed, the beginning of creation, there could be the Big Crunch, where the universe would end by re-collapsing on itself. But, even if there was the possibility of one unified theory of creation and dissolution, he himself admits that it is no more than,

> just a set of rules and equations. What is it that breathes fire into the equations and makes a universe for them to describe? The usual approach of science of constructing a mathematical model cannot answer the questions of why does the universe go to all the bother of existing? Is the

> unified theory so compelling that it brings about its own existence? Or does it need a creator, and, if so, does he have any other effect on the universe? And who created him?[24]

Brahman is the ground of all that exists, but why Brahman needs to create a universe so diverse, in which, on earth itself there are 1.4 million animal species and half a million species of plants, remains, as Shankara said, anirvachaniya, not entirely comprehensible. But, if this cosmic multiplicity is incomprehensible, the ground which gives rise to it, Brahman, is, according to Shankara, eternal, without a finite beginning or end. The universe, therefore, is also, as an emanation of Brahman, part of a beginning-less and endless cycle of creation. The attempt to give the observable universe a finite beginning, as best represented by the Big Bang theory, and a finite end, as would happen if the Big Crunch took place, begs the question: what existed before the Big Bang, and could not another universe emerge after the Big Crunch?

Indeed, scientists today are asking the same question. Even amidst the euphoria of new discoveries in quantum physics, British physicist, Sir Bernard Lovell wondered about what could be before beginnings or endings were identified by human calculation. 'There we reach the great barrier of thought,' he admitted, 'because we begin to struggle with the concepts of time and space before they existed in terms of our everyday experience. I feel as though I've suddenly driven into a great fog barrier where the familiar world has disappeared.'[25] Stephen Hawking, is himself assailed with doubt. The quantum theory of gravity, he argues,

> has opened up a new possibility, in which there would be no boundary to space-time and so there would be no need to

---

24 Stephen Hawking, *A Brief History of Time,* op. cit., pp.192-193.

25 A.C.B. Lovell, *The Individual and the Universe*, OUP, London, 1958, p. 9.

> specify the behaviour at the boundary. There would be no singularities at which the laws of science broke down and no edge of space-time at which one would have to appeal to God or some new law to set the boundary conditions of space-time. One could say: "The boundary condition of the universe is that it has no boundary." The universe would be completely self-contained, and not affected by anything outside itself. It would neither be created nor destroyed. It would just BE.[26]

Modern science is thus validating the basic Advaitic concept that, in conformity with the eternal nature of Brahman, the universe too is part of a successive cycle of manifestation and dissolution, and this process is eternal in nature. Stars die, and from their exploding debris new stars are born, as part of a continuous process. As Dr Mani Bhaumik explains in simple terms:

> The attraction of gravity starts to win when the stars nuclear fuel begins to diminish, as it does eventually in all stars. When this happens, gravity causes the star to begin contracting—to fall in on itself in a kind of replay of the process that occurred during its birth.....A star the size of our sun will eventually become a red giant, and finally give its outer shells back to the universe in the form of a planetary nebula, so that new stars and solar systems can be made.[27]
>
> A larger dying star, a supernova, will explode into oblivion, releasing a phenomenal amount of energy that could be several times the energy produced by our sun in its entire life. But in this explosive destruction, lie too the seeds of creation. The elements thrown into space by the blast gather with those of other expired stars to form giant molecular

---

26 ibid, p. 151.

27 Dr Mani Bhaumik, *The Cosmic Detective*, op. cit., pp. 22-23.

> gas clouds like the Eagle Nebula....These clouds are the seeds where new solar systems are born, many holding the possibility for the development of life.[28]

Therefore, all of us, says Dr Bhaumik are made of stardust and probably owe our very existence to an exploding star billions of years ago!

Even a black hole, a singularity of infinite density and curvature of space-time, at which point all known laws of science cease to apply and time itself stops, is bound by the same cycle of creation and destruction. Sooner or later it will lose mass, and when greatly reduced in size, it will, Hawking surmises, 'disappear completely in a tremendous final burst of emission, equivalent to the explosion of millions of H-bombs.'[29] That emission will, in turn, seed the creation of new galaxies.

The eternal cycle of creation or destruction, as evidenced by science, is thus, an endorsement of Shankaracharya's philosophical vision that, since Brahman itself is without a beginning or an end, the universe that emanates from it, in which it is both immanent and transcendent, is also without finite coordinates, and is anadi and anant, eternal. In fact, David Bohm, whose theory of the 'implicate order' we shall discuss later, says that:

> In our approach this 'big bang' is to be regarded as actually just a "little ripple". An interesting image is obtained by considering that in the middle of the actual ocean, myriads of small waves occasionally come together fortuitously with such phase relationships that they end up in a small region of space, suddenly to produce a very high wave which just appears as if from nowhere and out of nothing. Perhaps something like this could happen in the immense ocean of cosmic energy, creating a sudden wave pulse, from which

28 Ibid., p. 25.

29 Stephen Hawking, op. cit., p. 118.

> our "universe" would be born. This pulse would explode outward and break up into smaller ripples that spread yet further outward to constitute our "expanding universe".[30]

This analogy, of a timeless reality, that ebbs and declines in an unending cycle of creation and destruction, can be seen in the sub-atomic world of quantum physics too, where particles come into being and are extinguished in an unseen but ceaseless cycle. Some two hundred particles have by now been identified beyond the proton, the neutron and the electron. These exist, but many only for a period not longer than a millionth of a second. As mentioned earlier, some particles are not real in the conventional sense, but virtual entities that emerge and vanish into a void in a nano second. Particles like the proton, the electron and the photon (which represents the unit of electromagnetic radiation) are relatively stable but subject to annihilation through collision. The rest is characterised by incessant creation and simultaneous destruction through decay and instability.

Brahman, which is beyond the boundaries of time, then is witness to an eternal cycle of creation, maintenance and destruction—*shristi, sthithi,* and *pralaya*. In Hindu belief, this cycle is endless, and without a beginning or end. Srishti, creates; sthithi, maintains; pralaya, destroys, and then a new cycle begins again. The concept of an endless cycle of time corresponds perfectly with Einstein's theory of relativity, arguably the most significant scientific discovery of recent times.

Einstein established the equivalence of mass and energy. This means that all that we see as mass in the universe, from the largest galaxy to the smallest particle, is essentially energy that has assumed a certain mass, and if that mass mutates, or even visibly ceases to exist, its energy equivalent merely lapses back into its original state, or assumes another form. 'At the subatomic level of elementary particles there is no death in the sense of permanent

30 David Bohm, *Wholeness and the Implicate Order*, Routledge Classics, 1980, p. 244.

loss. The quantum vacuum, which is the underlying reality of all that is, exists eternally.'[31]

As recently as March 2013, in the Large Hadron Collider built by the European Organization for Nuclear Research, known by its French acronym CERN, scientists tentatively discovered the Higgs Boson (also called the 'God Particle'), which demonstrated that energy is neither created nor destroyed but simply converted into mass.

If we accept, as Shankara postulates, that Brahman is the constant, unchanging, ubiquitous and sole energy eternally pulsating through the universe, then it is easy to understand why, according to the equivalence between energy and mass, the finite world of nama-rupa emerges from it, and lapses back into it. In other words, nothing empirical ceases to exist, and nothing is ever born that did not exist in some form before, and, thus, the cycle of creation and destruction is an eternal continuum, with Brahman as the eternal causal nature (svabhava), or the unchanging universal (samanya), and all contingent products are effects—avastha or vishesha.

Scientists mostly express their conclusions in a dry, almost matter of fact way. But philosophers, and the imagery that illustrates their vision, are more poetic and evocative. If the reason why the empirical universe needs to exist, and exist only in a certain way, is, in the ultimate analysis, anirvachaniya or inexpressible and indefinable, as Shankara said and scientists today accept, then Hindu philosophy embellishes this finding with the grandeur of imagination.

The indefinable relationship of the physical universe to the ground from which it emanates, is depicted in the Hindu vision as leela, the joyous overflow of the fullness of Brahman, or more accurately, of Ishwara. Ishwara is Brahman reduced to the level of human comprehension in the form of a personal divinity. The universe is the play of Ishwara, a spontaneous expression of his

31 Danah Zohar, op. cit., p. 142.

benevolence. It may not be necessary or explicable, but it exists as his will, a sign of his unlimited exuberance, a festivity without reason, a celebration without purpose. In creating the world, God is at sport, revelling in his own plenitude, answerable only to himself, whimsically opaque, fulfilling his own desire-less creativity. Leela is the shadow on the cosmic canvas of the mesmerising light shed by the elusive powers of maya.

In giving form to his unbounded freedom of expression, Ishwara has no motivation (*prayojana*). Nor, is he in any way diminished in giving from himself. He is self-sufficiency itself, and that is precisely why he can create without cause or reason. As Shankara says in his bhashya on the *Brahma Sutra*, 'the activity of the Lord may be supposed to be mere sport (leela) proceeding from his own nature, without reference to any purpose.' Or, as he puts it more evocatively in the hymn to Dakshinamurti:

> bow to Him who, by the sheer power of His will, projects outside like a magician or a mighty Yogi this infinite universe which, in the beginning, rests without name or form, like the sprout in a seed, and after creation, by the power of time and space imagined through Maya, appears to be many, possessed of manifold shapes and hues.

Hindu belief holds Lord Krishna to be Leela Purushottam. In contrast to Lord Rama, who is Maryada Purushottam, the epitome of rectitude, Krishna weaves the magic of leela, in which the world is but a reflection of his playful omnipotence. In this role, he is the adorable child who steals butter, the lover who frolics with abandon with the gopis of Vrindavana, the warrior who participates in the epic war, the Mahabharata, and the saviour who counsels Arjuna on nishkama karma or duty without thought of reward. In other words, he is many in one, and one in all, impossible to define in one category alone. His very multifacetedness reflects his leela, as the God who revels in the sheer indefinability of his persona, and who creates the universe effortlessly, while almost at sport. To his countless devotees, he is accepted as both somber and playful, lover and ascetic, prankster and thinker, all-powerful and yet one who is punished for stealing butter!

If the comparison is to be made with the unpredictable diversities of quantum physics, Krishna is like a particle that is both a wave and a particle; a particle whose velocity and position can never be accurately measured; and, a particle whose existence can never be directly explained but whose measurable effects are beyond doubt!

Krishna is thus a metaphor for why the world is what it is: known, yet beyond complete explication. As one of the most lovable gods of Hinduism, he steps in confidently, in his contradictory splendour, where philosophers admit they have no answers, and scientists accept the limits of their knowledge. In that leelamayi world, where everything is suffused with the capricious benevolence of Ishwara, Krishna is the answer to questions that, at the human level, are unanswerable. As we have seen, Einstein would have liked God to be a little less versatile and a little more definable and predictable. 'God does not play dice,' he famously said, as we noted, but Hawking confirms just the opposite when he concedes that quantum physics 'introduces an unavoidable element of unpredictability or randomness into science.'[32] That wonderful randomness, which Shankara calls anirvachaniya, is leela, the play of the divine.

The same imaginative grandeur in Hindu thought is in evidence in describing the scientifically proven ceaseless flux of the universe, where birth and death follow each other in an unending and

32 ibid., p. 62.

beginning-less cycle, and there is no 'cosmological constant' as Einstein would have liked to believe.

Here the symbol of this cosmic flux is Shiva, also known as Nataraja, the Lord of Dance. In the tandava dance, he choreographs the cosmic cycle of creation, preservation and destruction. As immortalised in the Chola and Kurkihara bronzes, he is seen dynamically poised in the midst of his vigorously rhythmic portrayal of the endless swirl of the universe. Around him is a frame of fire, representing the pulsating energy permeating the universe; in his upper right hand is the drum, symbol of the primal sound of creation; in his upper left hand is a flame, pointing to the inevitability of destruction of all things transient; his lower right hand benevolently extends the promise of grace and redemption; and, his lower left hand points downward to the demon below his feet, indicative of the ignorance that we must conquer. His movements, while in perfect harmony, are so fast and vigorous that the tongue of flame in his hand creates the illusion of a circle of fire, and the sound of the drum appears to emanate from all quarters.

In the midst of this energetic dance, his face is the picture of calm, symbolic of his transcendence, where he is immanent in the dance of the cosmos, but totally above it. As Nataraja he, therefore, represents shrishti, sthithi, *samhara,* destruction; *tirobhava,* illusion; and, *anugraha,* grace.

The sheer loftiness of the spiritual imagination in creating such an image to represent the cosmic cycle of creation and destruction leaves one breathless. The great art historian and philosopher, Ananda Coomaraswamy says unhesitatingly that such a depiction of primal rhythmic energy is 'the clearest image of the activity of god which any art or religion can boast of.'[33] Fritjof Capra, himself a scholar of theoretical physics of considerable prominence,

33 A.K. Coomaraswamy, *The Dance of Shiva*, The Noonday Press, New York, 1969, p. 78.

concludes that Shiva's dance is the mythological counterpart of the dancing universe, representing the 'ceaseless flow of energy going through an infinite variety of patterns that melt into one another.'

'Modern physics,' he explains,

> has shown that the rhythm of creation and destruction is not only manifest in the turn of season and in the birth and death of all living creatures, but is also the very essence of inorganic matter. According to quantum field theory, all interactions between the constituents of matter take place through the emission and absorption of virtual particles. More than that, the dance of creation and destruction is the basis of the very existence of matter, since all material particles 'self-interact' by emitting and reabsorbing virtual particles. Modern physics has thus revealed that every subatomic particle not only performs an energy dance, but also is an energy dance; a pulsating process of creation and destruction.[34]

For Shankara, Shiva is, at the human level, the very incarnation of Brahman. His cosmic dance is thus the choreography of the universe enabled by the omnipresent, but nirguna, Brahman. In his hymn to Shiva, Shankara acknowledges, with devotional fervour, this role of Nataraja: 'Lord and Primeval Cause! From thee alone the world has sprung. Compassionate One! Thou who art Lord of all, in Thee Shiva, who dost reveal thyself through all things living and all without life! To Thee alone does the world at last return.'

The most remarkable congruence with Shankaracharya's philosophy is the recognition by leading scientists today that the energy that pervades the entire cosmos is actually nothing but unsullied and luminescent *consciousness*. Shankara asserted

34 Fritjof Capra, op. cit., p. 271.

that Brahman, although beyond all attributes, is consciousness personified (chaitanyam). In this form, Brahman has no specific determinations, either of merit or demerit from the human point of view, except that of pure being, which is characterised by chid or absolute awareness undetermined by any extraneous or causal factor. As Shankara writes in the *Vivekachudamani*: 'As the wave, the foam, the whirlpool and bubble etc. are all in essence but water, similarly the chit is all this, from the body up to the notion of 'I'. Everything is verily the chitta, homogenous and pure.'

From this Brahman consciousness arises the transient and the finite. They are its manifestations, like waves on the surface of the ocean, while the essential ground is the water from which the waves emanate. 'All this universe cognized by speech and mind is nothing but Brahman; there is nothing besides Brahman that exists. Are the pitcher, jug or jar known to be distinct from the earth or which they are composed?' Shankara, thus, clearly makes two categorical assertions: first, that Brahman, as chitta or undifferentiated consciousness, pervades the entire universe; and, two, that that consciousness is the ground from which the empirical, either physical objects, or the subtle mind, arises.

What is fascinating is that leading scientists today are saying the same thing. At the end of their deeply penetrating examination of the working of the universe, both at the macro and micro level, their vastly increased but still inconclusive knowledge of the who, what and why of the cosmos, has led them, finally, to posit the existence of a third dimension as the ground for all that they can observe, and that dimension is consciousness.

Max Planck (1858–1947), the German theoretical physicist who was amongst the founders of quantum physics, and a man who by temperament was skeptical about all 'non-scientific' speculations and relied greatly on 'logical' reasoning, was candid enough to admit towards the end of his life that consciousness is primary and matter only a derivative of it. In a speech on 'The Nature of Matter' at Florence in Italy, just a few years before he died, he said:

> As a man who has devoted his whole life to the most clear headed science, to the study of matter, I can tell you as a result of my research about atoms this much: There is no matter as such. All matter originates and exists only by virtue of a force which brings the particle of an atom to vibrate and holds this minute solar system of the atom together. We must assume behind this force the existence of a conscious and intelligent mind. The mind is the matrix of all matter.

Erwin Schrodinger, another pioneer of quantum physics, was deeply influenced by the philosophy of Vedanta. However, whatever his personal spiritual predilections, his scientific conclusion after all his pioneering research in science, led him to say in his book, '*What is Life? That individual consciousness is only a manifestation of a unitary consciousness pervading the universe* (emphasis mine). In that one conclusion, he was only paraphrasing the Upanashidic injunction: Tat tvam asi: That thou art, which was the foundational basis of Shankara's thought structure. Eugene Wigner echoed Schrodinger when he said that the laws of quantum theory could not be formulated 'in a fully consistent way without reference to consciousness.'[35]

Leading American theoretical physicist, Geoffrey Chew, now ninety-four years old, and the pioneer of the 'bootstrap' theory of quantum physics, which, inter alia, is eclectic about all theories that can provide a consistent model of the universe, admits that 'carried to its logical extreme, the bootstrap conjecture implies that the existence of consciousness along with all other aspects of

35 E.P. Wigner, *Symmetries and Reflections—Scientific Essays*, M.I.T. Press, Cambridge, 1970, p.172.

nature, is necessary for self-consistency of the whole.'[36] This was also the inference of scientists looking deep into the vast cosmos, far beyond the micro world of quantum physics. The great astrophysicist, Arthur Eddington had no hesitation in admitting that, 'All through the physical world runs that unknown content that must surely be the stuff of our own consciousness.'

Eddington's phrase, 'our own consciousness' is the key to the theory called the Anthropic principle. Essentially, this argues that the apparent laws of science are based on the fact that we exist, with 'conscious' minds to observe them. There is thus an integral link between the consciousness that we represent and the working of the universe. In other words, we are not the products of some mechanical evolutionary processes, but that process itself is designed to be part of the same consciousness of which we are the final product. Human beings are not objective observers but participants in the observation of scientific phenomena, and, therefore, the universe, as British mathematician Roger Penrose says, evolved in conformity with laws that consciousness was formatted to understand. The cosmos 'must have known that we are coming,' says physicist Freeman Dyson because science and a conscious observer cannot be separated. Even Hawking, who remains relentless in his search for that final unified theory to explain the universe, concedes that the anthropic principle, which actually introduces a non-measurable element into scientific equations, cannot be dismissed out of hand.

The world, according to Shankaracharya, was suffused with the consciousness of Brahman, and scientists today are far more open to accept this thesis for the simple reason that a wholly deterministic and explicable world is beyond their grasp.

The Judeo-Christian worldview persistently maintained that the world is a coherent whole, explicable in mechanical terms. But, in

---

36 G. F. Chew, 'Bootstrap: A Scientific Idea', Science volume 161 (23 May 1968), p. 763.

the light of the latest discoveries of modern science, 'the mechanical worldview could never really succeed. From the beginning, it was flawed by its inability to explain or account for consciousness.'[37] There has to be 'something', leading scientific minds are saying, which is beyond the detecting powers of telescopes and microscopes, and that 'something' alone can explicate an otherwise bewildering universe. American theoretical physicist, John Wheeler (1911–2008), who taught at Princeton University for most of his life, has posited the Participatory Anthropic Principle, in which he accepts that 'consciousness may play some role in bringing the universe into existence.'[38] Musing about how in the universe something can arise from nothing, he concluded that there has to be a 'conscious observer' to explicate the entire process. In a lecture in 1990 he went so far as to say that 'every item of the physical world has at bottom—a very deep bottom—in most instances, *an immaterial source and explanation.*' (emphasis mine). The biologist Edwin Chargaff also speaks about this 'immaterial', invisible force—which Shankara unhesitatingly calls Brahman. Chargaff writes that if a scientist 'has not experienced, at least a few times in his life, this cold shudder down his spine, this confrontation with an immense, invisible face whose breath moves him to tears, he is not a scientist.'[39]

Scientists, by training, shy away from becoming philosophers, but even when they do so, they hesitate to acknowledge the scientifically 'unverifiable' in direct terms. However, in spite of their scientific coyness, the implications of what they are saying, is directly corroborative of Shankara's assertions. If John Wheeler sought to provide scientific camouflage to his acceptance of consciousness by use of concepts like 'pre-geometry', American

---

37 Danah Zohar, op. cit., p. 234.

38 Science Show, *The Anthropic Universe*, 18 February 2008.

39 Quoted in Andrew Newberg et. al., *Why God Won't Go Away*, op. cit., p. 154.

scientist David Bohm (1917–1992), acknowledged widely as one of the most significant theoretical physicists of the twentieth century, spoke of 'pre-space', and articulated the concept of an 'implicate order', which, shorn of its scientific scaffolding, is a transparent and intuitive endorsement of Shankara's philosophy.

Bohm, who some say introduced 'unorthodox' ideas into quantum theory, and who admitted to being an admirer of Indian philosopher Jiddu Krishnamurti, coined the term 'implicate order' after observing the fundamentally inter-relatedness of the universe, and within this, the seemingly bizarre behaviour of sub-atomic particles. Both these phenomena could be explained only by the existence of 'unobserved forces'. What we take for reality, he said, are but 'abstract forms derived from a deeper reality in which what prevails is unbroken wholeness,'[40] a direct validation of Shankara's assertion that cosmic awareness is indivisible and without parts. This universe of unbroken wholeness,

> is the *implicate* or *enfolded* order. In the enfolded order, space and time are no longer the dominant factors determining the dependence or independence of different elements. Rather, an entirely different sort of basic connection of elements is possible, from which our ordinary notions of space and time, along with those of separately existent material particles, are abstracted as forms derived from the deeper order. These ordinary notions in fact appear in what is called the *explicate* or *unfolded* order, which is a special and distinguished form contained within the general totality of all the implicate order.[41]

The parallel with Shankara's argument that the empirical world

40 David Bohm, *Wholeness and the Implicate Order*, Routledge Classics, 1980, p. xviii.

41 ibid., p. xvii.

of nama-rupa—name and form—is but 'surface phenomena', and that underlying it is the deeper reality of Brahman—or the implicate order, as Bohm calls it, which is the ground from which all observable reality emerges—is stark. Bohm characterised surface phenomena as the 'explicate order', and sought to illustrate its difference with the implicate order through easily comprehensible examples. The images on our TV screen, he said, is the explicate order; the unseen signal enabling the image is the implicate order. In another analogy, he referred to a folded piece of paper in which small cuts are made. When the paper is unfolded, a widely separated pattern appears, but that is but the manifestation of the original cuts. The original cuts, Bohm argues, is the implicate order while the unfolded pattern represents the explicate order, the world of appearances as defined by Shankara.

Bohm illustrated his worldview by many more examples, understandable to an audience not familiar to the mathematical intricacies of quantum physics. In one of them, he speaks of a rectangular water tank full of water with transparent walls, and some fish, which is under observation by two television cameras placed at right angles to each other. The images projected by the two cameras on two screens, A and B, will show that,

> there is a certain relationship between the images appearing on the two screens. For example, on screen A we may see an image of a fish, and on screen B we will see another such image. At any given moment each image will generally *look* different from the other....Of course, we know that the two images do not refer to independently existent though interacting actualities (in which, one image could be said to "cause" related changes in the other. Rather, they refer to a single actuality, which is the images without the assumption that they causally affect each other). This actuality is of higher dimensionality than are the separate images on the screens; or, to put it differently, the images on the screens

> are two-dimensional *projections* (or facets) of a three-dimensional reality. In some sense, this three-dimensional reality holds these two two-dimensional projections within it. Yet, since these projections exist only as abstractions, the three-dimensional reality is neither of these, but rather it is something else, something of a nature beyond both.[42]

This, and other examples that Bohm uses to explicate his theory also bring out the validity of Shankara's theory of vivartavada, discussed earlier, that the essential cause (which, in his theory was the underlying ground of Brahman) can produce an effect without undergoing any change itself. Like the original tank of water, the basis of the universe remains unchanged. The effects it creates, as for instance in the duality of images being projected by two cameras placed at different positions, constitute the world of appearance, but these appearances do not change the original reality. If we substitute the appearance for the reality, it is because of the error of perception, avidya, and not because the cause has changed, or that the effect is, in essence, a separate entity from the cause.

Such a postulate is essentially different from the theory, held by some schools of Hindu philosophy, of *parinamavada*, wherein the cause itself changes while producing an effect. In studying the working of the cosmos, scientists like Bohm are now asserting, from the standpoint of science that the underlying cause of empirical phenomenon is unchanging and pervasive, and what we mostly—but erroneously—take to be real are but abstractions or effects, which do not impact the cause. The general nature of reality, as Bohm says, is then not one of *what is* to what is not. On the contrary, it 'is a relationship of certain phases of *what is* to other phases of *what is*, that are in different phases of enfoldment.'[43]

42 ibid., p. 238.
43 ibid., p. 258.

Bohm's long time co-worker on the theory of the implicate order was British quantum physicist Basil Hiley, Professor Emeritus at the University of London. He too maintained that mind and matter are subsumed by the deeper implicate order and no division between them exists. Hiley was categorical that this thesis could be proven by mathematical analysis.

Mani Bhaumik is even more emphatic in his endorsement of the Vedantic vision:

> In pre-space, the potentialities of consciousness and the primary field are united through mutual participation on a universal scale. Put another way, the essence of the implicate order is the *one source* that enfolds both the primary field (the common source of at least everything physical) and consciousness. Based upon this thesis, it would be logical to infer that *the one source of the world's great spiritual traditions is grounded in scientific theory.*[44]

Quite evidently, Shankara's thesis of Brahman as a consciousness pervading the universe has an increasing acceptance in the world of science. Shankara also believed that, as indicated in the Upanishads, there is, in each of us an *ansha* or part of that same consciousness in the form of our Atman or the real self. There is no difference between the two. Both are a continuum of the omnipresence of Brahman.

As human beings, caught in the snare of maya, and overwhelmed by ignorance, we lose sight of this real self, and consider the transient and material world that constitutes our finite lives to be all that matters. The Atman, asserts Shankara, remains untouched by our avidya; it is unsullied by our ego; unlike our phenomenal self, it is beyond our mind, senses, emotions and likes and dislikes. 'It does not change its character under any circumstances but

44 Mani Bhaumik, *Code Named God*, op. cit., p. 177.

maintains it. What appears or is produced by an external operative cause and is thus dependent on it is not the *nature* of the thing.'[45]

There is, thus, in every human being, the sakshin, the ever-witnessing self, that, as Shankara says, is *brahmatmak,* or of the nature of Brahman itself. This self reveals itself when we overcome our avidya, and as a consequence, the mind is quiescent and the ego is stilled, then it shines forth as our real and transcendent (*kutastha*) self, freed from our self-imposed upadhis or material, sensory and mental limitations. In that moment of the deepest calm, the Atman unites with what it was always a part, Brahman. To use Shankara's analogy, it is like space limited inside a jar escaping, once the jar is broken, to become one with the cosmic space, with which it was always identical in spite of its transient confinement.

The question is whether this philosophical vision is borne out by scientific research. The term 'neurotheology', which explores the possibility of a self within our self, was first used by Aldous Huxley in his novel *Island,* but more in a philosophical sense. Since then, there has been considerable work to scientifically establish the correlation between the brain and spiritual experience, an attempt by neurologists to try and 'understand how the human brain can at times transcend its evident limitations and experience a state of substantially heightened awareness, and a unity with the entire cosmos.'[46]

Neurologists concede that it is a difficult task to evaluate 'spiritual states'. Kevin Nelson, a leading proponent of brain-based theories, says in his book, *The Spiritual Doorway in the Brain: A Neurologists Search for the God Experience,* that his work 'irks some die-hard atheists, because it inextricably links

45 From Shankara's *Brahma Sutra Bhashya*, quoted by Kokileshwar Shastri, op. cit., p. 93.

46 A. Sayadmansour, *Neurotheology: The relationship between brain and religion, Iranian Journal of Neurology,* 2014: 13 (1), pp. 52-55.

spirituality with what it means to be human and makes it an empirical part of us, whether our reasoning brain likes it or not.'[47] But, fortunately, even sceptics accept that advanced brain imaging capabilities, and objectively devised yardsticks of measurement, have revolutionised the field of neurotheology, so that today, 'understanding the neurological foundations of spirituality is necessary for a contemporary understanding of what it means to be human.'[48]

Armed with these new technologies, many more neurologists and medical practitioners are affirming what Shankara said. Andrew Newberg, MD, is the director of research at the Myrna Brind Centre of Integrative Medicine and Professor of Emergency Medicine and Radiology at Thomas Jefferson University in Philadelphia. The late Eugene d'Aquili, MD, PhD was a clinical assistant professor at the Department of Psychiatry at the University of Pennsylvania. Together with journalist Vince Rause, they wrote a path-breaking book in 2001 called *Why God Won't Go Away: Brain Science and the Biology of Belief.* Echoing Shankara's thesis of the sakshin, representing the Atman in each of us, they write:

> There seems to be, within the human head, an inner, personal awareness, a free-standing observant self...Neurology cannot completely explain how such a thing can happen—how a nonmaterial mind can rise from mere biological functions; how the flesh and blood machinery of the brain can suddenly become "aware".[49]

The authors believe that the existence of such an aware self has its

---

47 Dr Kevin Nelson, *The Spiritual Doorway in the Brain: A Neurologist's Search for the God Experience*, see Prologue, Plume, 2012, p, 11.

48 ibid., p. 11.

49 Andrew Newberg et. al., op. cit., p. 32.

roots in the working of the autonomic nervous system, the limbic system, and in the complex analytical functions of the brain.

The human brain is an extraordinarily complex mechanism. It consists of billions of nerve cells, through which external data enters the cognitive system through billions of electrochemical energy inputs. Each part of the brain performs a specialised function, crunching a constant stream of sensory information, ceaselessly interpreting the external world; thoughts, images, perceptions and emotions incessantly flit around its neural pathways triggering the release of countless chemical neurotransmitters. But, if some of this ceaseless activity of the brain is 'blocked' through meditation, or in moments of deep surrender, or when the ego is stilled, is there another self that transcends the normal flux of our brain activity?

Newberg and D'Aquili believe that there is such a self. One of their ways to establish this is to map the brains of those who practice deep meditation. They write of one such person, Robert, who is about to begin his practiced meditation in a neurology lab in a university hospital. The moment Robert signals—by a gentle tug to a string being monitored in the examination room—that he is on the verge of entering his meditative climax, the doctors get to work.

They inject a radioactive material into Robert's left arm, and the moment his meditation is over, subject his brain to a SPECT (Single Photon Emission Computed Tomography) camera in the hospital's Nuclear Medicine department. The scans show that when Robert was at the deepest state of meditation, a significant part of his brain—which the doctors call the 'orientation association area'—was bathed in 'cool greens and blues'. In neurological terms, these colours indicate a substantial reduction in the brain's ceaseless activity. What excited the scientists was that since the orientation area is normally always in flux, why did meditation alter this, and if it did, what conclusions could be drawn from this fact?

At the end of many years of scientific research on this question, Newberg and D'Aquili came to the conclusion that 'spiritual experience, at its very root, is intimately interwoven with human biology,' and that there is 'evidence of a scientific process that has evolved to allow us humans to transcend material existence and acknowledge and connect with deeper, more spiritual part of ourselves perceived of *as an absolute, universal reality that connects us to all there is.*'[50] (emphasis mine)

The effects of meditation on the human body have been scientifically mapped: the blood pressure falls, the heartbeat slows down; stress hormones drop; and our immune system gets a boost. But, the far more important finding is that—entirely in conformity with what Shankara, and, indeed, several other schools of eastern philosophy assert—meditation, or moments of deep devotion and surrender, enable the brain to reconnect with its real self, that is always there but lies buried under the debris of the mind's artificial construct of our phenomenal self. When, by the removal of avidya, knowledge dawns of who we really are, we discover the identity of the Atman within us with the transcendent cosmic radiance of Brahman.

Is there scientific evidence of this reconnect between our self and the 'absolute and universal reality' that Newberg and D'Aquili speak of? Contrary to conventional thinking, latest neurology reveals that the brain has a remarkable ability to reinvent itself. It has the inherent faculty to learn from experience, and modify its neural components. Neurologists call this phenomena, 'neuroplasticity'.

Mani Bhaumik quotes the recent finding of neurobiologist Michael Ehlers at Duke University Medical Centre, that in the brain, 'synapses are completely turning over all their constituents multiple times a day—a stunning finding,' and that the entire

50 Andrew Newberg et. al., op. cit., pp. 8-9.

brain can be completely recycled on a bi-monthly basis.[51] If this is the case, can there not be a neurologically verifiable basis to Shankara's thesis that once the veil of ignorance about our real identity is removed, the brain has the potential to understand, and correcting its earlier error, realise the self within, and that self's identity with a transcendent reality?

In other words, neurologists are today daring to ask the question that only some years ago would have been considered unscientific: 'Could it be that the brain has evolved the ability to transcend material existence, and experience a higher plane of being that actually exists?'[52]

That 'higher plane', which mystics of many faiths have testified to, and Shankara posited as the lynchpin of his philosophy, was earlier dismissed by neurologists and psychologists as hallucinatory, or delusional or a sign of mental imbalance triggered by grief or distress, or even just plain neurotic. But now science is giving new credence to the accounts of those who testify to the experience of transcendence, where the mind, in a sense, overarches itself, and pole vaults to another level of consciousness. This heightened consciousness,

> is not necessarily created by the brain, but the brain has the ability to access the vast universal consciousness that underlies all of reality. Consciousness is primary to matter, and hence biology. The brain has consciousness like anything else in the universe and merely has a more sophisticated manner of experiencing and expressing it.[53]

In the University of Montreal, brain imager, Mario Beauregard

---

51 Mani Bhaumik, *Code Named God*, op. cit., p. 215.

52 Andrew Newberg et. al., op. cit., p. 140.

53 Andrew Newberg, *The Metaphysical Mind: Probing the Biology of Philosphical Thought.*

and Vincent Paquette have studied the mental activities of seven Carmalite nuns through electrodes attached to their brain. Their aim is to examine whether it is scientifically possible to map the blissful transcendence associated with the state of unio mystica—the sense of a mystical union with god. Their conclusion is that whenever the nuns have an intense spiritual experience, 'time slows down, and the self seems to dissolve into a larger entity that the nuns describe as God.'[54]

Dr Dean Hamer, a prominent geneticist who received his doctorate from Harvard University, argues in his book, *The God Gene: How Faith is Hardwired Into Our Genes,* that 'spirituality is among the most ubiquitous and powerful forces in human life.'[55] In his research at the National Institute of Health in America, he found that in a random survey, at least one-third of the people 'reported personal experiences in which they felt in contact with a divine and wonderful spiritual power.'[56]

Hamer's conclusion was that there is in each human being a *specific individual gene* that predisposes us to believe. This gene is primarily related to spirituality, not religion. As he writes, 'Spirituality is based in consciousness, religion in cognition. Spirituality is universal, whereas cultures have their own forms of religion. I would argue that the most important contrast is that spirituality is genetic, while religion is based on culture, traditions, beliefs and ideas.'[57]

One measurable characteristic of this genetic predisposition is the feeling of self-transcendence it bestows on the person who has a spiritual experience. In this moment of self-transcendence, which Abraham Maslow, the founder of 'humanist psychology'

---

54 *The Economist,* 4 March 2004.

55 Dean Hamer, *The God Gene: How Faith is Hardwired Into Our Genes,* Anchor Books, New York, p. 4.

56 ibid., p. 5.

57 ibid., p. 213.

in the 1960s, called a 'peak experience', an individual, writes Hamer, feels 'a sense of wholeness and unity with the universe, with everything and everywhere. There is an effortless letting go of the ego, a going beyond the self.'[58]

Hamer's theory was greatly influenced by the work of Robert Cloninger, a psychiatrist at Washington University Medical School in St. Louis, who developed the 'self-transcendence scale'. This scale has three separate but inter-related components: self-forgetfulness, transpersonal identification, and mysticism. Cloninger's surveys revealed that a majority of people had these components, and that those who had it had definitive degrees of all three. In terms of Shankara's philosophy, Cloninger's three components would correspond to the ability of an individual to go beyond his limited ego (self-forgetfulness), experience a feeling of unity with a larger totality—the universe or the cosmos (transpersonal identification), and have, on occasion, an intuitive insight into a realm beyond the normal empirical coordinates of our lives (mysticism).

Newberg and D'Aquili endorse this thesis of self-transcendence. They write: 'After years of research, however, our finding of various key brain structures and the way information is channeled along neural pathways led us to hypothesize that the brain possesses a neurological mechanism for self-transcendence. When taken to its extreme, this mechanism, would erase the mind's sense of self and undo any conscious awareness of an external world'.[59] Their categorical conclusion is that 'the state of absolute union that the mystics describe does in fact exist and the mind has developed the capacity to perceive it.'[60]

The scientists who wrote *Why God Won't Go Away* describe this transcendent state of absolute union—or in Shankara's terminology the realisation of the identity of the Atman and

58 ibid., p. 20.
59 ibid., p. 146.
60 ibid., p. 147.

Brahman—as Absolute Unitary Being (AUB). In that state, they assert, the signals to the ever active 'orientation association area', which is the hallmark of our routine self, are 'deafferentiated' or reduced in a transformative way. The result is that the self, or the inherent transcendence within us, reasserts itself. This does not nullify awareness, but takes it to an unimaginably higher level.

> Deafferentation does not deprive the mind of awareness, it simply frees that awareness of the usual subjective sense of self, and from all sense of the spatial world in which that self could be. The result of such a lack of output, almost certainly would be a *state of pure awareness,* an awareness stripped of ego, focused on nothing, oblivious to the passage of time and physical sensation. This awareness would be neurobiologically incapable of differentiating between subject and object, between the limited personal self and the external, material world. It would perceive and interpret reality *as a formless unified whole, with no limits, no substance, no beginning, and no end.* All the assembled constructs of the conscious mind—the emotions, memories, thoughts and unformed intuitions by which we know our selves—would come undone, *and dissolve into this underlying pure awareness.*[61] (emphasis mine)

This scientific inference is a remarkable scientific endorsement of what the Upanishadic seers, and Shankara, said. Pure awareness, chitta, Shankara stressed, is the distinguishing sign of Brahman. When the mind is deeply still, and has overcome the limitations of the false sense of ego and the distractions of the sensory world, it enables the Atman within us to unite with this underlying pure awareness. As Shankara writes in the *Vivekachudamani:* 'Through the complete cessation of Egoism, through the stoppage of the

61 ibid., pp. 150-151.

diverse mental waves due to it, and through the discrimination of the inner Reality, one realizes that Reality as "I am Thou"—Tat Tvam Asi.'[62]

This realisation can come, as neurologists testify, through a conscious attempt to control the incessant flux of the mind, through meditation, yoga, prayer, bhakti, surrender, and constant vigilance of the mental processes. At the vyavaharik, or practical level, these practices have Shankara's approval too. But Shankara does not rule out the possibility—indeed, even the likelihood—of this realisation dawning in one moment of intuitive liberation. Brahmanubhava, where the individual suddenly transcends the ego, and perceives himself as part of a larger, universal reality, with all notions of the phenomenal 'I' dissolving at the very moment of this revolutionary realisation, happens, neurologists say, when the 'normal rational thought processes give way to more intuitive ways of understanding—-In a sense, all mystical experiences are spontaneous—even the mystics who dedicate their lives to the pursuit of spiritual union can't anticipate when it will occur.'[63] This is exactly what Shankara said about the actual experience of brahmanubhava. That experience is *sakshatkara*, one of direct perception, or *samyagdarshana* (perfect intuition).

Shankara said that Brahman is sat (truth), chitta (awareness) and ananda (bliss)—satchidananda. In the *Nirvana Shatakam*, Shankara emphasises that nothing else is real about us, or matters, in an ontological sense, except the realisation of chidananda—bliss and awareness—and once this is known, we become one with Shiva—*Shivoham! Shivoham!* The Absolute Unitary Being, which Newberg and his co-authors recognise, is synonymous with Brahman. Those who experience it know that is of the nature of bliss. The moment the mind shuts out its

---

62 *Vivekachudamani,* translated by Swami Madhavananda, The Advaita Ashrama, Mayavati, Almora, 1921, p. 138.

63 Andrew Newberg et. al., op. cit., pp. 101, 134.

natural and sterile chatter, and awakens to a heightened level of awareness, in which all distinctions of object and subject and personal and external disappear, and there is an intense feeling of complete peace, wholeness and fulfillment, a sense of being one with the entire cosmos, the consequence has to be bliss. Meditation, Mani Bhaumik, says is 'also the mind's most blissful state, as evidenced by the significant rise of the neurotransmitter serotonin in the brain chemistry of deep meditators. Serotonin is the same neurotransmitter that the popular anti-depressant Prozac manipulates....the mind in deep meditation reaches a crossover point where all the momentum favours a quantum leap into perfect coherence.'[64]

Those who experience this bliss, recognise it as a 'higher reality', surpassing, without a semblance of doubt, the empirical world that is their normal accoutrement. Neurologists cannot scientifically measure the intensity of that bliss, which as Shankara himself says is indescribable, but they accept that those who experience it consider it as palpable and real. In fact, Newberg and D'Aquili go so far as to concede that 'informed speculation tells us that it's possible that AUB may be as real, if not more fundamentally real than what we perceive as "ordinary" reality, *one from which all objective and subjective perspectives of the world are derived.*'[65] There could be no clearer scientific confirmation of Shankara's assertion that Brahman is the only real, and that everything else is derived from it.

It must have required great courage of conviction, and deep spiritual and philosophical insight for Shankaracharya to build on the insights of the Upanishads, a structure of thought, over a millennium ago, that saw the universe and our own lives within it with a clairvoyance that is being so amazingly endorsed by science today. Philosophers and scientists normally inhabit separate

64 Mani Bhaumik, *Code Named God*, op. cit., pp. 212-213.
65 Andrew Newberg et. al., op. cit., p. 178.

worlds. The seeker after spiritual truth pursues his quest beyond mathematical equations; the explorer of the material world is hesitant to go beyond what is empirically verifiable. And yet, sometimes, these separate worlds coalesce. Scientists are unable to come up with final answers to questions they thought are answerable. It is then that they, gingerly, begin to step towards the universe of philosophers.

Can there be explanations of the working of this vast and complex universe that are beyond the horizon of scientific analysis and observation? To be sure, scientists are not easily swayed. For them to move from the verifiable to the conceptual is akin to a betrayal of their own training and methodology. The metaphysical concept that attracts them must be of a nature that is itself a product of exceptional rigour of thought. Shankaracharya's Vedantic philosophy has that uncompromising consistency and logic, where, certain fundamental postulates, almost like mathematical equations, are stated with a certitude that is evidence of the 'third eye' that opens only to those who look deep within.

The irony is that most leading scientists, particularly outside India, but also within, have little knowledge of the structure of Shankaracharya's philosophy, and the transparent interface it has with scientific discoveries today. It can only be hoped that a reading of this chapter will impel them to discover the depths of Hinduism's greatest thinker and his remarkable philosophical prescience, and give credit where it is due, albeit belatedly.

EPILOGUE: THE LEGACY

There is no doubt that the philosophy of Vedanta as propounded by Shankaracharya makes him the most important thinker in the exceptional philosophical lineage of Hinduism. In the centuries that followed his elucidation of an absolute monism based on the insights of the Upanishads, there was, as can be expected, both an acceptance of his basic tenets, *and* an understandable reaction to the uncompromising 'intellectualism' of his vision. As a consequence, Hinduism has ever since, never denied the existence of Brahman, as a supreme, attribute-less and omnipresent reality pervading the universe, or rejected the fact that our finite world, in relation to that supreme reality, is of subordinate value.

However, there has been a concerted effort to somehow unite the unrelenting non-dualism of Shankaracharya with a theism that is more appealing to ordinary people craving for the grace of a personal god in their search for solace and assurance.

It is important to keep in mind that this effort does not negate the logic or cerebral strength of Shankara's philosophy. It merely seeks to 'reduce' it to a level that could accommodate religious practice and devotion at the altar of a more comprehensible and less remote divinity. It is to the lasting—but not uncharacteristic—credit of Hinduism, that this effort was made not arbitrarily, nor by fiat or simplistic denial, but through the use of logic and reasoning moored in a philosophical context.

Given the sheer integrity of Shankara's reasoning, and his refusal to deviate from the consequences of that reasoning, the task was not easy. In fact, on many occasions, the philosophical arguments put by later Hindu thinkers against his philosophical tenets, appear to be contrived, or wanting in varying degrees from the point of logical consistency. But, the human need to move away from the notion of a persistently transcendent and aloof Brahman, to a theism more responsive to our daily lives, was so great that, gradually, on the hard rock of Shankara's philosophical structure there sprouted a lush undergrowth of what is, in emotional terms, possibly a more fulfilling theism, where, essentially the focus moves from Brahman to Ishwara, and from logic to devotion.

Ramanuja was born in Sriperumbudur, South India in the year 1017 CE—and whose millennium was celebrated in 2017—some two hundred years after the death of Shankara. Even as a child, he acquired a mastery of the Vedanta doctrine, and adopting the life of a sanyasin, settled down in Srirangam. He wrote several highly regarded treatises on Vedanta, and seminal commentaries on the *Brahma Sutra* and the *Bhagavad Gita*. Although, he did not seek to consciously differ from Shankara, he is ultimately associated with the doctrine of Vishista Advaita, or qualified non-dualism, which was different from Shankara's unyielding non-dualism, and moulded Advaita towards a personalised theism.

Ramanuja did not contest Shankara's assertion that Brahman is supreme, all-knowing, omnipotent and omnipresent, characterised by the experience of sat (being), chitta (consciousness), and ananda (bliss). However, he did not support Shankara's assertion that Brahman is attribute-less. He argued that pure consciousness is an untenable construct. A thing without any attributes is as good as being non-existent, and if it has attributes, it cannot be pure consciousness. It is not possible 'for the mind to apprehend an undifferentiated object. What is known is necessarily known as characterised in some way.'[1] Shankara's inference that Brahman is 'nirguna' is, Ramanuja asserts, a misreading of the Upanishads. What the Upanishads actually intend to indicate is that 'some qualities are denied while there are still others characterizing it.'[2]

If Brahman, although supreme, is not without attributes, then it must be determinate, a whole, no doubt, but with verifiable elements. These, according to Ramanuja, are the individual souls, their bodies, inanimate matter and, overseeing them all, Ishwara or God. The absolute, therefore, is not unqualified and indeterminate, but has internal differences (*svagatabheda*), which are real and have separate autonomy (*chidachidvishishtha*). They may be dependent on Brahman, but are not subsumed into 'nothingness' by it.

It follows then that the empirical world is not an illusion. To say that it is purely phenomenal, a product of the illusionary powers of maya, is wrong. Nor can it be dismissed as a product of avidya or nescience. To explain the empirical as 'inexpressible' or anirvachaniya, as Shankara does, is illogical. There is nothing logically inconsistent in accepting that the infinite can give rise to the finite, or that there can be diversity within unity, and a coherence between a whole and its parts.

As a follow up to this argument, Ramanuja articulated his own theory of causation, *satkaryavada*. This was different to Shankara's theory—vivartavada, which we have discussed earlier. Basically, vivartavada does not accept that the effect is different from the cause. The effect could represent the one, unchanging cause in a different form—like a pot does clay—but that does not make it, in essence, different from the cause. This theory was different to that of parinamavada, espoused by other schools of Hindu philosophy, that the cause actually undergoes a change when giving rise to the effect.

---

1 M. Hiriyana, *Outlines of Indian Philosophy*, George, Allen & Unwin, Mumbai, 1973, p. 386.

2 ibid., p. 387.

Ramanuja postulates a third variant. The cause, he argues, can be the eternal basis, *adhara*, but the effect, even while dependent on it, *adheya*, can have its own independently verifiable attributes, *visheshana*. Brahman is, indeed, the essential substance or *dravya* underlying all reality, and the inner self, *sarvantaratmatvam,* of all things, but individual human beings, jiva, and all other empirical phenomena, are its visheshana—adjectives or attributes—which are *distinct* from it. In other words, if Brahman is the supreme personality, Ishwara or God is its perfect manifestation, and the soul, as embodied in human beings, are imperfect entities. It is the role of Ishwara to guide the imperfect to the perfect, and the perfect to the supreme.

At one stroke then, Ramanuja, while not disputing the supremacy of Brahman, gave to human beings an autonomy, in which they could, through their efforts and the grace of Ishwara, strive towards salvation. In such a saguna world of attributes, Ramanuja's chosen path for salvation was not jnana or knowledge as Shankara emphasised, nor karma or action as the mimamshaks advocated and Shankara decried, but bhakti or devotion.

In fact, on the foundations of his philosophical divergence with Shankara, Ramanuja built an elaborate and appealing edifice of the art of complete surrender, *prapatti,* to the grace, prasada, of Ishwara. What is more, he invested considerable thought to the elaboration of what constituted bhakti. At one level, it was, as is commonly understood, the exhilaration of devotion. At another, it required the conscious acquisition of certain virtues, such as *vimoka,* the constant longing for god, *abhaysa*, the continuous thinking about god, dana or charity, daya or compassion, *arjavam* or integrity, satyam or truthfulness, and ahimsa or non-violence. Simple devotion, at the level of prayers or visiting temples, is a lower form of bhakti. But, bhakti, reinforced by such virtues, and emotionally exalted by prapatti, the complete surrender to god, is, argues Ramanuja, the surest path to salvation, and has the sanction of the Upanishads, the *Bhagavad Gita,* and the *Brahman Sutras.*

Ramanuja's greatest contribution thus was not the denial of Brahman, but the inclusion within its pervasive supremacy, of the validity of devotion to a personal god, and in so doing, provide, for ordinary mortals, an alternative form of spirituality to the remote intellectual aloofness of the nirguna Brahman of Shankara. In the structure of Advaitic thought, he provided the philosophical key to open the gates of bhakti.

As Dr S. Radhakrishnan writes:

> The sense of personal communion with God involves a real fellowship with an "other" divine personality. The nirguna Brahman, which stares at us with frozen eyes regardless of our selfless devotion and silent suffering, is not the god of religious insight. Shankara's method, according to Ramanuja, leads him to a void, which he tries to conceal by a futile play of concepts. His nirguna Brahman is a blank....[3]

With Brahman as the background, Ramanuja's focus became Ishwara, a personalised god, accessible to his devotees. For him, he was Vishnu, who symbolised to perfection the supreme spirit, and subsumed within himself the other two members of the Hindu divinity—Brahma and Shiva. In contrast to Shankara's partiality to Shiva—although this was never exclusive and he wrote devotional stotras to Vishnu as well—Ramanuja unleashed a wave of Vaishnava devotion that has left a very marked impact on the evolution of Hinduism.

In the Vaishnava tradition, the world was dependent on the grace of Vishnu, in his role of supporter (*prakari*), controller (*niyanta*), and the sole refuge (*seshi*). The relation of man to such an Ishwara was not one of inhibition. God became a friend, a parent, a child, a confidante, and even a beloved. Through his grace, in any relationship of devotion chosen by a devotee, he

---

3 S. Radhakrishnan, op. cit., p. 638.

was the guarantor of moksha, guiding the dependent soul beyond its mortal barriers. Once these barriers were broken, the liberated soul could reach heaven. Ramanuja goes beyond the normal restraints of philosophy to actually essay such a heaven, where a congregation of liberated souls enjoy the pleasures of crystal-clear streams, fruit laden trees, music and delicious food, and a wonderful climate all through the year.

Ramanuja's Vaishnava theism gave philosophical backing to earlier traditions of Vishnu worship as evidenced in the *Vishnu Purana*, the *Harivamsha* and the *Bhagwata Purana*, as also the later poet-saints called the Alwars in South India. However, once Ramanuja laid the philosophical framework for a Vishnu-focussed theism, his thought process was taken much further by later thinkers like Madhava, Nimbarkar, Vallabha and Chaitanya.

Madhava was born in 1199 CE in a village near Udupi in Karnataka. A scholar like Ramanuja, he wrote learned commentaries on the *Brahma Sutra*, the *Gita* and the Upanishads, and a gloss on the *Bhagwata Purana*. Unlike Ramanuja's Vishista Advaita, which was a qualified monism, Madhava was openly dualistic in his approach. For him, god, souls, and the world were eternally three different entities. The Upanishadic statement, Tat tvam asi did not mean that the soul and Brahman are identical, but only that the soul has qualities *similar* to Brahman.

Madhava concedes that Brahman is the embodiment of supreme perfection, but asserts that Vishnu, as its embodiment, is unfettered in his powers as the creator, maintainer and destroyer of the world. Lakshmi, Vishnu's consort, is co-eternal with him and represents his creative energy. A devotee's only way to salvation is through uninhibited bhakti, for only devotion can move the Lord to extend his grace. Madhava takes Ramanuja's emphasis on bhakti to another level of fervour. A devotee is encouraged to brand his body with Vishnu's symbols, and carry out all the rites, pilgrimages and sacrifices, making worship, in thought and practice, the only means to moksha.

Nimbarka, a Telugu Brahmin who lived a little earlier than Madhava, postulated a theory of Dvait Advaita, or dualistic non-dualism. This theory specifically refutes the predicateless character of Brahman, and breaks further from Shankara by arguing that Brahman undergoes actual change, *parinama,* while creating the dependent yet autonomous entities of jiva and prakriti. What is created is both different from Brahman, and yet not entirely different since its existence is dependent on it. Further, that the material cause of creation is the power of Shakti inherent within Brahman; this interdependent world of similar yet different entities is governed by Ishwara, the supreme god, which Nimbarka, as part of the Vaishnava school, identifies with Krishna. As stressed by Ramanuja, and reiterated later by Madhava, Nimbarka also believes that bhakti and prapatti, total devotion and surrender infused with love, are the means for the realisation of God or Brahmansakshatkara.

Like Nimbarka, Vallabha, born in 1401 CE, was also a Telugu Brahmin from South India who moved to the north, and Chaitanya, who was born at Nadia in West Bengal (or, by another tradition, at Sylhet, now in Bangladesh) in 1486, and spent a great deal of his life in Odisha, completed the process of transmuting the nirguna Brahman to a flourishing theism centred around Vishnu, and his avatar, Krishna.

Vallabha articulated the theory of Shuddh Advaita, or pure non-dualism. The world, and the jivas within it, are real; they may be the emanation of the supreme Brahman, but Brahman itself is personified in an all-powerful Krishna, the creator of the world, and mukti from the shackles of samsara can only be achieved through eternally and selflessly serving him. Krishna's abode is the celestial Vrindavana, and a devotee can remove the veil of avidya only by immersing himself in his unqualified love.

Chaitanya carried forward this theism to a new level of devotional fervour. By his time, Jayadeva, the author of the *Gitagovinda* (twelfth century CE), had elevated the worship of

Radha-Krishna to a cult. The impact of the sensual love poetry of the *Gitagovinda* was like a tidal wave, and acquired unprecedented popularity all over India, particularly in Bengal. The work began to be sung and performed in Vaishnava temples as a matter of ritual.

From the fourteenth to the sixteenth centuries, a host of poets carried forward the legacy of Jayadeva. However, unlike Jayadeva, these poets wrote in the language spoken by the common man.

Chandidasa, who lived at the confluence of the fourteenth and fifteenth centuries, wrote in his native Bengali. Vidyapati (1352–1448), a younger contemporary of Chandidasa, lived in Mithila, Bihar, and wrote in Maithali. Surdas wrote in Braj. Braj was also the choice of expression of Bihari (1595–1664). All these poets acquired immense popularity because their compositions had a sensuous simplicity, deriving strength from the local idiom and turn of phrase. To the masses they provided a scripture that could be comprehended without effort and was thoroughly enjoyable for its lyrical informality. There was a directness of appeal in their language that evoked an immediate response.

Not surprisingly, the development of kirtans, the fast-tempoed singing of community devotional songs, had a direct correlation with the popularity of these works. By this time, the *Gitagovinda* had also been translated into other regional languages. The cumulative result was that personal theism, as represented by the love lore of Radha and Krishna, moved out from the rarefied chambers of philosophers, into the homes and rituals of ordinary people.

Chaitanya's fervent Vaishanava bhakti was undoubtedly influenced by these developments. Krishna was the prime focus of his devotion. His divinity, he postulated in a manner similar to Vallabha, was characterised by several shaktis, the three principal ones being: jiva shakti, maya shakti and swarupa shakti. Individual souls were emanations of his jiva shakti; the manifest world was a creation of his maya shakti; the expression of the essential nature of his own bliss was swarupa shakti. The relations between these shaktis or energies was one of *achintyabhedabheda*—inconceivable oneness and difference—wherein each was different, but all were one with Krishna. Vrindavana, where he frolicked in abandon with the gopis and with Radha, were the spontaneous creations of Krishna's swarupa shakti. The most important component of this was unblemished joy (*hladini* shakti). Radha was the specific embodiment of hladini shakti. Thus she was not only a part of Krishna's essential self, but the most joyous aspect of it.

Chaitanya's theism also projected Vrindavana as a reflection and continuation of Krishna's eternal paradise—Goloka. Krishna's leela in Vrindavana—the rasa or circular dance with the gopis, and his dalliance with Radha—was not merely something that happened during his avatar on earth; such activity was an intrinsic part of the Lord's godhead and was being enacted ceaselessly in his eternal heavenly estate.

> By the Bhagwat's inscrutable power (achintya prabhava), therefore, his highest paradise, which is situated beyond all the Lokas (divine domains), also exists on the phenomenal earth. The terrestrial Goloka or Vrindavana is thus not essentially different but really identical to the celestial Goloka or Vrindavana, and the Lord Krishna exists eternally in both places with the same retinue.[4]

Chaitanya was called Mahaprabhu, and was regarded by his followers as an avatar of Krishna himself. For him, Krishna was the supreme absolute truth; displaying the pure love for him was the ultimate goal for all devotees, and the purpose of life was to receive his lovable blessing. The devotional outpouring that he

---

4 S.K. De, *Early History of the Vaishnava Faith and Movement in Bengal from Sanskrit and Bengali Sources*, Kolkata, 1961, p. 334.

inspired—and sanctified—was huge, and influenced even Swami Ramakrishna Paramhamsa several centuries later.

The aftermath of Shankara's austere but rigorously logical explication of the universe was, at one level, a derogation of his thought structure, but at another, its validation. The progressive dilution of his attribute-less notion of Brahman towards a more accessible personal theism, was, quite clearly, a rebellion from the remoteness of his unyielding, yet relentlessly consistent logic. But the fact that this happened was, I suspect, not something that would have surprised him. It was precisely for this reason that he segmented the jnana marga at two levels: para vidya, or higher knowledge, where the primary concern was the metaphysical comprehension of the absolute; and apara vidya, lower knowledge, where bhakti, worship, yoga, prayer, surrender, ritual and devotion were given legitimacy, as part of the preparatory steps to move from apara to para vidya.

What followed him was, therefore, something to which he had himself given sanction. Indeed, going beyond, he himself practiced a deeply moving theism that led him to write some of the most evocative stotras to the principal deities of the Hindu pantheon. However, the significant point is that this theism that he himself practiced, did not deflect him, even for a moment, from the basic tenets of the Advaitic vision, and the concept of Brahman that was central to it.

The struggle between Shankara's monism, and Ramanuja's theism, neither compromised the former, nor invalidated the latter. Shankara's Brahman was, for lay devotees, much too intellectualised a construct. It did not provide the assurance that human insecurity, need and fulfilment seek in the here and now. For instance, some tangible concept of the absolute to identify with; a divinity that they can internalise in personal terms; the solidarity of faith—not in a concept—but in a deity that is comprehensible and not merely the consequence—however compelling—of logic alone. Shankara understood this and, therefore, accepted theistic ritual and practice *without* diluting his essential monism. Ramanuja, to my mind, understood the logic underpinning Shankara's notion of Brahman, but was keen to find a way to provide philosophical legitimacy to theism, with all its pageantry of worship and ritual and bhakti, *without* devaluing it as apara vidya.

The basic fact is that Ramanuja—undoubtedly one of the great minds of Hinduism—and the thinkers that followed him, were guided by the need to make spirituality more religious, whereas Shankara was motivated by the desire to make religion more spiritual. In this sense, the Brahman of Advaita, and the Vishnu of Ramanuja, were two sides of the same coin of human yearning. One catered to human vulnerability and fulfilment in the life lived now, the other to the search of the human intellect for ultimate truths. One paved the path for the grace of the almighty, the other for the cosmic secrets that lay behind the reality of the supreme. Both had their own relevance, and there is little point served in picking holes in the logic of Ramanuja in order to prove the logical superiority of Shankara.

Shankara exalted religion to philosophy, while Ramanuja tempered philosophy to the level of religion. That is why Shankara did not consider theism wrong, nor did Ramanuja—or any of the thinkers that followed him—ever negate the concept of Brahman. As Dr S. Radhakrishnan writes:

> Shankara and Ramanuja are the two great thinkers of the Vedanta, and the best qualities of each were the defects of the other. Shankara's apparently arid logic made his system unattractive religiously; Ramanuja's beautiful stories of the other world, which he narrates with the confidence of one who has personally assisted at the origination of the other

> world, carry no conviction. Shankara's devastating dialectic, which traces all—God, man and the world—to one ultimate consciousness, produces not a little curling of the lips in the followers of Ramanuja.[5]

Shankara's greatness lay in understanding the human need for religious practice, but not allowing this to impede his exploration of the mysteries of the universe. For sheer profundity of thought, he was in this unflagging pursuit, without a peer. The greatness of his legacy of thought not only stands undiminished with the passage of time, but has grown in value, even as it is being validated by the latest discoveries of science.

The tragedy is that in the land that gave birth to this unparalleled genius, very few are aware of the greatness of his contribution, and its stunning relevance to the newly emerging vision of the cosmos, and what sustains it. Even those who are entrusted with preserving his corpus of thought are often more distracted by the ritual of religion—which has its own place—than the grandeur of his metaphysical insights.

Can Hindus, and Indians as a whole, once again rediscover the worth of Shankara, and say to the world that here, indeed, was a thinker who, in the attenuated life that he lived, gave to the world, and to humanity as a whole, a vision of the absolute and the universe that, for sheer audacity has few equals in the history of ideas of the human race?

---

5 S. Radhakrishnan, op. cit., p. 673.

A SELECT ANTHOLOGY

Bhashya Text
Shankaracharya's Commentary on the Bhagavad Gita

The Gita, consisting of seven hundred shlokas in eighteen chapters, is embedded in the Mahabharata, probably written around 500 BCE. Along with the Upanishads, and the Brahma Sutra, it is considered to be one of the three foundational texts that delineate the Hindu philosophical world-view.

Shankara wrote an extensive commentary or bhashya on the Gita, explaining the meaning of each of its verses. The essential message of the Gita, which is karma yoga or nishkama karma—action without thought of reward—was greatly valued by Shankara. Although he differed with the mimamshaks on their exclusive emphasis on action—including the performance of rituals—as per Vedic injunctions, he believed that action, when performed in a spirit of surrender and without thought of reward, was a valid preparatory step to understand and experience the supreme reality of Brahman.

We have selected the lucid translation by A. Madhava Shastri, done as far back as 1901, for—as Shastri himself states—he has endeavoured to present Shankara's bhashya in a manner 'as clearly intelligible to a general reader, without unnecessarily departing from the original, even as regards the structure of the sentence.'

The portion selected deals with those stanzas of the Gita that bring out the essence of its meaning, and provide the requisite scope for Shankara to express his views on each of them.

Prasāde sarvaduḥkhānāaṃ hānirasyopajāyate |
Prasannacetaso hyasu buddhiḥ paryavatiṣṭhte ||

(In peace there is an end of all miseries; for, the reason of the tranquil-minded soon becomes steady.)

Bhashya of Acharya Shankara: On the attainment of peace, there is an end to all the devotee's miseries such as pertains to the body and the mind. For, the reason (buddhi) of the pure-minded man soon becomes steady, pervading on all sides like the akasha; i.e., it remains steadfast, in the form of the self.

The sense of the passage is this: The man whose heart is pure and whose mind is steady has achieved his object. Wherefore the devout man should resort only to those sense-objects which are indispensable and not forbidden by the shastras, with the senses devoid of love and hatred.

Tranquillity is thus extolled:

Nāsti buddhirayuktasya na chāyuktasya bhāvanā |
Na Chābhāvayataḥ śāntiraśāntasya kutaḥ sukham ||

(There is no wisdom to the unsteady, and no meditation to the unsteady, and to the unmeditative no peace; to the peaceless, how can there be happiness?)

Bhashya of Acharya Shankara: To the unsteady, to the man who cannot fix the mind in contemplation, there can be no wisdom (buddhi), no knowledge of the true nature of the self. To the unsteady, there can be no meditation, no intense devotion to self-knowledge. So, to him who is not devoted to self-knowledge, there can be no peace, no tranquillity. To the peaceless man, how can there be happiness? Verily, happiness consists in the freedom of the senses from thirst for sensual enjoyment, not in the thirst (*trishna*) for objects. This last is mere misery indeed. While there is thirst, there can be no trace of happiness; we cannot so much as smell it.

(Question): Why is there no knowledge for the unsteady?

(Answer): Listen:

Indriyāṇāṁ hi caratāṁ yanmano'nuvidhīyate |
Tadasya harati prajñāṁ vāyurnāvamivāmbhasi ||

(For, the mind which yields to the roving senses carries away his knowledge, as the wind {carries away} a ship on water.)

Bhashya of Acharya Shankara: For, the mind which yields to the senses engaged in their respective objects, i.e., the mind which is altogether engrossed in the thought of the various objects of the senses, destroys the devotee's discriminative knowledge of the self and the not-self.

How? As the wind carries away a ship from the intended course of the sailors and drives her astray, so the mind carries away the devotee's consciousness from the self and turns it towards sense-objects.

The Lord concludes by reaffirming the same proposition:

Tasmādyasya mahābāho nigṛhītāni sarvaśaḥ |
Indriyāṇīndriyārthebhyastasya prajñā pratiṣṭhitā ||

(Therefore, O mighty-armed, his knowledge is steady whose senses have been entirely restrained from sense-objects.)

Bhashya of Acharya Shankara: It has been shown that evil arises from the senses pursuing sense-objects. Wherefore, that devotee's knowledge is steady whose senses have been restrained from sense-objects (such as sound) in all forms, subjective and objective.

In the case of the man who possesses discriminative knowledge and whose knowledge has become steady, his experience of all matters, temporal and spiritual (*laukika* and *vaidika*, sensuous and supersensuous), ceases on the cessation of nescience (avidya); for, it is the effect of nescience; and nescience ceases because it is opposed of knowledge. To make this clear, the Lord proceeds:

Yā niśā sarvabhūtānāṁ tasyāṁ jāgarti saṁyamī |
Yasyāṁ jāgrati bhūtāni sā niśā paśyato muneḥ ||

(What is night to all beings; therein the self-controlled one is awake. Where all beings are awake, that is the night of the sage who sees.)

Bhashya of Acharya Shankara: To all beings, the supreme reality is night. Night is by nature *tamasic*, and, as such, causes confusion of things. The reality is accessible only to a man of steady knowledge. Just as what is day to others becomes night to night-wanderers, so, to all beings who are ignorant and who correspond to the night-wanderers, the supreme reality is dark, is like night; for it is not accessible to those whose minds are not in it. With reference to that supreme reality, the self-restrained yogin who has subdued the senses, and who has shaken off the sleep of avidya, is fully awake. When all beings are said to be awake, i.e., when all beings, who in reality sleep in the night of ignorance, imbued with the distinct notions of perceiver and things perceived, are as it were mere dreamers in sleep at night—that state is night in the eye of the sage who knows the supreme reality: for, it is nescience itself.

Wherefore works are enjoined on the ignorant, not on the wise. Wisdom (vidya) arising, nescience (avidya) disappears as does the darkness of the night at sunrise. Before the dawn of wisdom, nescience presents itself in various forms—as action, means and results, and is regarded as authoritative, and becomes the sources of all action. When it is regarded as of no authority, it cannot induce action. A man engages in action regarding it as his duty— regarding that action is enjoined by such an authority as the Veda, but not looking upon all this duality as mere illusion, as though it were night. When he has learnt to look upon all this dual world as a mere illusion, as though it were night, when he has realised the self, his duty consists not in the performance of action, but in the renunciation of all action. Our Lord will accordingly show that such a man's duty consists in devotion to wisdom, in *jnana-nishtha*.

(Objection): In the absence of an injunction (*pravartaka pramana vidhi*) one cannot have recourse to that course either.

(Answer): This objection does not apply; for, the knowledge of Atman means the knowledge of one's own self. There is indeed no need of an injunction impelling one to devote oneself to one's Atman for the very reason that Atman is one's very self. And all organs of knowledge (*pramanas*) are so called because they ultimately lead to knowledge of the self. When the knowledge of the true nature of the self has been attained, neither organs of knowledge nor objects of knowledge present themselves to consciousness any longer. For, the final authority, (viz., the Veda), teaches that the self is in reality no percipient of objects, and while so denying, (i.e., as a result of that teaching), the Veda itself ceases to be an authority, just as the dream-perception (ceases to be an authority) in the waking state. In ordinary experience, too, we do not find any organ of knowledge necessitating further operation (on the part of the knower) when once the thing to be perceived by that organ has been perceived.

The Lord proceeds to teach, by an illustration, that that devotee only who is wise, who has abandoned desires, and whose wisdom is steady, can attain moksha, but not he who, without renouncing, cherishes a desire for objects of pleasure.

Āpūryamāṇamacalapratiṣṭhaṁ samudramāpaḥ praviśanti yadvat |
Tadvatkāmā yaṁ praviśanti sarve sa śāntimāpnoti na kāmakāmī ||

(He attains peace, into whom all desires enter as waters enter the ocean, which filled from all sides, remains unaltered; but not he who desires objects.)

Bhashya of Acharya Shankara: The ocean is filled with waters flowing from all sides. Its state is unaltered, though waters flow into it from all sides: it remains all the while within its bounds without change. That sage into whom in this manner desires of all sorts enter from all sides without affecting him—as waters enter into the ocean—even in the presence of objects; in whose self they are absorbed, and whom they do not enslave; that sage attains peace (moksha), but not the other who has a longing for external objects.

Because it is so, therefore,

Vihāya kāmānyaḥ sarvānpumāṁścarti niḥspṛhaḥ |
Nirmamo nirahaṅkāraḥ sa śāntimadhigacchati ||

(That man attains peace, who, abandoning all desires, moves about without attachment, without selfishness, without vanity.)

Bhashya of Acharya Shankara: That man of renunciation, who, entirely abandoning all desires, goes through life content with the bare necessities of life, who has no attachment even for those bare necessities of life, who regards not as his even those things which are needed for the mere bodily existence, who is not vain of his knowledge—such a man of steady knowledge, that man who knows Brahman, attains peace (nirvana), the end of all the misery of samsara (mundane existence). In short, he becomes the very Brahman.

This devotion to knowledge is extolled as follows:

Eṣā brāmī sthitiḥ pārtha naināṁ prāpya vimuhyati |
Sthitvā"syāmantakāle'pi brahma nirvāṇamṛcchati ||

(This is the Brahmic state, O son of Pritha. Attaining to this, none is deluded. Remaining in this state even at the last period of life, one attains to the felicity of Brahman.)

Bhashya of Acharya Shankara: This foregoing state—to renounce all and to dwell in Brahman—is the divine state, the state of Brahman. It pertains to and has its being in Brahman. On reaching this state, one is no longer deluded. Remaining in this state even at the last period of life, one attains moksha, the felicity of Brahman. And it needs no saying that he who renounces while yet a student and dwells in Brahman throughout life, attains the felicity of Brahman, the Brahma-nirvana.

The Prakarana Texts

The Prakarana is a document that is related to a main theme of a major text, in which the author is free to make comments upon, or refer to, one or more of the major texts. This definition of a Prakarana text is given in the Parashara Upapurana:

Shastraikadeshasambaddham shastrakaryantare sthitam |
Ahuh prakaranam nama shastrabhedam vichakshanah ||
– *Parashara Upapurana–18.21–22*

Atmabodha
(Self-knowledge)

Atmabodha, meaning self-knowledge or self-awareness, is a short—consisting only of sixty-eight verses or shlokas—but exceptionally readable and lucid work of Shankaracharya. In a sense, it is a simple summary of his entire Vedantic structure of thought, intended, it would seem, as a basic primer for his students and followers. The text follows a clearly elaborated doctrine, starting with knowledge as the key to liberation, the nature of the Atman within us, the assertion of the pervasive and attribute-less nature of Brahman, and the path towards the realisation of the complete identity between the Atman and Brahman.

The first translation of Atmabodha into English was done in 1812 by J. Taylor under the title, The Knowledge of Spirit. Another translation by Reverend J.F. Kearns was published in The Indian Antiquary in 1876. We have chosen the translation by Swami Nikhilananda of the Sri Ramakrishna Math, published in 1947.

Tapobhiḥ kṣīṇapāpānāṃ śāntānāṃ vītarāgiṇām |
Mumukṣūṇāmapekṣyo'yamātmabodho vidhīyate ||

(I am composing the Atmabodha, or self-knowledge, to serve the needs of those who have been purified through the practice of austerities, and who are peaceful in heart, free from cravings, and desirous of liberation.)

Bodho'nyasādhanebhyo hi sākṣānmokṣaikasādhanam |
Pākasya vahnivajjñānaṃ vinā mokṣo na sidhyati ||

(As fire is the direct cause of cooking, so knowledge and not any other form of discipline is the direct cause of liberation; for liberation cannot be attained without knowledge.)

Saṃsāraḥ svapnatulyo hi rāgadveṣādisaṅkulaḥ |
Svakāle satyavadbhāti prabodhe satyasadbhavet ||

(The world, filled with attachments and aversions, and the rest, is like a dream; it appears to be real as long as one is ignorant, but becomes unreal when one is awake.)

Anādyavidyānirvācyā kāraṇopādhirucyate |
Upādhitritayādanyamātmānamavadhārayet ||

(Avidya, or nescience, indescribable and beginning-less, is called the cause, which is an upadhi {self-limiting adjunct} superimposed on Atman. Know for certain that Atman is other than the three upadhis.)

Prakāśo'rkasya toyasya śaityamagneryathoṣṇatā |
Svabhāvaḥ saccidānandanityanirmalatātmanaḥ ||

(The nature of Atman is eternity, purity, reality, consciousness, and bliss, just as luminosity is the nature of the sun, coolness of water, and heat of fire.)

Ātmano vikriyā nāsti buddherbodho na jātviti |
Jīvaḥ sarvamalaṃ jñātvā jñātā draṣṭeti muhyati ||

(Atman never undergoes change, and the buddhi is never endowed with consciousness. But man believes Atman to be identical with the buddhi and falls under such delusions as that he is the seer and the knower.)

Rajjusarpavadātmānaṃ jīvaṃ jñātvā bhayaṃ vahet |
Nāhaṃ jīvaḥ parātmeti jñātañcennirbhayo bhavet ||

(The soul regarding itself as a jiva is overcome by fear, just like the man who regards a rope as a snake. The soul regains fearlessness by realising that it is not a jiva but the supreme soul.)

Niṣidhya nikhilopādhīnneti netīti vākyataḥ |
Vidyādaikyaṃ mahāvākyairjīvātmaparamātmanoḥ ||

(By negating all the upadhis through the help of the scriptural statement, 'It is not this, it is not this,' realise the oneness of the individual soul and the supreme soul by means of the great Vedic aphorisms.)

Nityaśuddhavimuktaikamakhaṇḍānandamadvayam |
Satyaṃ jñānamanantaṃ yatparaṃ brahmāhameva tat ||

(I am verily that supreme Brahman, which is eternal, stainless, and free; which is one, indivisible, and non-dual; and which is of the nature of bliss, truth, knowledge, and infinity.)

Evaṃ nirantarābhyastā brahmaivāsmīti vāsanā |
Haratyavidyāvikṣepān rogāniva rasāyanam ||

(The impression of 'I am Brahman', thus created by uninterrupted reflection, destroys ignorance and its distractions, as *rasayana* medicine destroys diseases.)

Jñātṛjñānajñeyabhedaḥ pare nātmani vidyate |
Cidānandaikarūpatvāddīpyate svayameva tat ||

(The supreme self, on account of its being of the nature of exceeding bliss, does not admit of the distinction of the knower, knowledge, and the object of knowledge; it alone shines.)

Tatvasvarūpānubhavādutpannaṃ jñānamaṃjasā |
Ahaṃ mameti cājñānaṃ bādhate digbhramādivat ||

(The knowledge produced by the realisation of the true nature of reality destroys immediately the ignorance characterised by the notions of 'I' and 'mine' as the sun the mistake regarding one's direction.)

Samyagvijñānavān yogī svātmanyevākhilaṃ jagat |
Ekaṃ ca sarvamātmānamīkṣate jñānacakṣuṣā ||

(The yogi endowed with complete enlightenment sees, through the eye of knowledge, the entire universe in his own self and regards everything as the self and nothing else.)

Ātmaivedaṃ jagatsarvamātmano'nyanna vidyate |
Mṛdo yadvadghaṭādīni svātmānaṃ sarvamīkṣate ||

(The tangible universe is verily Atman; nothing whatsoever exists that is other than Atman. As pots and jars are verily clay and cannot be anything but clay, so, to the enlightened, all that is perceived is the self.)

Yaddṛṣṭvā nāparaṃ dṛśyaṃ yadbhūtvā na punarbhavaḥ |
Yajjñātvā nāparaṃ jñeyaṃ tadbrahmetyavadhārayet ||

(Realise that to be Brahman which, when seen, leaves nothing more to be seen, having become which one is not born again into the world of becoming and which, when known, leaves nothing else to be known.)

Atadvyāvṛttirūpeṇa vedāntairlakṣyate'dvayam |
Akhaṇḍānandamekaṃ yattatadbrahmetyavadhārayet ||

(Realise that to be Brahman which is non-dual, indivisible, one, and blissful, and which is indicated by Vedanta as the irreducible substratum after the negation of all tangible objects.)

Yadbhāsā bhāsyate'rkādi bhāsyairyattu na bhāsyate |
Yena sarvamidaṃ bhāti tadbrahmetyavadhārayet ||

(Realise that to be Brahman by the light of which luminous orbs like the sun and moon are illumined, but which cannot be illumined by their light, and by which everything is illumined.)

Jagadvilakṣaṇaṃ brahma brahmaṇo'nyanna kiṃcana |
Brahmānyadbhāti cenmithyā yathā marumarīcikā ||

(Brahman is other than the universe. There exists nothing that is not Brahman. If any object other than Brahman appears to exist, it is unreal like a mirage.)

Sarvagaṃ saccidātmānaṃ jñānacakṣurnirīkṣate |
Ajñānacakṣurnekṣeta bhāsvantaṃ bhānumandhavat ||

(Though Atman is reality and consciousness, and ever present everywhere, yet it is perceived by the eye of wisdom alone. But one whose vision is obscured by ignorance does not see the radiant Atman, as the blind do not see the resplendent sun.)

Śravaṇādibhiruddīptajñānāgniparitāpitaḥ |
Jīvassarvamalānmuktaḥ svarṇavaddyotate svayam ||

(The jiva free from impurities, being well heated in the fire of knowledge kindled by heating and so on, shines of himself, like gold.)

Digdeśakālādyanapekṣya sarvagaṃ
Śītādihṛnnityasukhaṃ niraṃjanam |
Yassvātmatīrthaṃ bhajate viniṣkriyaḥ
Sa sarvavitsarvagato'mṛto bhavet ||

(He who, renouncing all activities, worships in the sacred and stainless shrine of Atman, which is independent of time, place, and distance; which is present everywhere; which is the destroyer of heat and cold, and the other opposites; and which is the giver of eternal happiness, becomes all-knowing and all-pervading and attains, hereafter immortality.)

Tattvabodha

For anyone wishing to understand the essential tenets of Shankaracharya's philosophy and the Advaita vision, the Tattvabodha, which broadly translates to 'the knowledge of truth', is mandatory reading. In it, Shankara, as the teacher, puts down the questions that pertain to different aspects of the Vedantic doctrine, and provides the answers. These questions, and the answers, are in the form of a hypothetical dialogue between a student and his teacher. The answers simplify, for both the ordinary reader and the student of Philosophy, the complex terminologies used by Shankara in more elaborate expositions, such as his commentary on the Brahma Sutra. The questions and answers follow a carefully thought-out structure, guiding the reader through an analysis of the jiva or the individual, to the process of creation or shrishti, leading up to the nature of one's real identity, and, finally, to the freedom that comes from moksha or liberation.

The opening shloka is in the nature of an invocation or mangalacharya to the guru. The rest of the text is in prose.

Vāsudevendrayogīndraṃ natvā jñānapradaṃ gurum ।
Mumukṣūṇāṃ hitārthāya tattvabodhobhidhīyate ॥

(Having saluted Shri Vasudevendra, the king of yogis, the guru who is the bestower of knowledge, *Tattvabodha* is expounded for the benefit of the seekers.)

Sādhanacatuṣṭayasampannādhikāriṇāṃ mokṣasādhanabhūtaṃ
Tattvavivekaprakāraṃ vakṣyāmaḥ ॥

(We shall explain to those who are endowed with the four-fold qualifications, the mode of discrimination which is the means of liberation.)

Sādhanacatuṣṭayam
(The four-fold qualifications)

Sādhanacatuṣṭayaiṃ kim?
Nityānityavastuvivekaḥ । *Ihāmutrārthaphalabhogavirāgaḥ* ।
Śamādiṣaṭkasampattiḥ । *Mumukṣutvaṃ ceti* ।

(What are the four-fold qualifications? The capacity to discriminate between the permanent and the impermanent, dispassion to the enjoyment of the fruits of one's actions here and hereafter, the group of six accomplishments {inner wealth} beginning with *sham* and the yearning for liberation.)

Nityānityavastuvivekaḥ
(Discrimination)

Nityānityavastuvivekaḥ kaḥ?
Nityavastvekaṃ brahma tadvyatiriktaṃ sarvamanityam ।
Ayameva nityānityavastuvivekaḥ ।

(What is meant by discrimination between the permanent and the impermanent? The reality alone is eternal; everything else is ephemeral. This conviction alone is the discrimination between the permanent and the impermanent.)

Virāgaḥ
(Dispassion)

Virāgaḥ kaḥ?
ihasvargabhogeṣu icchārāhityam ।

(What is dispassion? The absence of the desire for the enjoyments {of the fruits of one's actions} in this world and in heaven.)

Śamādisādhanasampattiḥ
(The six-fold wealth)

Śamādisādhanasampattiḥ kā?
Śamo dama uparamastitikṣā śraddhā samādhānaṃ ca iti ।

(What is the inner starting with Sham? They are sham, *dam, uparam, titiksha, shraddha* and *samadhana*.)

Śamaḥ kaḥ? mano nigrahaḥ ।
Damaḥ kaḥ? cakṣurādibāhyendriyanigrahaḥ ।
Uparamaḥ kaḥ? svadharmānuṣṭhānameva ।

Titikṣā kā? śītoṣṇasukhaduḥkhādisahiṣṇutvam ।
Śraddhā kīdṛśī? guruvedāntavākyādiṣu viśvāsaḥ śraddhā ।
Samādhānaṃ kim? cittaikāgratā ।

(What is sham? It is control or mastery over the mind. What is dam? It is the control of the external sense organs such as the eyes etc. What is uparam or uparati? It is the strict observance of one own's dharma {duty}. What is titiksha? It is endurance of heat and cold, pleasure and pain etc. What is the nature of shraddha? Faith in the words etc., of the guru and Vedanta {scriptures} is shraddha. What is samadhana? It is the single pointedness of the mind.)

Mumukṣutvaṃ
(Liberation)

Mumukṣutvaṃ kim?
mokṣo me bhūyād iti icchā ।

(What is *mumukṣutvaṃ?* Let me attain liberation. This intense desire is mumukṣutvaṃ.)

Etat sādhanacatuṣṭayam ।
Tatastattvavivekasyādhikāriṇo bhavanti ।

(This is the four-fold qualification. Thereafter, they become fit for the enquiry into the truth.)

Tattvaviveka
(Enquiry into truth)

Tattvavivekaḥ kaḥ? Ātmā satyaṃ tadanyat sarvaṃ mithyeti ।

(What is enquiry into the truth? It is the firm conviction that the self is real and all, other than that is unreal.)

Ātmā kaḥ?
Sthūlasūkṣmakāraṇaśarīrādvyatiriktaḥ pañcakośātītaḥ san avasthātrayasākṣī saccidānandasvarūpaḥ san yastiṣṭhati sa ātmā ।

(What is the self? That which is other than the gross, subtle and causal bodies, beyond the five sheaths, the witness of the three states of consciousness and of the nature of existence-consciousness-bliss is the self.)

Śarīratrayam

(The three bodies)

The gross body

Sthūlaśarīraṃ kim? pañcīkṛtapañcamahābhūtaiḥ kṛtaṃ satkarmajanyaṃ sukhaduḥkhādibhogāyatanaṃ śarīram asti jāyate vardhate vipariṇamate apakṣīyate vinaśyatīti ṣaḍvikāravadetatsthūlaśarīram ।

(That which is made up of the five great elements that have undergone the process of *panchikarana*, born as a result of the good actions of the past, the counter of experiences like joy, sorrow etc., and subject to the six modifications namely, to potentially exist, to be born, to grow, to mature, to decay and to die is the gross body.)

The subtle body

Sūkṣmaśarīraṃ kim? Apañcīkṛtapañcamahābhūtaiḥ kṛtaṃ satkarmajanyaṃ sukhaduḥkhādibhogasādhanaṃ pañcajñānendriyāṇi pañcakarmendriyāṇi pañcaprāṇādayaḥ manaścaikaṃ buddhiścaikā evaṃ saptadaśākalābhiḥ saha yattiṣṭhati tatsūkṣmaśarīram ।

(What is the subtle body? That which is composed of the five great elements which have not undergone grossification, born of the good actions of the past, the instrument for the experience of joy, sorrow etc., constituted of seventeen items, namely, the five sense organs of perception, the five sense organs of action, five *pranas*, the mind and the intellect is the subtle body.)

(The five sense organs of perception)

Śrotraṃ tvak cakṣuḥ rasanā ghrāṇam iti pañca jñānendriyāṇi | śrotrasya digdevatā | tvaco vāyuḥ | cakṣuṣaḥ sūryaḥ | rasanāyā varuṇaḥ | ghrāṇasya aśvinau | iti jñānendriyadevatāḥ | śrotrasya viṣayaḥ śabdagrahaṇam | tvaco viṣayaḥ sparśagrahaṇam | cakṣuṣo viṣayaḥ rūpagrahaṇam | rasanāyā viṣayaḥ rasagrahaṇam | ghrāṇasya viṣayaḥ gandhagrahaṇam iti |

(The five sense organs of perception are the ears, skin, eyes, tongue and nose. The presiding deities of the sense organs of perception are space of the ears, air of the skin, the sun of the eyes, water of the tongue and the Ashvini kumaras of the nose. The field of experience of the sense organs of perception are—cognition of sound for the ear; cognition of touch for the skin; cognition of sight for the eyes; cognition of taste for the tongue and cognition of smell for the nose.)

(The five sense organs of action)

vākpāṇipādapāyūpasthānīti pañcakarmendriyāṇi | vāco devatā vahniḥ | hastayorindraḥ | pādayorviṣṇuḥ | pāyormṛtyuḥ | upasthasya prajāpatiḥ | iti karmendriyadevatāḥ | vāco viṣayaḥ bhāṣaṇam | pāṇyorviṣayaḥ vastugrahaṇam | pādayorviṣayaḥ gamanam | pāyorviṣayaḥ malatyāgaḥ | upasthasya viṣayaḥ ānanda iti |

(The five sense organs of action are—speech, the hands, the legs, the anus and the genitals. The presiding deities of the organs of action are—agni (fire) of speech, *Indra* of the hands, *Vishnu* of the legs, *Yama* of the anus and *Prajapati* of the genitals. The function of speech is to speak, that of the hands to grasp things, of the legs locomotion, of the anus elimination of waste and the genitals, pleasure {procreation}.)

The causal body

kāraṇaśarīraṃ kim? anirvācyānādyavidyārūpaṃ śarīradvayasya kāraṇamātraṃ satsvarūpā'jñānaṃ nirvikalpakarūpaṃ yadasti tatkāraṇaśarīram ।

(That which is inexplicable, beginning-less, in the form of ignorance, the sole cause of the two bodies {gross and subtle}, ignorant of one's own true nature, free from duality—is the causal body.)

The three states

Avasthātrayaṃ kim? Jāgratsvapnasuṣuptyavasthāḥ ।

(What are the three states? They are the waking, dream and deep sleep states.)

Jagrat Avastha
(The waking state)

Jāgradavasthā kā? śrotrādijñānendriyaiḥ śabdādiviṣayaiśca jñāyate iti yat sā jāgradāvasthā । *sthūla śarīrābhimānī ātmā viśva ityucyate* ।

(What is the waking state? The state of experience in which the sense objects like sound are perceived through the sense organs like the ears, is the waking state. The self, identification with the gross body, is then called *vishva*).

Svapna Avastha
(The dream state)

Svapnāvasthā keti cet? jāgradavasthāyāṃ yaddṛṣṭaṃ yad śrutam tajjanitavāsanayā nidrāsamaye yaḥ prapañcaḥ pratīyate sā svapnāvasthā | *sūkṣmaśarīrābhimānī ātmā taijasa ityucyate* |

(For the question, what is the dream state, the explanation is: the word that is projected while in sleep from the impressions born of what was seen and heard in the waking state is called the dream state. The self identified with the subtle body is called *taiijas*).

Sushupti Avastha
(The deep sleep state)

Attha suṣuptyavasthā kā? ahaṃ kimapi na jānāmi sukhena mayā nidrā'nubhūyata iti suṣuptyavasthā | *kāraṇaśarīrābhimānī ātmā prājña ityucyate* |

(Then what is the deep sleep state? That state about which one says later 'I did not know anything, I enjoyed a good sleep,' is the deep sleep state. The self identified with the causal body is called prana.)

Pañca kośāḥ
(The five sheaths)

Pañca kośāḥ ke? annamayaḥ prāṇamayaḥ manomayaḥ vijñānamayaḥ ānandamayaśceti |

(What are the five sheaths? They are Annamaya, Pranamaya, Manomaya, Vijnanamaya and Anandamaya.)

Annamayaḥ kośaḥ
(The food sheath)

Annamayaḥ kaḥ? annarasenaiva bhūtvā annarasenaiva vṛddhiṃ prāpya annarūpapṛthivyāṃ yadvilīyate tadannamayaḥ kośaḥ sthūlaśarīram I

(That which is born from the essence of food, grows by the essence of food and merges into the earth, which is of the nature of food is called the food sheath or the gross body.)

Prāṇamayaḥ kośaḥ
(The vital air sheath)

Prāṇamayaḥ kaḥ? prāṇādyāḥ pañcavāyavaḥ vāgādīndriyapañcakaṃ prāṇamayaḥ kośaḥ I

(What is *Prāṇamayaḥ kośaḥ*? The five physiological functions like prana, etc., and the five organs of action like speech etc., together form the vital air sheath.)

Manomayaḥ kośaḥ
(The mental sheath)

Manomayaḥ kośaḥ kaḥ? manaśca jñānendriyapañcakaṃ militvā yo bhavati sa manomayaḥ kośaḥ I

(What is *Manomayaḥ kośaḥ*? The mind and the five sense organs of perception together form the mental sheath.)

Vijñānamayaḥ kośaḥ
(The intellectual sheath)

Vijñānamaya kaḥ? buddhijñānendriyapañcakaṃ militvā yo bhavati sa vijñānamaya kośaḥ |

(What is *Vijñānamayaḥ kośaḥ*? The intellect and the five sense organs of perception together is the intellectual sheath. It is subtle, and pervades the former three sheaths. It controls the other three. It constitutes the intellect and the five sense organs or perception. The five senses are common to both the mental and intellectual sheaths as perception involves both the mind and the intellect.)

Ānandamayaḥ kośaḥ
(The bliss sheath)

Ānandamayaḥ kaḥ? evameva
kāraṇaśarīrabhūtāvidyāsthamalinasattvaṃ
priyādivṛttisahitaṃ sat ānandamayaḥ kośaḥ | *etatkośapañcakam* |

(What is *Anandamaya kośaḥ*? Established in ignorance, which is of the form of the causal body, of impure nature, united with thoughts like priya etc., is the bliss sheath. These are the five sheaths.)

Pañcakośātita
(Beyond the five sheaths)

Madīyaṃ śarīraṃ madīyāḥ prāṇāḥ madīyaṃ manaśca madīyā buddhirmadīyaṃ ajñānamiti svenaiva jñāyate tadyathā madīyatvena jñātaṃ kaṭakakuṇḍala gṛhādikaṃ svasmadbhinnaṃ tathā pañcakośādikaṃ svasmadbhinnam madīyatvena jñātamātmā na bhavati |

(Just as bangles, earrings, house etc., known as 'mine' are all other than knower 'me', so too, the five sheaths etc., are known by the self as my body, my pranas, my mind, my intellect, and my knowledge and are therefore not the self.)

Ātman

(The nature of the self)

Ātmā tarhi kaḥ? saccidānandasvarūpaḥ | *satkim? kālatraye'pi tiṣṭhatīti sat* | *citkim? jñānasvarūpaḥ* | *ānandaḥ kaḥ? sukhasvarūpaḥ* | *evaṃ saccidānandasvarūpaṃ svātmānaṃ vijānīyāt* |

(Then what is the self? It is of the nature of existence, consciousness, bliss. What is existence? That which remains unchanged in the three periods of time {past, present and future} is existence. What is consciousness? It is of the nature of absolute knowledge. What is bliss? It is of the nature of absolute happiness. Thus one should know oneself to be of the nature of existence-consciousnes—bliss.)

Jagat

(The universe)

Atha caturviṃśatitattvotpattiprakāraṃ vakṣyāmaḥ |

(Now we shall explain the evolution of the twenty-four factors.)

Maya

Brahmāśrayā sattvarajastamoguṇātmikā māyā asti

(Depending on Brahman, maya exists, which is of the nature of the three qualities of *sattva*, *rajas* and *tamas*.)

The evolution of the five elements

Tataḥ ākāśaḥ sambhūtaḥ | ākāśād vāyuḥ | vāyostejaḥ | tejasa āpaḥ | adbhyaḥ pṛthivī |

(From that {maya}, space was born. From space, air. From air, fire. From fire, water. From water, earth.)

The evolution of the sattva aspect
(The organs of perception)

Eteṣāṃ pañcatattvānāṃ madhye ākāśasya sātvikāṃśāt śrotrendriyaṃ sambhūtam | vāyoḥ sātvikāṃśāt tvagindriyaṃ sambhūtam | agneḥ sātvikāṃśāt cakṣurindriyaṃ sambhūtam | jalasya sātvikāṃśāt rasanendriyaṃ sambhūtam | pṛthivyāḥ sātvikāṃśāt ghrāṇendriyaṃ sambhūtam |

(Among these five great elements, out of the sattvic aspect of space, the organ of hearing, the ear, evolved. From the sattvic aspect of air, the organ of touch, the skin, evolved. From the sattvic aspect of fire, the organ of sight, the eye, evolved. From the sattvic aspect of water, the organ of taste, the tongue evolved. From the sattvic aspect of earth, the organ of smell, the nose, evolved.)

(The inner instruments)

Eteṣāṃ pañcatattvānāṃ samaṣṭisātvikāṃśāt manobuddhyahaṅkāra cittāntaḥkaraṇāni sambhūtāni | saṅkalpavikalpātmakaṃ manaḥ | niścayātmikā buddhiḥ | ahaṃkartā ahaṃkāraḥ | cintanakartṛ cittam | manaso devatā candramāḥ | buddhe brahmā | ahaṃkārasya rudraḥ | cittasya vāsudevaḥ |

(From the total sattvic aspect of these five elements, the inner instrument of the mind, intellect, ego and memory are formed. The mind is of the nature of indecision. The intellect is of the nature of decision. The ego is of the nature of the notion of doership. Memory is of the nature of thinking or recollection. The presiding deity of the mind is the moon, of the intellect, Brahma, of the ego, Rudra and of memory, Vasudeva.)

The evolution of the rajas aspect

Eteṣāṃ pañcatattvānāṃ madhye ākāśasya rājasāṃśāt vāgindriyaṃ sambhūtam | *vāyoḥ rājasāṃśāt pāṇīndriyaṃ sambhūtam* | *vanheḥ rājasāṃśāt pādendriyaṃ sambhūtam* | *jalasya rājasāṃśāt upasthendriyaṃ sambhūtam* | *pṛthivyā rājasāṃśāt gudendriyaṃ sambhūtam* | *eteṣāṃ samaṣṭirājasāṃśāt pañcaprāṇāḥ sambhūtāḥ* |

(Among these five elements, from the rajas aspect of space, the organ of speech is formed. From the rajas aspect of air, the organ of grasping, the hands are formed. From the rajas aspect of fire, the organ of locomotion, the legs are formed. From the rajas aspect of water, the organ of procreation is formed. From the rajasic aspect of earth, the anus is formed. From the total rajas aspect of these five elements, the five vital airs, pranas are formed.)

The evolution of the tamasic aspect

Eteṣāṃ pañcatattvānāṃ tāmasāṃśāt pañcīkṛtapañcatattvāni bhavanti | *pañcīkaraṇaṃ katham iti cet* | *eteṣāṃ pañcamahābhūtānāṃ tāmasāṃśasvarūpam ekamekaṃ bhūtaṃ dvidhā vibhajya ekamekamardhaṃ pṛthak tūṣṇīṃ vyavasthāpya aparamaparamardhaṃ caturdhāṃ vibhajya svārdhamanyeṣu ardheṣu svabhāgacatuṣṭayasaṃyojanaṃ kāryam* | *tadā pañcīkaraṇaṃ bhavati* |

etebhyaḥ pañcīkṛtapañcamahābhūtebhyaḥ sthūlaśarīraṃ bhavati |
evaṃ piṇḍabrahmāṇḍayoraikyaṃ sambhūtam |

(From the tamas aspect of these five elements, the grossified five elements are born. If it is asked how this *panchikarana* takes place, it is as follows.

- The tamas aspect of each of the five elements divides into two equal parts.
- One half of each remains intact.
- The other half of each gets divided into four equal parts.
- Then to the intact half of one element, one-eight portion from each of the other four elements gets joined.
- Then panchikarana is completed.
- From these five grossified elements, the gross body is formed.

Thus, there is identity between the microcosm and the macrocosm.)

Jiva and Ishwara

Sthūlaśarīrābhimāni jīvanāmakaṃ brahmapratibimbaṃ bhavati | sa eva jīvaḥ prakṛtyā svasmāt īśvaraṃ bhinnatvena jānāti | avidyopādhiḥ san ātmā jīva ityucyate | māyopādhiḥ san īśvara ityucyate | evaṃ upādhibhedāt jīveśvarabhedadṛṣṭiḥ yāvatparyantaṃ tiṣṭhati tāvatparyantaṃ janmamaraṇādirūpasaṃsāro na nivartate | tasmātkāraṇānna jīveśvarayorbhedabuddhiḥ svīkāryā |

(The reflection of Brahman, which identifies itself with the gross body, is called the jiva. This jiva by nature takes Ishwara to be different from himself or herself. The self conditioned by ignorance {maya} is called Ishwara. So long as the notion that the jiva and Ishwara are different remains, which is due to the difference in the conditioning, till then, there is no redemption from samsara which is of the form of repeated birth, death etc. Due to that reason, the notion that the jiva is different from Ishwara should not be accepted.)

An enquiry into the statement: That Thou Art

Nanu sāhaṃkārasya kiṃcijjñasya jīvasya nirahaṃkārasya sarvajñasya īśvarasya tattvamasīti mahāvākyāt kathamabhedabuddhiḥ syādubhayoḥ viruddhadharmākrāntatvāt |

(But the jiva is endowed with ego and his knowledge is limited, whereas, Ishwara is without ego and is omniscient. Then how can there be identity, as stated in the mahavakya, 'That thou art', between these two who are possessed of contradictory characteristics?)

Iti cenna | *sthūlasūkṣmaśarīrābhimānī tvaṃpadavācyārthaḥ* | *upādhivinirmuktaṃ samādhidaśāsampannaṃ śuddhaṃ caitanyaṃ tvaṃpadalakṣyārthaḥ* | *evaṃ sarvajñatvādiviśiṣta īśvaraḥ tatpadavācyārthaḥ* | *upādhiśūnyaṃ śuddhacaitanyaṃ tatpadalakṣyārthaḥ evaṃ ca jīveśvarayo caitanyarūpeṇā'bhede bādhakābhāvaḥ* |

(If there is such a doubt, no {it is not so}. That literal meaning of the word 'thou' is the one identified with the gross and subtle bodies. The implied meaning of the word 'thou' is pure awareness which is free from all conditionings and which is appreciated in the state of samadhi. So also the literal meaning of the word 'That' is Ishwara having omniscience etc.; the implied meaning of the word that is the pure awareness, free from all conditionings. Thus there is no contradiction regarding the identity between the jiva and Ishwara from the standpoint of awareness.)

Jīvanmuktaḥ
(Man of realisation)

Evaṃ ca vedāntavākyaiḥ sadgurūpadeśena ca sarveṣvapi bhūteṣu yeṣāṃ brahmabuddhirutpannā te jīvanmuktāḥ ityarthaḥ I

(Thus by the words of Vedanta and the teachings of the satguru, those in whom the vision of the truth is born in all beings, are liberated while living {jīvanmuktaḥ}.)

Nanu jīvanmuktaḥ kaḥ? yathā deho'haṃ puruṣo'haṃ brāhmaṇo'haṃ śūdro'hamasmīti dṛḍhaniścayastathā nāhaṃ brāhmaṇaḥ na śūdraḥ na puruṣaḥ kintu asaṃgaḥ saccidānandasvarūpaḥ prakāśarūpaḥ sarvāntaryāmī cidākāśarūpo'smīti dṛḍhaniścayarūpo'parokṣajñānavān jīvanmuktaḥ I

(Then who is a jīvanmuktaḥ? Just as one has firm belief 'I am the body'; 'I am a man'; 'I am a Brahmin'; 'I am Shudra', in the same way one who by his immediate knowledge {aparoksha jnana} has firmly ascertained, 'I am not a Brahmin'; 'I am not a Shudra'; I am not a man' but 'I am unattached' and of the nature of existence-consciousness-bliss, effulgent, the indweller of all and the formless awareness is a jīvanmuktaḥ.)

Brahmaivāhamasmītyaparokṣajñānena nikhilakarmabandhavinirmuktaḥ syāt I

(By immediate knowledge that I am Brahman alone, one becomes free from bondage of all karmas.)

Karma
(The actions)

Karmāṇi katividhāni santīti cet āgāmisañcitaprārabdhabhedena trividhāni santi |

(If one is asked—how many kinds of karmas are there, {the reply is} there are three kinds of karmas, viz., *agami*, *sanchita* and *prarabdha*.)

Agami karma

jñānotpattyanantaraṃ jñānidehakṛtaṃ puṇyapāparūpaṃ karma yadasti tadāgāmītyabhidhīyate |

(The results of actions, good or bad performed by the body of the realised soul {jnani} after the dawn of knowledge is known as agami.)

Sanchita karma

Sañcitaṃ karma kim? anantakoṭijanmanāṃ bījabhūtaṃ sat yatkarmajātaṃ pūrvārjitaṃ tiṣṭhati tat sañcitaṃ jñeyam |

(The result of actions performed in {all} previous births which are in seed form to give rise to endless crores of births in future is called sanchita {accumulated} karma.)

Prarabdha karma

Prārabdhaṃ karma kimiti cet | *idaṃ śarīramutpādya iha loke evaṃ sukhaduḥkhādipradaṃ yatkarma tatprārabdhaṃ bhogena naṣṭaṃ bhavati prārabdhakarmaṇāṃ bhogādeva kṣaya iti* |

(Having given birth to this body, the actions which give result in this very world, in the form of happiness or misery and which can be destroyed only by enjoying or suffering them is called prarabdha karma.)

Freedom from the bondage of actions

Sañcitaṃ karma brahmaivāhamiti niścayātmakajñānena naśyati I

(Sanchita karma is destroyed by the firm knowledge, 'I am Brahman alone'.)

Āgāmi karma api jñānena naśyati kiṃca āgāmi karmaṇāṃ nalinīdalagatajalavat jñāninām sambandho nāsti I

(The agami karma is also destroyed by knowledge and the wise man is not affected by it—as a lotus leaf is not affected by the water on it {*padma patram ivambhasa*}.)

Kiṃca ye jñāninaṃ stuvanti bhajanti arcayanti tānprati jñānikṛtaṃ āgāmi puṇyaṃ gacchati I *ye jñāninaṃ nindanti dviṣanti duḥkhapradānaṃ kurvanti tānprati jñānikṛtaṃ sarvamāgāmi kriyamāṇaṃ yadavācyaṃ karma pāpātmakaṃ tadgacchati suhṛdaḥ puṇyakṛtaṃ durhṛdaḥ pāpakṛtyaṃ gṛhṇanti* I

(Further, to those who praise, serve and worship the wise man, go the results of the actions done by the wise man. To those who criticise, hate or cause pain to the wise man go the results of all unpraiseworthy and sinful actions done by the wise man.)

Conclusion

Tathā cātmavitsaṃsāraṃ tīrtvā brahmānandamihaiva prāpnoti I *tarati śokamātmavit iti śruteḥ* I *tanuṃ tyajatu vā kāśyāṃ śvapacasya*

gṛhe'thavā | jñānasamprāptisamaye mukto'sau vigatāśayaḥ | iti smṛteśca |

(Thus the knower of the self, having crossed samsara, attains supreme bliss here itself. The *shruti* affirms—the knower of the self goes beyond all sorrow. Let the wise man cast off his body in Kashi or in the house of a dog-eater {it is immaterial} because at the time of gaining knowledge {itself} he is liberated, being freed from all the results of his actions. So assert the *smritis* too.)

Vivekachudamani

Vivekdachudamani, which translates to 'crest jewel of discrimination', consists of 580 verses, focused on the need for viveka or discrimination. This discrimination is required to distinguish between the real and the unreal, the eternal and the transient, and the ephemeral and the permanent.

Like Shankara's other Prakarana or introductory texts to Vedanta, the Vivekachudamani also is in the nature of a summarised presentation of the essential tenets of Advaita philosophy. In it he explains, through short stanzas, the entire gamut of his basic concepts relating to the nature of the jiva; the importance of knowledge and its limitations as well; the role of avidya or ignorance; the nature of maya and the three elements or gunas that constitute it; the identity of the Atman with Brahman; the non-dual paramountcy of Brahman, and the way to experience it.

The text opens with an invocation to Govinda, which could be Lord Krishna, or Govindapada, his Guru at Omkareshwar in whose ashrama he first mastered the essentials of Vedanta. Shankara then proceeds to explain, step by step, the path to self-realisation, including the characteristics of a jīvanmuktaḥ, a person who has achieved the state of enlightened wisdom.

A detailed Sanskrit commentary on 515 verses of the work was written by the former pontiff of Sringeri, Sri Chandrasekhara Bharati. A Tamil translation and commentary was penned by the great sage Ramanna Maharishi in the last century. English translations by Christopher Isherwood and Swami Chinmayananda are also available. We have selected the English translation—perhaps the first—by Swami Madhavananda in 1921.

jantūnāṃ narajanmadurlabhamataḥ puṃstvaṃ tato vipratā
Tasmādvaidikadharmamārgaparatā vidwatvamasmātparam |
Ātmānātmavivecanaṃ svanubhavo brahmātmanā saṃsthitir-
Muktirno śatajanmakoṭisukṛtaiḥ puṇyairvinā labhyate ||

(For all beings a human birth is difficult to obtain, more so is a male body, rarer than that is Brahminhood, rarer still is the attachment to the path of Vedic religion; higher than this is erudition in the scriptures; discrimination between the self and not self, realisation, and continuing in a state of identity with Brahman—these come next in order. {This kind of} mukti is not to be attained except through the well-earned merits of a hundred crore of births.)

Labdhvā kathaṃcitnnarajanma durlabhaṃ
Tatrāpi puṃstvaṃ śrutipāradarśanam |
Yastvātmamuktau na yateta mūḍhadhīḥ
Sa hyātmahā svaṃ vinihantyasadgrahāt ||

(The man who having by some means obtained a human birth, with a male body and mastery of the Vedas to boot, is foolish enough not to exert for self-liberation verily commits suicide, for he kills himself by clinging to things unreal.)

Vadantu śāstrāṇi yajantu devān
Kurvantu karmāṇi bhajantu devatāḥ ।
Ātmaikyabodhena vināpi muktir-
Na sidhyati brahmaśatāntare'pi ॥

(Let people quote scriptures and sacrifice to the gods, let them perform rituals and worship the deities, there is no liberation for anyone without the realisation of one's identity with the Atman, no not even in the lifetime of a hundred Brahman put together.)

Na yogena na sāṅkhyena karmaṇā no na vidyayā ।
Brahmātmaikatvabodhena mokṣaḥ sidhyati nānyathā ॥

(Neither by yoga, nor by sankhya, nor by work, nor by learning, but by the realisation of one's identity with Brahman is liberation possible, and by no other means.)

Vīṇāyā rūpasaundaryaṃ tantrīvādanasauṣṭhavam ।
Prajārañjanamātraṃ tanna sāmrājyāya kalpate ॥

(The beauty of the veena and the skill of playing on its chords serve sincerely to please some persons; they do not suffice to confer sovereignty.)

Vāgvaikharī śabdajharī śāstravyākhyānakauśalam ।
Vaiduṣyaṃ viduṣāṃ tadvadbhuktaye na tu muktaye ॥

(Loud speech consisting of a shower of words, the skill expounding scriptures, and likewise erudition—these merely bring on a little personal enjoyment to the scholar but are no good for liberation.)

Avijñāte pare tattve śāstrādhītistu niṣphalā ।
Vijñāte'pi pare tattve śāstrādhītistu niṣphalā ॥

(The study of scriptures is useless as long as the highest truth is unknown, and it is equally useless when the highest truth has already been known.)

Śabdajālaṃ mahāraṇyaṃ cittabhramaṇakāraṇam |
Ataḥ prayatnājjñātavyaṃ tattvajñaistattvamātmanaḥ ||

(The scriptures consisting of many words are a dense forest which causes the mind to ramble merely. Hence the man of wisdom should earnestly set about knowing the true nature of the self.)

Ajñānasarpadaṣṭasya brahmajñānauṣadhaṃ vinā |
Kimu vedaiśca śāstraiśca kimu mantraiḥ kimauṣadhaiḥ ||

(For one who has been bitten by the serpent of ignorance the only remedy is the knowledge of Brahman; of what avail are the Vedas and scriptures, mantras and medicines to such a one?)

Avyaktanāmnī parameśaśaktiḥ
Anādyavidyā triguṇātmikā parā |
Kāryānumeyā sudhiyaiva māyā
Yayā jagatsarvamidaṃ prasūyate ||

(Avidya or maya, called also undifferentiated, is the power of the Lord. It is without a beginning, is made up of the three gunas and is superior to the effects {as their cause}. She is to be inferred by one of clear intellect only from the effects she produces.)

Sannāpyasannāpyubhayātmikā no
Bhinnāpyabhinnāpyubhayātmikā no |
Sāṅgāpyanaṅgā hyubhayātmikā no
Mahādbhutā'nirvacanīyarūpā ||

(She is neither existence nor non-existence nor partaking of both characters; neither same nor different nor both; neither composed of parts nor an indivisible whole nor both; she is most wonderful and cannot be described in words.)

Śuddhādvayabrahmavibodhanāśyā
Sarpabhramo rajjuvivekato yathā |
Rajastamaḥ sattvamiti prasiddhā
Guṇāstadīyāḥ prathitaiḥ svakāryaiḥ ||

(This maya can be destroyed by the realisation of the pure Brahman, the one without a second, just as the mistaken idea of a snake is removed by the discrimination of the rope. She has her gunas known as rajas, tamas, and sattva, named after their respective functions.)

Kāmaḥ krodho lobhadambhādyasūyā
Haṅkārerṣyāmatsarādyāstu ghorāḥ |
Dharmā ete rājasāḥ pumpravṛttir
Yasmādeṣā tadrajo bandhahetuḥ ||

(Lust, anger, avarice, arrogance, spite, egoism, envy and jealousy etc.—these are the dire attributes of rajas, from which this worldly tendency of man is produced. Therefore rajas is a cause of bondage.)

Eṣā'vṛtirnāma tamoguṇasya
Śaktiryayā vastvavabhāsate'nyathā |
Saiṣā nidānaṃ puruṣasya saṃsṛter
Vikṣepaśakteḥ pravaṇasya hetuḥ ||

(*Avriti* or the veiling power is power of tamas which makes things appear other than what they are. It is this that causes man's repeated transmigrations, and starts the action of the projecting power {vikshepa}.)

Prajñāvānapi paṇḍito'pi caturo'pyatyantasūkṣmātmadṛg-
Vyālīḍhastamasā na vetti bahudhā sambodhito'pi sphuṭam
Bhrāntyāropitameva sādhu kalayatyālambate tadguṇān
Hantāsau prabalā durantatamasaḥ śaktirmahatyāvṛtiḥ ǀ

(Even wise and learned men, and men who are clever and adept in the vision of the exceedingly subtle Atman, are overpowered by tamas and do not understand the Atman even though clearly explained in various ways. What is simply superimposed by delusion, they consider as true, and attach themselves to its effects. Alas! How powerful is the great avriti shakti of dreadful tamas.)

Abhāvanā vā viparītabhāvanā-
Sambhāvanā vipratipattirasyāḥ ǀ
Saṃsargayuktaṃ na vimuñcati dhruvaṃ
Vikṣepaśaktiḥ kṣapayatyajasram ǀǀ

(Absence of right judgement, or contrary judgement, want of definite belief and doubt—these certainly never desert one who has any connection with this 'veiling power', and then the 'projecting power—vikshepa' gives ceaseless trouble.)

Ajñānamālasyajaḍatvanidrā-
Pramādamūḍhatvamukhāstamoguṇāḥ ǀ
Etaiḥ prayukto na hi vetti kiñci-
Nnidrāluvatstambhavadeva tiṣṭhati ǀǀ

(Ignorance, lassitude, dullness, sleep, inadvertence and stupidity etc., are attributes of tamas. One tied to these does not comprehend anything but remains like one asleep or like a stock or stone.)

Viśuddhasattvasya guṇāḥ prasādaḥ
Svātmānubhūtiḥ paramā praśāntiḥ ǀ

Tṛptiḥ praharṣaḥ paramātmaniṣṭhā
Yayā sadānandarasaṃ samṛcchati ||

(The traits of pure sattva are cheerfulness, the realisation of one's own self, supreme peace, contentment, bliss, and steady devotion for the Atman, by which the aspirant enjoys bliss everlasting.)

Bījaṃ saṃsṛtibhūmijasya tu tamo dehātmadhīraṅkuro
Rāgaḥ pallavamambu karma tu vapuḥ skandho'savaḥ śākhikāḥ |
Agrāṇīndriyasaṃhatiśca viṣayāḥ puṣpāṇi duḥkhaṃ phalaṃ
Nānākarmasamudbhavaṃ bahuvidhaṃ bhoktātra jīvaḥ khagaḥ ||

(Of the tree of samsara ignorance is the seed, the identification with the body is its sprout, attachment its tender leaves, work its water, the body its trunk, the vital forces its branches, the organs its twigs, the sense-objects its flowers, various miseries due to diverse works are its fruits, and the individual soul is the bird on it.)

Satyaṃ jñānamanantaṃ brahma viśuddhaṃ paraṃ svataḥsiddham |
Nityānandaikarasaṃ pratyagabhinnaṃ nirantaraṃ jayati ||

(Brahman is existence, knowledge, the absolute, pure, supreme, self-existent, eternal and indivisible bliss, not different {in reality} from the individual soul, and devoid of interior or exterior—there it reigns triumphant.)

Yadidaṃ sakalaṃ viśvaṃ nānārūpaṃ pratītamajñānāt |
Tatsarvaṃ brahmaiva pratyastāśeṣabhāvanādoṣam ||

(All this universe which appears as of diverse forms through ignorance is nothing else but Brahman, which is absolutely free from all the limitations of human thought.)

Ataḥ paraṃ brahma sadadvitīyaṃ
Viśuddhavijñānaghanaṃ nirañjanam |
Praśāntamādyantavihīnamakriyaṃ
Nirantarānandarasasvarūpam ||

(Hence whatever there manifests, viz., this universe, is supreme Brahman itself, the real, the one without a second, pure, the essence of knowledge, the taintless, pacified, devoid of beginning and end, beyond activity, the essence of bliss absolute.)

Nirastamāyākṛtasarvabhedaṃ
Nityaṃ sukhaṃ niṣkalamaprameyam |
Arūpamavyaktamanākhyamavyayaṃ
Jyotiḥ svayaṃ kiñcididaṃ cakāsti ||

(Transcending all the diversities created by maya or nescience, eternal, ever beyond the reach of pain, indivisible, unconditioned, formless, undifferentiated, nameless, immutable, self-luminous.)

Jñātṛjñeyajñānaśūnyamanantaṃ nirvikalpakam |
Kevalākhaṇḍacinmātraṃ paraṃ tattvaṃ vidurbudhāḥ ||

(Sages realise the supreme principle, Brahman, in which there is no differentiation of knower, knowledge and known, infinite, transcendent, the essence of knowledge, the absolute.)

Aheyamanupādeyaṃ manovācāmagocaram |
Aprameyamanādyantaṃ brahma pūrṇamahaṃ mahaḥ ||

(Which can be neither thrown away nor taken up, which is beyond the reach of mind and speech, immeasurable, without beginning and end, the whole, one's very self, and of surpassing glory.)

Mṛtkāryaṃ sakalaṃ ghaṭādi satataṃ mṛnmātramevāhitaṃ
Tadvatsajjanitaṃ sadātmakamidaṃ sanmātramevākhilam |

Yasmānnāsti sataḥ paraṃ kimapi tatsatyaṃ sa ātmā svayaṃ
Tasmāttattvamasi praśāntamamalaṃ brahmādvayaṃ yatparam ||

(All modifications of earth, such as the jar etc., which are always accepted by the mind as real, are (in reality) nothing but earth. Similarly this entire universe which is produced from the real Brahman, is Brahman itself and nothing but Brahman. Because there is nothing else whatever but Brahman, and that is the only self-existent reality, our very self; therefore thou art that pacified, pure, supreme Brahman, the one without a second.)

Yatra bhrāntyā kalpitaṃ tadviveke
Tattanmātraṃ naiva tasmādvibhinnam |
Svapne naṣṭaṃ svapnaviśvaṃ vicitra
Svasmādbhinnaṃ kinnu dṛṣṭaṃ prabodhe ||

({What is} erroneously supposed to exist in something is, when the truth about it has been known, nothing but that substratum, and not at all different from it: the diversified dream universe {appears and} passes away in the dream itself. Does it appear on waking as something distinct from one's own self?)

Santyanye pratibandhāḥ puṃsaḥ saṃsārahetavo dṛṣṭāḥ |
Teṣāmevaṃ mūlaṃ prathamavikāro bhavatyahaṅkāraḥ ||

(Other obstacles are also observed to exist for men, which lead to transmigration. The root of them, for the above reasons, is the first modification of nescience they call egoism.)

Yāvatsyātsvasya sambandho'haṅkāreṇa durātmanā |
Tāvanna leśamātrāpi muktivārtā vilakṣaṇā ||

(So long as one has any relation with this wicked ego, there should not be the least talk about liberation, which is unique.)

Ahaṅkāragrahānmuktaḥ svarūpamupapadyate |
Candravadvimalaḥ pūrṇaḥ sadānandaḥ svayamprabhuḥ ||

(Free from the clutches of egoism, man attains to his real nature, as the moon from those of the planet Rahu. He becomes pure, infinite, eternally blissful and self-luminous.)

Yo vā pure so'hamiti pratīto
Buddhyā praklṛptastamasā'timūḍhayā |
Tasyaiva niḥśeṣatayā vināśe
Brahmātmabhāvaḥ pratibandhaśūnyaḥ ||

(That which has been created by the buddhi, extremely deluded by nescience and which is perceived in this body as 'I am such and such'—when that egoism is totally destroyed, one attains an unobstructed identity with the Brahman.)

Āśāṃ chinddhi viṣopameṣu viṣayeṣveṣaiva mṛtyoḥ kṛti-
Styaktvā jātikulāśrameṣvabhimatiṃ muñcātidūrātkriyāḥ |
Dehādāvasati tyajātmadhiṣaṇāṃ prajñāṃ kuruṣvātmani
Tvaṃ draṣṭāsyamano'si nirdvayaparaṃ brahmāsi yadvastutaḥ ||

(Sever thy craving for sense-objects which are like poison, for it is the very image of death, and giving up thy very image of death, and giving up thy pride of caste, family and order of life, fling actions to a distance; give up thy identification with such unreal things as the body and the rest, and fix thy mind on the Atman. For thou art really the witness, the Brahman, unshackled by the mind, the one without a second, and supreme.)

Lakṣye brahmaṇi mānasaṃ dṛḍhataraṃ saṃsthāpya bāhyendriyaṃ
Svasthāne viniveśya niścalatanuścopekṣya dehasthitim |
Brahmātmaikyamupetya tanmayatayā cākhaṇḍavṛttyā'niśaṃ
Brahmānandarasaṃ pibātmanimudā śūnyaiḥ kimanyairbhṛśam ||

(Fixing the mind firmly on the ideal, Brahman, and restraining the external organs in their respective centres; with the body held steady, and taking no thought for its maintenance; attaining the identity with Brahman; and being one with it, always drink joyfully of the bliss of Brahman in thy own self, without a break. What is the purpose of other things which are entirely hollow?)

Anātmacintanaṃ tyaktvā kaśmalaṃ duḥkhakāraṇam |
Cintayātmānamānandarūpaṃ yanmuktikāraṇam ||

(Giving up the thought of the not-self which is evil and productive of misery, think of the self, the bliss absolute, which conduces to liberation.)

Vedāntasiddhāntaniruktireṣā
Brahmaiva jīvaḥ sakalaṃ jagacca |
Akhaṇḍarūpasthitireva mokṣo
Brahmādvitīye śrutayaḥ pramāṇam ||

(The verdict of all discussion on Vedanta is the jiva and the whole universe is nothing but Brahman, and that liberation means abiding in Brahman, the indivisible entity. The shrutis themselves are authority {for the statement} that Brahman is one without a second.)

Iti guruvacanācchrutipramāṇāt
Paramavagamya satattvamātmayuktyā |
Praśamitakaraṇaḥ samāhitātmā
Kvacidacalākṛtirātmaniṣṭhato'bhūt ||

(Realising the supreme truth at a blessed moment, through the above instructions of the guru, the authority of the scriptures and his own reasoning, with his senses pacified and the mind concentrated, {the disciple} became immovable in form and perfectly established in the Atman.)

Sarvādhāraṃ sarvavastuprakāśaṃ
Sarvākāraṃ sarvagaṃ sarvaśūnyam ।
Nityaṃ śuddhaṃ niścalaṃ nirvikalpaṃ
Brahmādvaitaṃ yattadevāhamasmi ।।

(I am verily that Brahman, the one without a second, which is the support of all, which illumines all things, which has infinite forms, is omnipresent, devoid of multiplicity, eternal, pure, unmoved, and absolute.)

Yatpratyastāśeṣamāyāviśeṣaṃ
Pratyagrūpaṃ pratyayāgamyamānam ।
Satyajñānānantamānandarūpaṃ
Brahmādvaitaṃ yattadevāhamasmi ।।

(I am verily that Brahman, the one without a second, which transcends the endless differentiations of maya, is the inmost essence of all, beyond the range of consciousness, which is truth, knowledge, infinitude, and bliss-absolute.)

Cintāśūnyamadainyabhaikṣamaśanaṃ pānaṃ saridvāriṣu
Svātantryeṇa niraṅkuśā sthitirabhīrnidrā śmaśāne vane ।
Vastraṃ kṣālanaśoṣaṇādirahitaṃ digvāstu śayyā mahī
Sañcāro nigamāntavīthiṣu vidāṃ krīḍā pare brahmaṇi ।।

(Men of realisation have their food without anxiety or humiliation, by begging, and their drink from the water of rivers; they live freely and independently, and sleep without fear in cremation grounds or forests; their clothing may be the quarters themselves, which need no washing and drying, or any bark, etc., the earth is their bed; they roam in the avenue of Vedanta; while their pastime is in the supreme Brahman.)

Saṃsārādhvani tāpabhānukiraṇaprodbhūtadāhavyathā-
Khinnānāṃ jalakāṅkṣayā marubhuvi bhrāntyā paribhrāmyatām ।

Atyāsannasudhāmbudhiṃ sukhakaraṃ brahmādvayaṃ darśaya
tyeṣā śaṅkarabhāratī vijayate nirvāṇasandāyinī ||

(For those who are afflicted, in the way of the world, by the burning pain due to the sunshine of threefold misery; who through delusion wander about in a desert in search of water; for them here is the triumphant message of Shankara pointing out, within easy reach, the comforting ocean of nectar, the Brahman, the one without a second to lead them on to liberation.)

Bhaja Govindam/Charpatpanjarika Stotra

Bhaja Govindam (Praise Govinda/Repeat the name of Govinda), is one of the most popular hymns penned by Shankara, that is still sung and recited by millions of Hindus every day. It consists of seventeen stanzas in rhyme. The hymn is steeped in the emotion of bhakti, urging the need for devotion to the Lord as against mechanical acquisition of conventional knowledge.

The legend is that Shankara spontaneously composed this hymn in Varanasi on being irritated by the sound of a student loudly trying to learn the rules of grammar by rote. Its basic refrain is that surrender yourself to Govinda, the Lord, for the rules of grammar will not profit you once the hour of death draws near.

This composition, like many others, written by Shankara, wherein he underlines the importance of devotion and surrender, and pours his heart out in obeisance to a deity in the Hindu pantheon, may surprise those who associate him only with the jnana marga or the path of knowledge to salvation. The jnana marga was, indeed, the path that Shankara believed to be the most efficacious in the search for knowledge of Brahman, and consequently of moksha.

However—and this is the important point—he never proscribed prayer and worship animated by the spirit of self-surrender and bhakti. The conventional modes of religious practice, if sufficiently suffused by the yearning for spiritual grace, had his sanction. Under the rubric of apara vidya, or practical knowledge—as against apara vidya or transcendental knowledge—Shankara endorsed such outpourings of devotion as a preparatory step to the para knowledge of Brahman.

The Bhaja Govindam invokes a strong mood of vairagya or renunciation given the transience of the reasons of human pride. We surround ourselves with coordinates of assurance—family, children, wealth, fame, youth, and considering them permanent, spend a lifetime seeking to preserve the inherently ephemeral and momentary, while shutting our eyes to the inevitability of death. It is only when death approaches do we understand the mirage we treasured, and by then, very often, it is too late to pursue the path of jnana that alone can give us lasting happiness and contentment.

For Shankara then, the learning of grammar, as an end in itself, without realising the nature of our finite lives, is a metaphor to highlight the imperative need to acquire that wisdom in the light of which alone we can achieve lasting happiness. Surrender to a personal God—in this case Govinda or Krishna—is the first step in moving towards that wisdom.

Charpatpanjarika Stotra
(Hymn of renunciation)

Dinayāminyau sāyaṃ prātaśśiśiravasantau punarāyātaḥ |
Kālaḥ krīḍati gacchatyāyustadapi na muñcatyāśāvāyuḥ ||
Bhaja govindaṃ bhaja govindaṃ bhaja govindaṃ mūḍhamate |
Saṃprāpte sannihite kāle nahi nahi rakṣati ḍukṛñkaraṇe ||

(Sunrise and sunset, daylight and darkness, winter and springtime, come and go; even the course of time is playful; life itself soon ebbs away; but man's vain hope, alas! Goes onward, tirelessly onward evermore. Worship Govinda, worship Govinda, worship Govinda, foolish one! Rules of grammar profit nothing once the hour of death draws nigh.)

Agre vahniḥ pṛṣṭhe bhānū rātrau cubukasamarpitajānuḥ |
Karatalabhikṣastarutalavāsastadapi na muñcatyāśāpāśaḥ ||
Bhaja govindaṃ bhaja govindaṃ bhaja govindaṃ mūḍhamate |
Saṃprāpte sannihite kāle nahi nahi rakṣati ḍukṛñkaraṇe ||

(Seeking for warmth, the penniless beggar closely crouches before his fire, or sits with only the sun to warm him; nightly he lays himself down to slumber, curling up to keep out the cold; hungrily eats his beggar's portion out of the bowl his hands provide him; takes up his dwelling under a tree: still is his heart a helpless prisoner bound with the chains of empty hope, worship Govinda, worship Govinda, worship Govinda, foolish one! Rules of grammar profit nothing once the hour of death draws nigh.)

Yāvadvittopārjanaśaktastāvannijaparivāro raktaḥ |
Pascājjīvati jarjaradehe vārtāṃ ko'pi na pṛcchati gehe ||
Bhaja govindaṃ bhaja govindaṃ bhaja govindaṃ mūḍhamate |
Saṃprapte sannihite kāle nahi nahi rakṣati dukṛñ karane ||

(While a man supports his family, see what loving care they show! But when his ageing body falters, nearing the time of dissolution, none, not even his nearest kin, will think to ask him how he fares. Worship Govinda, worship Govinda, worship Govinda, foolish one! Rules of grammar profit nothing once the hour of death draws nigh.)

Jaṭilo muṇḍī luñchitakeśaḥ kāṣāyambarabahukṛtaveṣaḥ |
paśyannapi ca na paśyati mūḍho udaranimitto bahukṛtaveṣaḥ ||
Bhaja govindaṃ bhaja govindaṃ bhaja govindaṃ mūḍhamate |
Saṃprāpte sannihite kāle nahi nahi rakṣati ḍukṛñkaraṇe ||

(Many are those, whose locks are matted, many whose heads are closely shaved, many who pluck out all their hair; some of them wearing robes of ochre, some of them clad in other colours—all these things for their stomachs' sake. Seeing truth revealed before them, still the deluded see it not. Worship Govinda, worship Govinda, worship Govinda, foolish one! Rules of grammar profit nothing once the hour of death draws nigh.)

Bhagvaḍgītā kiñcidadhitā gaṅgājalalavakaṇikā pītā |
sakṛdapi yasya murārisamarcā tasya yamaḥ kiṃ kurute carcām ||
Bhaja govindaṃ bhaja govindaṃ bhaja govindaṃ mūḍhamate |
Saṃprāpte sannihite kāle nahi nahi rakṣati ḍukṛñkaraṇe ||

(Let a man but read from the *Gita*, drink of the Ganges but a drop, worship but once the Lord Almighty, and he will set at rest forever all his fear of the king of death. Worship Govinda, worship Govinda, worship Govinda, foolish one! Rules of grammar profit nothing once the hour of death draws nigh.)

Aṅgaṃ galitaṃ palitaṃ muṇḍaṃ daśanavihīnaṃ jātaṃ tuṇḍam |
Vṛddho yāti gṛhītvā daṇḍaṃ tadapi na muñcatyāśapiṇḍam ||
Bhaja govindaṃ bhaja govindaṃ bhaja govindaṃ mūḍhamate |
Saṃprāpte sannihite kāle nahi nahi rakṣati ḍukṛñkaraṇe ||

(Feeble has grown the old man's body, toothless his gums and bald his head; but there he goes, upon his crutches, clinging firmly to fruitless hope! Worship Govinda, worship Govinda, worship Govinda, foolish one! Rules of grammar profit nothing once the hour of death draws nigh.)

Bālastāvatkrīḍasaktaḥ taruṇastāvattruṇīraktaḥ |
Vṛddhastāvatccintāmagnaḥ pare brahmaṇi ko'pi na lagnaḥ ||
Bhaja govindam bhaja govindam bhaja govindam mūdhamate |
Saṃprāpte sannihite kāle nahi nahi rakṣati ḍukṛñkaraṇe ||

(Lost in play is the carefree stripling, lost in his sweetheart's charms, the youth; the old man broods upon his sorrows; none there is, alas! Whose spirit yearns to be lost in the Parabrahman. Worship Govinda, worship Govinda, worship Govinda, foolish one! Rules of grammar profit nothing once the hour of death draws nigh.)

Punarapi jananaṃ punarapi maraṇam punarapi jananījaṭhare śayanam |
Iha saṃsāre bahudustāre kṛpayāpāre pāhi murāre ||
Bhaja govindaṃ bhaja govindaṃ bhaja govindaṃ mūḍhamate |
Saṃprāpte sannihite kāle nahi nahi rakṣati ḍukṛñkaraṇe ||

(Birth unceasing! Death unceasing! Ever to pass through a mother's womb! Hard to cross is the world's wide ocean: Lord, redeem me through Thy mercy! Worship Govinda, worship Govinda, worship Govinda, foolish one! Rules of grammar profit nothing once the hour of death draws nigh.)

Punarapi rajanī punarapi divasaḥ punarapi pakṣaḥ punarapi māsaḥ |
Punarapyayanaṃ punarapi varṣe tadapi na muñcatyāśāmarṣam ||
Bhaja govindaṃ bhaja govindaṃ bhaja govindaṃ mūḍhamate |
Saṃprāpte sannihite kāle nahi nahi rakṣati ḍukṛñkaraṇe ||

(Day follows day, night follows night, new moon, full moon, ever returning: summer and winter see the planet ever inclining on its axis; year follows year unfailingly. But, though a changeless law of recurrence grips the world in relentless sway, still there is none who dare abandon expectation's empty promise. Worship Govinda, worship Govinda, worship Govinda, foolish one! Rules of grammar profit nothing once the hour of death draws nigh.)

Vayasi gate kaḥ kāmavikāraśśuṣke nīre kaḥ kāsāraḥ I
Kṣīṇe vitte kaḥ parivāro jñāte tattve kassaṃsāraḥ II
Bhaja govindaṃ bhaja govindaṃ bhaja govindaṃ mūḍhamate I
Saṃprāpte sannihite kāle nahi nahi rakṣati ḍukrñkaraṇe II

(Youth being fled, what good is passion? Water gone, what use is a lake? Where to be found our friends and kinsmen once the money's all exhausted? Where is the world, when truth is known? Worship Govinda, worship Govinda, worship Govinda, foolish one! Rules of grammar profit nothing once the hour of death draws nigh.)

Nārīstanabharanābhīdeśaṃ dṛṣṭvā māyāmohāveśam I
Etanmāṃsavasādivikāraṃ manasi vicintaya vāraṃ vāram II
Bhaja govindaṃ bhaja govindaṃ bhaja govindaṃ mūḍhamate I
Saṃprāpte sannihite kāle nahi nahi rakṣati ḍukrñkaraṇe II

(Lust at the sight of a woman's body springs from ignorance, springs from error; inwardly reason, over and over, bodies are flesh and blood and fat. Worship Govinda, worship Govinda, worship Govinda, foolish one! Rules of grammar profit nothing once the hour of death draws nigh.)

Kastvaṃ ko'haṃ kuta āyātaḥ kā me jananī ko me mātaḥ I
Iti paribhāvaya sarvamasāraṃ viśvaṃ tyaktvā svapravicāram II
Bhaja govindaṃ bhaja govindaṃ bhaja govindaṃ mūḍhamate I
Saṃprāpte sannihite kāle nahi nahi rakṣati ḍukṛñkaraṇe II

(Who am I? And who are you? What is the place from which I come? Who is my mother? Who my sire? Pondering thus, perceive them all as fancies only, without substance; give up the world as an idle dream. Worship Govinda, worship Govinda, Worship Govinda, foolish one! Rules of grammar profit nothing once the hour of death draws nigh.)

Geyaṃ gītānāmsahasraṃ dhyeyaṃ śrīpatirūpamajasram |
Neyaṃ saccanasaṅge cittaṃ deyaṃ dīnajanāya ca vittam ||
Bhaja govindaṃ bhaja govindaṃ bhaja govindaṃ mūḍhamate |
Saṃprāpte sannihite kāle nahi nahi rakṣati ḍukṛñkaraṇe ||

(Every day recite from the *Gita*; chant the thousand names of Vishnu, cherishing Him within your heart. Take delight to be with the holy; give your riches away to the poor. Worship Govinda, worship Govinda, worship Govinda, foolish one! Rules of grammar profit nothing once the hour of death draws nigh.)

Yāvajjīvo nivasati dehe tāvatpṛcchati kuśalam gehe |
Gatavati vāyau dehāpāye bhāryā bibhyati tasminkāye ||
Bhaja govindaṃ bhaja govindaṃ bhaja govindaṃ mūdhamate |
Saṃprāpte sannihite kāle nahi nahi rakṣati ḍukṛñkaraṇe ||

(While man's soul remains in his body, fondly his family wish him well; but when the life breath leaves its dwelling, even his wife will flee in fear. Worship Govinda, worship Govinda, worship Govinda, foolish one! Rules of grammar profit nothing once the hour of death draws nigh.)

Sukhataḥ kṛiyate rāmābhogaḥ pascādhanta śarīre rogaḥ |
Yadyapi loke maraṇaṃ śaraṇaṃ tadapi na muñcati pāpācaraṇam ||
Bhaja govindaṃ bhaja govindaṃ bhaja govindaṃ mūḍhamate |
Saṃprāpte sannihite kāle nahi nahi rakṣati ḍukṛñkaraṇe ||

(He who yields to lust for pleasure leaves his frame a prey to disease; yet, though death is the final ending, none forswears his sinfulness. Worship Govinda, worship Govinda, worship Govinda, foolish one! Rules of grammar profit nothing once the hour of death draws nigh.)

Rathyākarpaṭaviracitakanthaḥ puṇyāpuṇyavivarjitapanthaḥ |
Nāhaṃ na tvaṃ nāyaṃ lokastadapi kimarthaṃ kṛiyate śokaḥ ||

Bhaja govindaṃ bhaja govindaṃ bhaja govindaṃ mūḍhamate |
Saṃprāpte sannihite kāle nahi nahi rakṣati ḍukṛñkaraṇe ||

(Rags cast off along the highway serve as a garment for the monk; freed from vice and freed from virtue, onward he wanders; in his sight nor I nor you nor the world exists. Why, when so give way to sorrow? Worship Govinda, worship Govinda, worship Govinda, foolish one! Rules of grammar profit nothing once the hour of death draws nigh.)

Kurute gaṅgāsāgaragamanaṃ vrataparipālanamathavā dānam |
Jñānavihīne sarvamanena muktirna bhavati janmaśatena ||
Bhaja govindaṃ bhaja govindaṃ bhaja govindaṃ mūḍhamate |
Saṃprāpte sannihite kāle nahi nahi rakṣati ḍukṛñkaraṇe ||

(Though, for the sake of his salvation, man may go on a pilgrimage to Ganga-sagara, keep his vows, and give to the poor, failing the knowledge of the highest, nothing of this assures him freedom even in the span of a hundred lives. Worship Govinda, worship Govinda, worship Govinda, foolish one! Rules of grammar profit nothing once the hour of death draws nigh.)

Dwadashapanjarika Stotra

This beautiful and short composition consisting of twelve stanzas, which translates to 'a cudgel for delusion', is meant to jolt the spiritual aspirant into realising that the world around him that he takes as real, is actually, because of its fragility and transience, but a delusion, and as unstable as 'raindrops on a lotus leaf'. To nurture attachment to such a world, and to allow the emotions of ego, anger, pride that are a natural consequence to such attachment, to govern our lives, is the delusion that must be conquered. A clear understanding of who we actually are, accompanied by surrender and devotion, are the tools to overcome this delusion.

In its tone and content, this stotra is similar to the Bhaja Govindam, and enjoys great popularity for both its intense brevity and the emotions of vairagya or non-attachment, and bhakti, it evokes.

Mūḍha jahīhi dhanāgamatṛṣṇāṃ kuru sadbuddhiṃ mansi vitṛṣṇām |
Yallabhase nijakarmopāttaṃ vittaṃ tena vinodaya cittam ||

(Renounce, o fool, your ceaseless thirst for hoarding gold and precious gems; content yourself with what may come through deeds performed in earlier lives; devote your mind to righteousness and let dispassion be your law.)

Arthamanarhaṃ bhāvaya nityaṃ nāsti tatassukhaleśassatyam |
Puttrādapi dhanabhājām bhītissarvatraisā vihitā rītiḥ ||

(Remember, riches bring but grief; truly, no joy abides in them. A rich man even fears his son: this is his portion everywhere.)

Kā te kānta kaste putrassaṃsāro'yamatīva vicitraḥ |
Kasya tvaṃ kaḥ kuta āyātaḥ tattvaṃ cintaya tadiha bhrātaḥ ||

(Who is your wife? And who your child? Strange indeed is this mortal world! Who are you? And who is your own? Where is the region whence you come? Brother, ponder on these things.)

Mā kuru dhanajanayauvanagarvaṃ harati nimeṣātkālassarvam |
Māyāmayamidamakhilaṃ hitvā brahmapadaṃ tvaṃ praviśa viditvā ||

(Boast not of youth, or friends, or wealth: swifter than eyes can wink, by time each one of these is stolen away. Abjure the illusion of the words and join yourself to timeless truth.)

Kāmaṃ krodhaṃ lobhaṃ mohaṃ tyaktātmānaṃ bhāvaya ko'haṃ |
Ātmajñānavihīnā mūḍhāste pacyante narakaniguḍhāḥ ||

(Give up the curse of lust and wrath; give up delusion, give up greed; remember who you really are. Fools are they that are blind to self: cast into hell, they suffer there.)

Suramandiratarumūlanivāsaśśayyā bhūtalamajinaṃ vāsaḥ |
Sarvaparigrahabhogatyāgaḥ kasya sukhaṃ na karoti virāgaḥ ||

(Make of a temple or tree your home, clothe yourself in the skin of a deer, and use the bare earth for your bed. Avoiding gifts and sense delights, could any fail to be content, blest with dispassion such as this?)

Śatrau mitre putre bandhau mā kuru yatnaṃ vigrahasandhau |
Bhava samacittassarvatra tvaṃ vāñchasyacirādyadi viṣṇutvam ||

(Be not attached to friend or foe, to son or kinsman, peace or war; if you aspire to Vishnu's realm, look upon all things equally.)

Tvayi mayi cānyatraiko viṣṇuḥ vyarthaṃ kupyasi mayyasahiṣṇuḥ |
Sarvasminnapi paśyātmānaṃ sarvatrotsṛja bhedjñānam ||

(Vishnu alone it is who dwells in you, in me, in everything; empty of meaning is your wrath, and the impatience you reveal. Seeing yourself in everyone, have done with all diversity.)

Prāṇāyāmaṃ pratyāhāraṃ nityānityavivekavicāram |
Jāpyasamānasamādhividhānaṃ kurvavadhānaṃ mahadavadhānam ||

(Control the self, restrain the breath, sift out the transient from the true, repeat the holy name of God, and still the restless mind within. To this, the universal rule, apply yourself with heart and soul.)

Nalinīdalagatajalamatitaralaṃ tadvajjīvitamatiśayacapalam |
Viddhi vyādhyabhimānagrastaṃ lokaṃ śokahataṃ ca samastam ||

(Uncertain is the life of man as raindrops on a lotus leaf; the whole of humankind is prey to grief and ego and disease: remember this unfailingly.)

Kā te'ṣṭādaśadeśe cintā vātula kiṃ tava nāsti niyantā |
Yastvāṃ haste sudṛḍhanibaddhaṃ bodhayati prabhavādiviruddham ||

(Why do all things distress your mind? Has reason quite abandoned you? Have you no guide to hold you firm, instructing you of life and death?)

Gurucaraṇāmbujanirbharabhaktaḥ saṃsārādacirādbhava muktaḥ |
Indriyamānasaniyamādevaṃ drakṣyasi nijahṛdayasthaṃ devam ||

(Cherish your guru's lotus feet and free yourself without delay from the enslavement of this world; curb your senses and your mind and see the Lord within your heart.)

Dwādaśapañjarikāmaya eṣaḥ śiṣyāṇāṃ kathito hyupadeśaḥ |
Yeṣāṃ citte naiva vivekaste pacyante narakamanekam ||

(These dozen stanzas I have penned to spur my pupils on their way: unless a man pursues the real, his pangs surpass the pangs of hell.)

Kaupina Panchakam

This work must be the shortest compositions of Shankara. It is a sanyasin's passionate appreciation of the life of renunciation, where his only possession is the loin-cloth (kaupina), and free from all worldly desires, he is set free to lead the life of a wandering mendicant. Each stanza movingly essays the sheer sense of freedom that comes to the person who has transcended the attachments that are the inevitable accessories of a normal life, and even though it consists only of five stanzas, by the time one finishes reading it, there is a genuine sense of empathy for the life of a sanyasin that Shankara chose for himself.

It is important to remember that Shankara did not mandatorily advocate a life of a sanyasin. He believed that the jnana marga, the path of knowledge, was open to all, including the householder. It was also his belief that the experience of Brahman, brahmanubhava, could come to any one at any time, whether he or she is a sanyasin or not. The sanyasin's life was Shankara's personal choice, and his unalloyed contentment in that life, comes through movingly in this stotra.

Vedāntvākeṣu sadā ramanto
Bhikṣānnamātreṇa ca tuṣṭimantaḥ |
Viśokamantaḥkaraṇe carantaḥ
Kaupīnavantaḥ khalu bhāgyavantaḥ ||

(Roaming ever in the grove of Vedanta,
Ever pleased with his beggar's morsel,
Wandering onward, his heart free from sorrow,
Blest indeed is the wearer of the loin-cloth.)

Mūlaṃ taroḥ kevalamāśrayantaḥ
Pāṇidwayaṃ bhoktumamantrayantaḥ |
Kanthāmiva śrīmapi kutsayantaḥ
Kaupīnavantaḥ khalu bhāgyavantaḥ ||

(Sitting at the foot of a tree for shelter,
Eating from his hands his meagre portion,

Spurning wealth like a patched up garment,
Blest indeed is the wearer of the loin-cloth.)

Svānandabhāve parituṣṭimantaḥ
Suśāntasarvendriyavṛttimantaḥ |
Aharniśam brahmasukhe ramantaḥ
kaupīnavantaḥ khalu bhāgyavantaḥ ||

(Satisfied fully by the bliss within him,
Curbing wholly the cravings of his senses,
Delighting day and night in the bliss of Brahman,
Blest indeed is the wearer of the loin-cloth.)

Dehādibhāvaṃ parivartayantaḥ
Svātmānamātmanyavalokayantaḥ |
Nāntaṃ na madhyaṃ na bahiḥ smarantaḥ
kaupīnavantaḥ khalu bhāgyavantaḥ ||

(Witnessing the changes of mind and body,
Naught but the self within him beholding,
Heedless of outer, of inner, of middle,
Blest indeed is the wearer of the loin-cloth.)

Brahmākṣaraṃ pāvanamuccaranto
Brahmāhamasmīti vibhāvayantaḥ |
Bhikṣāśino dikṣu paribhramantaḥ
kaupīnavantaḥ khalu bhāgyavantaḥ ||

(Chanting Brahman, the word of redemption,
Meditating only on 'I am Brahman',
Living on alms and wandering freely,
Blest indeed is the wearer of the loin-cloth.)

Guru Ashtakam

This is another short hymn written by Shankara—just eight stanzas—in tribute to the guru. The basic refrain of the composition is to stress that, even if a person has all that the world can offer, what is its intrinsic value compared to the bliss that comes in surrendering to an enlightened guru. The last two lines of each stanza reiterate this point: 'Yet if the mind be not absorbed in the Guru's lotus feet, what will it avail you, what, indeed, will it avail?' In the original Sanskrit, the last line, dramatically repeats the question to him who is bereft of a guru even though he may have everything he desires: 'Tatah kim, tatah kim, tatah kim, tatah kim,' which literally translates to 'what then, what then, what then, what then?'

Shankara believed strongly in the role of the right preceptor in an individual's search for spiritual solace. Typically, he did not consider this to be indispensable. There could be some who intuitively experience the bliss of Brahman; but, for most people, in their pursuit of the right knowledge to achieve that goal, and even in areas beyond the realm of knowledge, the paroksha and aparoksha, direct and indirect, guidance of a true guru has a very important role. Shankara himself began his spiritual journey by first identifying the guru he wanted to learn from; he travelled at a very young age from Kaladi in Kerala to Omkareshwar on the Narmada to learn at the feet of the guru who he had chosen—Govindapada. By all accounts, he lived the life of a disciple in Govindapada's hermitage for several years, before moving on to Varanasi. All his life he acknowledged his indebtedness to his guru.

Śarīraṃ surūpaṃ sadā rogamuktaṃ
Yaśascāru citraṃ dhanaṃ merutulyam |
Manaścenna lagnaṃ guroraṅghripadme
Tataḥ kiṃ tataḥ kiṃ tataḥ kiṃ tataḥ kim ||

(Though your body be comely and remain in perfect health,
Though your name be unsullied and mountain high your hoarded gold,
Yet if the mind be not absorbed in the guru's lotus feet,
What will it all avail you? What, indeed, will it all avail?)

Kalatraṃ dhanaṃ putrapautrādisarvaṃ
Gṛhaṃ bāndhavāḥ sarvametadhi jātam |
Manaścenna lagnaṃ gurorаṅghripadme
Tataḥ kiṃ tataḥ kiṃ tataḥ kiṃ tataḥ kim ||

(Even if fortune blesses you with riches and a virtuous wife,
With children and their children, with friendship and the joys of home,
Yet if the mind be not absorbed in the guru's lotus feet,
What will it all avail you? What, indeed, will it all avail?)

Ṣaḍaṅgādi vedo mukhe śastravidyā
Kavitvādi gadyaṃ supadyaṃ karoti |
Manaścenna lagnaṃ guroraṅghripadme
Tataḥ kiṃ tataḥ kiṃ tataḥ kiṃ tataḥ kim ||

(Though the lore of the Vedas takes up its dwelling on your tongue,
Though you be learned in scripture, gifted in writing prose and verses,
Yet if the mind be not absorbed in the guru's lotus feet,
What will it all avail you? What, indeed, will it all avail?)

Videśeṣu mānyaḥ svadeśeṣu dhanyaḥ
Sadācāravṛteṣu matto na cānyaḥ |
Manaścenna lagnaṃ guroraṅghripadme
Tataḥ kiṃ tataḥ kiṃ tataḥ kiṃ tataḥ kim ||

(Even if you are honoured at home and famed in foreign lands,
Given to pious deeds, and ever averse to wickedness,
Yet if the mind be not absorbed in the guru's lotus feet,
What will it all avail you? What, indeed, will it all avail?)

Kṣamā maṇḍale bhūpabhūpālvaṛndaiḥ
Sadāsevitaṃ yasya pādāravindam |
Manaścenna lagnaṃ guroraṅghripadme
Tataḥ kiṃ tataḥ kiṃ tataḥ kiṃ tataḥ kim ||

(Though you became, at last, the emperor of the universe,
Though you possess for servants the mightiest of the kings of earth,
Yet if the mind be not absorbed in the guru's lotus feet,
What will it all avail you? What, indeed, will it all avail?)

Yaśaścedgataṃ dikṣu dānapratāpāt
Jagaḍvastu sarvaṃ kare yatprasādāt |
Manaścenna lagnaṃ guroraṅghripadme
Tataḥ kiṃ tataḥ kiṃ tataḥ kiṃ tataḥ kim ||

(Even if every nation resound with your beneficence,
Yet if the mind be not absorbed in the lotus feet of him,
By grace of whom, alone, everything in this world is won.
What will it all avail you? What, indeed, will it all avail?)

Na bhogo na yogo na vā vājimedhe
Na kāntāsukhe naiva vitteṣu cittam |
Manaścenna lagnaṃ guroraṅghripadme
Tataḥ kiṃ tataḥ kiṃ tataḥ kiṃ tataḥ kim ||

(Though you pursue no pleasures, derive no joy from wealth or wife,
Reject the powers of yoga, and scorn the fruit of sacrifice,

Yet if the mind be not absorbed in the guru's lotus feet,
What will it all avail you? What, indeed, will it all avail?)

Araṇye na vā svasya gehe na kārye
Na dehe mano vartate me tvanarghye |
Manaścenna lagnaṃ guroraṅghripadme
Tataḥ kiṃ tataḥ kiṃ tataḥ kiṃ tataḥ kim ||

(Even if you be ready to dwell in the forest as at home,
No more attached to work, untrammeled by an ugly form,
Yet if the mind be not absorbed in the guru's lotus feet,
What will it all avail you? What, indeed, will it all avail?)

Gurorasṭakaṃ yaḥ paṭhetpuṇyadehī
Yatirbhūpatirbrahmacāri ca gehī |
Labhedvāñchitārthaṃ padaṃ brahmasaṇjñaṃ
Guroruktavākye mano yasya lagnam ||

(Of novices and monks, of rulers and of worldly men,
That noble soul who ponders these verses in the guru's praise,
And to the guru's teaching applies his mind with constant zeal,
He will attain to Brahman, the treasure coveted by all.)

Nirvana Shatakam

This composition of Shankara, consisting of six shlokas—hence the name shatakam—must rank among the most famous lines he has penned. In many ways, the Nirvana Shatakam, also known as the Atman Shatakam, is a remarkable summation in the most compressed manner possible, of the very essence of the non-duality of the Advaita doctrine.

The theme of the Shatakam is to deny the existence of everything—the mind, the ego, the senses, the elements, the body, the emotions, the entire gamut of human relations, all religious rituals, pilgrimages, mantras, the four conventional goals or purusharthas, dharma, artha, kama and moksha, the Vedas themselves, and even the guru—only to assert that the only thing that matters is bliss and awareness, the attributes of the one and only pervasive reality: Brahman. One who realises Brahman becomes, Shankara asserts, Shiva himself—and hence the refrain at the end of each shloka: I am Shiva! I am Shiva!

The impact of the Shatakam on the attentive listener can be dramatic. Suddenly, the world as is known peels away, layer by layer, belief by belief, leaving only the ultimate and irreducible residue, Brahman. There is, as each shloka plays out, a genuine sense of deep transcendence, and a feeling of the bliss and awareness that is the inevitable consequence of the spiritual overarching of our mortal accoutrements.

To assert the non-dual Advaita vision with such emphasis, and to so categorically deny the existence—in ontological terms—of everything else, must have required great clarity, courage and conviction. There is a tradition that believes that the first three stanzas of this work were narrated by the young Shankara when he reached his guru, Govindapada, at Omkareshwar. According to this belief, Govindapada asked Shankara, 'Who are you?' In reply, Shankara is supposed to have recited the first three stanzas, whereupon Govindapada accepted him as his disciple. To my mind, though, such a remarkable composition could only have been composed by Shankara later in life, as a lyrical consequence of years of study and spiritual insight.

Whatever the truth, the Nirvana Shatakam is a truly remarkable composition, and definitely ranks as my favourite among all his Prakarana texts.

Manobuddhyahankāracittāni nāhaṃ
na ca śrotrajihve na ca ghrāṇanetre |
Na ca vyoma bhumirna tejo Na vāyus
cidānandarūpaḥ śivo'haṃ śivo'ham ||

(I am neither the mind, intelligence, ego, nor chitta, neither the ears nor the tongue, nor the senses of smell and sight; neither ether nor air, nor fire nor water nor earth: I am eternal bliss and awareness—I am Shiva! I am Shiva!)

Na ca prāṇasaṃjño na vai pañcavāyur
na vā saptadhāturna vā pañcakośaḥ |
Na vākpaṇipādaṃ na copasthapāyū
Cidanāndarūpaḥ śivo'haṃ śivo'ham ||

(I am neither the prana, nor the five vital breaths, neither the seven elements of the body, nor its five sheaths, nor hands nor feet nor tongue, nor other organs of action: I am eternal bliss and awareness—I am Shiva! I am Shiva!)

Na me dwesarāgau na me lobhamohau
mado naiva me naiva mātsaryabhāvaḥ |
Na dharmo na cārtho na kāmo na mokṣas
cidānandarūpaḥ śivo'ham śivo'ham ||

(Neither greed nor delusion, loathing nor liking, have I; nothing of pride or ego, of dharma or liberation; neither desire of the mind nor object for its desiring: I am eternal bliss and awareness—I am Shiva! I am Shiva!)

Na puṇyaṃ na pāpam na saukhyaṃ na duḥkhaṃ
na mantro na tīrthaṃ na veda na yajñāḥ |
Ahaṃ bhojanaṃ naiva bhojyaṃ na bhoktā
cidānandarupaḥ śivo'haṃ śivo'ham ||

(Nothing of pleasure and pain, of virtue and vice, do I know, of mantra or sacred place, of Vedas or sacrifice; neither am I the eater, the food nor the act of eating: I am eternal bliss and awareness—I am Shiva! I am Shiva!)

Na mṛtyurna śankā na me jātibhedaḥ
pitā naiva me naiva mātā na janma |
Na bandhurna mitraṃ gururnaiva śiṣyaś-
cidānandarūpaḥ śivo'haṃ śivo'ham ||

(Death or fear I have none, nor any distinction of castes; neither father nor mother, nor even a birth, have I; neither friend nor comrade, neither disciple nor guru: I am eternal bliss and awareness—I am Shiva! I am Shiva!)

Ahaṃ nirvikalpo nirākārarūpo
vibhutvācca sarvatra sarvendriyāṇām |
Na cāsangataṃ naiva muktirna meyaś-
cidānandarūpaḥ śivo'ham śivo'ham ||

(I have no form or fancy: the all-pervading am I; everywhere I exist, and yet am beyond the sense; neither salvation am I, nor anything to be known: I am eternal bliss and awareness—I am Shiva! I am Shiva!)

Manishapanchakam

The Manishpanchakam is a set of five verses. The Sanskrit word manisha means firm conviction. Panchakam means five. Hence, Manishapanchakam—five verses, each indicating Shankara's firm conviction.

This Prakarana text is pivotal to assess Shankara's approach and attitude to social issues, and their interface with his Advaitic philosophy. (This is discussed in detail on page 21). In essence, what the Manishapanchakam establishes is that Shankara, in asserting that Brahman alone exists, and all else is subordinate or illusionary, devalued man-made social distinctions such as those of caste. For a person who has understood the reality of Brahman, human labels of 'lower' or 'upper' caste have no relevance.

This work, it is believed, was composed when Shankara was residing in Kashi. According to legend, one day Shankara, while on his way to the temple, came across a person of the lowest caste (chandala). Since 'lower castes' were supposed to socially 'defile' those of higher castes, the chandala was asked to move out of the way. But, the chandala instead asked Shankara how can there be any social discrimination when all human beings, and, indeed, the entire universe, is nothing but the reflection of Brahman, the one and only real. When confronted with this question, Shankara is believed to have recited the Manishapanchakam.

The significant point is that each verse ends by reiterating Shankara's 'firm conviction' that, for a person who has attained self-knowledge, there is no relevance of social hierarchies.

Sociologists will quibble whether the Manishapanchakam is enough to establish Shankara's disdain of the caste system and other upper caste orthodoxies, but this text is certainly emphatic in demonstrating his philosophical egalitarianism. In any case, it is noteworthy that, in a period of deeply entrenched social orthodoxies and discrimination, Shankara, in conformity with the logical inference of the Advaita doctrine, had the courage to publicly articulate his views to the contrary.

Jāgratsvapnasuṣuptiṣu sphuṭatarā yā saṃvidujjṛmbhate
Yā brahmādipipīlikāntatanuṣu protā jagatsākṣiṇī ।

Saivāhaṃ na ca dṛśyavastviti dṛḍhaprajñāpi yasyāsti ce-
Ccāṇḍālo'stu sa tu dvijo'stu gururityeṣā manīṣā mama ||

(That consciousness which shines clearly in the states of waking, dream, and deep sleep, that witness of the world which interpenetrates all beings from Brahma down to an ant—that, verily, I am, and not the seen object—he to whom there is such firm knowledge is the preceptor, be he chandala or Brahmin. This is my conclusive view.)

Brahmaivāhamidaṃ jagacca sakalaṃ cinmātravistāritaṃ
Sarvaṃ caitadavidyayā triguṇayā'śeṣaṃ mayā kalpitam |
Itthaṃ yasya dṛḍhā matiḥ sukhatare nitye pare nirmale
Cāṇḍālo'stu sa tu dvijo'stu gururityeṣā manīṣā mama ||

(I am Brahman alone. And, this entire world has been spread out by pure consciousness. All this, without residue, has been superimposed by me through nescience which consist of the three gunas {sattva, rajas, and tamas}. Thus, he in whom there is firm knowledge in respect of the eternal, blemishless supreme {Brahman} which is unexcellable bliss, is the preceptor, be he a chandala or a Brahmin. This is my conclusive view.)

Śaśvannaśvarameva viśvamakhilaṃ niścitya vācā guror-
Nityaṃ brahma nirantaraṃ vimṛśatā nirvyājaśāntātmanā |
Bhūtaṃ bhāti ca duṣkṛtaṃ pradahatā saṃvinmaye pāvake
Prārabdhāya samarpitaṃ svavapurityeṣā manīṣā mama ||

(The entire universe constantly perishes. Determining thus through the teaching of the preceptor, he who contemplates ceaselessly the eternal Brahman, has his mind rendered guileless and quiescent, gets the evil results of his past and future deeds burnt up in the fire of knowledge, and offers up his body to prarabdha {i.e,. karma that is responsible for the present embodiment}. This is my conclusive view.)

Yā tiryaṅnaradevatābhirahamityantaḥ sphuṭā gṛhyate
Yadbhāsā hṛdayākṣadehaviṣayā bhānti svato'cetanāḥ |
Tāṃ bhāsyaiḥ pihitārkamaṇḍalanibhāṃ sphūrtiṃ sadā bhāvaya
Nyogī nirvṛtamānaso hi gururityeṣā manīṣā mama ||

(That {pure consciousness} which is realised within clearly as 'I' by animals, men and gods; that by whose light the mind, the sense-organs, the body, and the objects, which are by themselves non-intelligent, shine; that which is {hidden} like the solar orb that is covered by what are illumined by it {viz., the clouds}—contemplating that effulgence always, the yogi becomes filled with the supreme happiness in this mind. That one is the preceptor. This is my conclusive view.)

Yatsaukhyāmbudhileśaleśata ime śakrādayo nirvṛtā
Yaccitte nitarāṃ praśāntakalane labdhvā munirnirvṛtaḥ |
Yasminnityasukhāmbudhau galitadhīrbrahmaiva na brahmavid
Yaḥ kaścitsa surendravanditapado nūnaṃ manīṣā mama ||

(That ocean of bliss, by taking a very small drop of which Indra and other gods become happy; that by gaining which in the mind that has become perfectly quiescent without modification, the ascetic experiences happiness; that ocean of eternal bliss, by dissolving the mind into which, one remains even as Brahman, and not merely as a knower of Brahman—he {who knows this}, whoever he may be, is the one whose feet are adored by {even} the king of the gods. Surely, this is my conclusive view.)

Dashashloki

This composition in ten verses—dasha shloka—is similar to the Nirvana Shatakam, and like it, a summation, in typically Shankara's way, of the unyielding non-dual vision of Advaita. Like in the Nirvana Shatakam, in the Dashashloki too, Shankara's attempt is to deny everything else only to unequivocally assert the sole reality of Brahman. Each verse lists the number of things that have no worth, and each verse ends, like in the Nirvana Shatakam, with the assertion, 'Shiva kevaloh ham' (Only Shiva am I). The new elements in this composition is Shankara's recognition that the state of deep sleep or sushupti, when the mind is at its most still, is akin to the real nature of the Atman or self within us. He also adds in this work the fourth state of consciousness, beyond even sushupti, that of turiya, where the individual, awake or asleep, is in this world, but has completely and joyfully transcended all its constraining coordinates. In one of the verses he negates too the other schools of thought, including specifically the sankhya, the Buddhist, the mimanshaka and the Jaina.

Given the similarity of thought and structure between the Nirvana Shatakam and Dashashloki, it is not surprising that some scholars believe that it was the latter that Shankara recited when asked by Govindapada: 'Who are you?' This debate need not, however, detain us, for it is certain that whatever Shankara's reply was to his guru's question, it was sufficiently impressive for him to be immediately accepted as a disciple.

Na bhūmirna toyaṃ na tejo na vāyuḥ
Na khaṃ nendriyaṃ vā na teṣāṃ samūhaḥ |
Anekāntikatvāt suṣuptyekasiddaḥ
Tadeko'vaśiṣṭaḥ śivaḥ kevalo'ham ||

(I am not the earth nor water, neither fire nor air, I am not space. Neither am I any of the faculties nor am I their aggregrate. {I am not any of these} as they are all uncertain. I am proved however in the sole experience of deep sleep. That one, the residue, the auspicious, the only one, am I.)

Na varṇā na varṇāśramācāradharmā
Na me dhāraṇādhyānayogādayopi |
Anātmāśrayāhaṃmamādhyāsahānāt
Tadeko'vaśiṣṭaḥ śivaḥ kevalo'ham ||

(The castes are not for me, nor the observances and duties attached to the castes and the stages of life. Even the steadying of the mind, concentration, self-communion and other courses are not for me. For the mistaken senses of I and mine which rested on the non-self have been abandoned. That one, the residue, the auspicious, that alone, am I.)

Na mātā pitā vā na devā na lokā
Na vedā na yajñā na tīrtha bruvanti |
Suṣuptau nirastātiśūnyātmakatvāt
Tadeko'vaśiṣṭaḥ śivaḥ kevalo'ham ||

(There is no mother nor father; no gods nor regions of experience; no scriptures nor sacrificial sites; and no sacred place—so say the sages. For, in the state of deep sleep, all these are negatived and that state is completely devoid {of any object of perception}. That one, the residue, the auspicious, that alone, am I.)

Na sākhyaṃ na śaivaṃ na tatpāñcarātraṃ
Na jainaṃ na mīmāṃsakādermataṃ vā |
Viśiṣṭānubhūtyā viśuddhātmakatvāt
Tadeko'vaśiṣṭaḥ śivaḥ kevalo'ham ||

(There is no sankhya nor Shaiva, nor that Pancharatra nor Jaina. The conception of the mimanshaka and others does not exist. For, through the direct realisation of what is qualified, the self is known as of the nature of the absolutely pure. That one, the residue, the auspicious, that alone, am I.)

Na cordhva na cādho na cāntarna bāhyaṃ
Na madhyaṃ na tiryaṃ na pūrvā'parā dik |
Viyadvyāpakatvādakhaṇḍaikarūpaḥ
Tadeko'vaśiṣṭaḥ śivaḥ kevalo'ham ||

(There is neither above nor below, neither inside nor outside, no middle nor crosswise, no direction, east or west. For it is all-pervasive like space. It is partless and homogeneous in its nature. That one, the residue, the auspicious, that alone, am I.)

Na śuklaṃ na kṛṣṇaṃ na raktaṃ na pītaṃ
Na kubjaṃ na pīnaṃ na hrasvaṃ na dīrgham |
Arūpaṃ tathā jyotirākārakatvāt
Tadeko'vaśiṣṭaḥ śivaḥ kevalo'ham ||

(It is neither white nor black, neither red nor yellow, neither dwarfish nor stout, neither short nor long. As it is of the nature of light, it is shapeless also. That one, the residue, the auspicious, that alone, am I.)

Na śāstā na śāstraṃ na śiṣyo na śikṣā
Na ca tvaṃ na cāhaṃ na cāyaṃ prapañcaḥ |
Svarūpāvabodho vikalpāsahiṣṇuḥ
Tadeko'vaśiṣṭaḥ śivaḥ kevalo'ham ||

(There is no ruler nor rule, no pupil nor training.There is no you nor I. This universe is not, for the realisation of the true nature of the self does not tolerate any distincion. That one, the residue, the auspicious, that alone, am I.)

Na jāgran na me svapnako vā suṣuptiḥ
Na viśvau na vā taijasaḥ prājñako vā |

Avidyātmakatvāt trayāṇaṃ turīyaḥ
Tadeko'vaśiṣṭaḥ śivaḥ kevalo'ham ||

(There is no waking state for me nor dream or deep sleep. I am not visva{the self identified with the experiencer of the waking state}, nor taijasa {identified with dream state}, nor prajna {identified with deep sleep}. I am really the fourth {turiya}. That one, the residue, the auspicious, that alone, am I.)

Api vyāpakatvāt hitatvaprayogāt
Svataḥ siddhabhāvādananyāśrayatvāt |
Jagat tucchametat samastaṃ tadanyat
Tadeko'vaśiṣṭaḥ śivaḥ kevalo'ham ||

(All this universe which is other than the self is worthless {having no existence of its own} for it is well known that the self is all-pervasive, recognised as the reality and that its existence is self-proven and does not depend upon anything else. That one, the residue, the auspicious, that alone, am I.)

Na caikaṃ tadanyad dvitīyaṃ kutaḥ syāt
Na kevalatvaṃ na cā'kevalatvam |
na śunyaṃ na cāśūnyamadvaitakatvāt
Kathaṃ sarvavedāntasiddhaṃ bravīmi ||

(It is not one, for how can there be a second distinct from it? Aloneness cannot be attributed to it nor even not-aloneness. It is neither a void nor a non-void. When it does not admit of a second entity, in what manner can I speak about it though it is established by all the Upanishads?)

Saundarya Lahari

This somewhat controversial text is Shankara's tribute to Devi or Shakti, the Mother Goddess, depicted here as Parvati, the consort of Shiva. These compositions reveal Shankara's profound and abiding preoccupation with tantric forms of worship. The reasons for this association are discussed in detail in pages, 82, 135, 136 & 138. Suffice to add here that Shankara did not find any contradiction between his philosophical commitment to Brahman at the paramarthik or ontological level, and to his worship of Shiva as the embodiment of the spirit of Brahman at the vyavaharik or practical level, with the Devi as the latent energy within Brahman.

Saundarya Lahari literally translates to 'the wave of beauty' and is specifically tantric in content. In fact, some scholars regard it as a tantric textbook, co-relating each of its hundred verses to different pujas and worship of the Sri Chakra. For instance, stanza eleven of the Saundarya Lahari explicitly pays homage to the Sri Chakra. For the tantric sadhaka, each verse has a double entendre indicating a mantra to depict a diagrammatic section of the yantra, that is the Sri Chakra as a whole. The systematic repetition of the mantra, accompanied by meditation on the yantra, leads to a mood of devotion and mental concentration, that are as good as any other practical means sanctioned by Shankara to achieve the metaphysical goal of brahmanubhava, or the experience of Brahman.

We have discussed earlier Shankara's exposure to Kashmiri Shaivism, which is unmistakably tantric in its approach. In this conceptualisation, Brahman is Shiva, the omnipresent, formless energy, and Shakti is the power latent in Him. Shiva is chitta, the pure attribute-less consciousness within all of us, and Shakti is chidrupini, the power inherent in that consciousness, from which all creation is made possible. Shankara's acceptance of the Shakti cult is not in doubt. In all the four mathas set up by him—and in the 'disputed' fifth at Kanchi—there are prominent temples to the Devi, and in each of them there is a special place given to the Sri Chakra.

The language of Saundarya Lahari, especially in the depiction of the physical attributes of the Devi, is quite overtly sensual. This has led some scholars to cast a doubt whether Shankara, the celibate sanyasin, could have written such a text. However, the dominant opinion is that Shankara is, indeed, the author of this text. In fact, so well established was Shankara's association with the shakti cult—and by extension to tantra—that many authorities recognise him as Sri Chakra Pratishtapana Acharya, the master who established the Sri Chakra.

Śivaḥ śaktyā yukto yadi bhavati śaktaḥ prabhavituṃ
Na cedevaṃ devo na khalu kuśalaḥ spanditumapi |
Atastvāmārādhyāṃ hariharaviriñcādibhirapi
Praṇantuṃ stotuṃ vā kathamakṛtapuṇyaḥ prabhavati ||

(If the auspicious one is united with his power, he is able to create. If he is not thus, he is not capable of stirring even. Hence how can one without virtue, prostrate or praise you, who is venerated by the three deities of creation, protection, and destruction?)

Kvaṇatkāñcīdāmā karikalabhakumbhastananatā
Parikṣīṇā madhye pariṇataśaraccandravadanā |
Dhanurbāṇān pāśaṃ sṛṇimapi dadhānā karatalaiḥ
Purastādāstāṃ naḥ puramathiturāhopuruṣikā ||

(Let the gracious one, the pride of the Destroyer of Tripura appear before us, her face shining like the full autumnal moon, her body slightly bent by the weight of her pitcher-like breasts resembling the temples of the elephant, her hands holding the bow, the arrows, the rope and the goad.)

Mahīṃ mūlādhāre kamapi maṇipūre hutavahaṃ
Sthitaṃ svādhiṣṭhāne hṛdi marutamākāśamupari |
Mano'pi bhrūmadhye sakalamapi bhitvā kulapathaṃ
Sahasrāre padme saha rahasi patyā viharase ||

(In the thousand-petalled lotus, *sahasrara*, you sport with your lord in secret, having traversed the entire path of kundalini, viz., the element of earth in Muladhara, water in Manipura, fire in Svadhisthana, air in Anahata, ether above it in Vishuddhi and the mind in Ajna between the eyebrows.)

Sudhādhārāsāraiścaraṇayugalāntarvigalitaiḥ
Prapañcaṃ siñcantī punarapi rasāmnāyamahasaḥ |
Avāpya svāṃ bhūmiṃ bhujaganibhamadhyuṣṭavalayaṃ
Svamātmānaṃ kṛtvā svapiṣi kulakuṇḍe kuhariṇi ||

(Oh! Glorious one, I drenching all the veins with the nectar dripping from your feet, from the dizzy heights you descend to your abode and turning yourself into a serpentine coil sleep in the fine hole of the lotus-root—like Muladhara.)

Caturbhiḥ śrīkaṇṭhaiḥ śivayuvatibhiḥ pañcabhirapi
Prabhinnābhiḥ śambhornavabhirapi mūlaprakṛtibhiḥ |
Catuścatvāriṃśadvasudalakalāśratrivalaya-
Trirekhābhiḥ sārdhaṃ tava śaraṇakoṇāḥ pariṇatāḥ ||

(Oh! Supreme power, your angles of abode become forty-four in number with four wheels of auspiciousness, five different wheels of power, nine basic roots of nature, and three encircling lines encasing eight and sixteen petals.)

Naraṃ varṣīyāṃsaṃ nayanavirasaṃ narmasu jaḍaṃ
Tavāpāṅgāloke patitamanudhāvanti śataśaḥ |
Galadveṇībandhāḥ kucakalaśavisrastasicayā
Haṭhāt truṭyatkāñcyo vigalitadukūlā yuvatayaḥ ||

(Oh! Supreme power, hundreds of youthful women their hair-knots loosened, upper garments falling from their pot-like breasts, their girdles broken, their silken saris slipping, pursue a decrepit ugly, old man indifferent to the art of love, on whom your kind glance has fallen.)

Mukhaṃ binduṃ kṛtvā kucayugamadhastasya tadadho
Harārdhaṃ dhyāyedyo haramahiṣi te manmathakalām |
Sa sadyaḥ saṃkṣobhaṃ nayati vanitā ityatilaghu
Trilokīmapyāśu bhramayati ravīndustanayugām ||

(Oh! Queen of the Destroyer, that he who can meditate on your Kamakala treating your face as a point, below that the pair of your breasts, and further below the womb can forthwith captivate women is an easy trifle, for such a one can quickly conquer the three worlds, whose breasts are as it were the sun and the moon.)

Tvayā hṛtvā vāmaṃ vapuraparitṛptena manasā
Śarīrārdhaṃ śambhoraparamapi śaṅke hṛtamabhūt |
Yadetattvadrūpaṃ sakalamaruṇābhaṃ trinayanaṃ
Kucābhyāmānamraṃ kuṭilaśaśicūḍālamakuṭam ||

(Your form, bent by the weight of breasts is all-crimson, three-eyed and crescent-crested; this, I feel, is due to your taking over the other half, being dissatisfied with the left half of the body of the creator of bliss, already stolen by you.)

Japo jalpaḥ śilpaṃ sakalamapi mudrāviracanā
Gatiḥ prādakṣiṇyakramaṇamaśanādyāhutividhiḥ |
Praṇāmassaṃveśassukhamakhilamātmārpaṇadṛśā
Saparyāparyāyastava bhavatu yanme vilasitam ||

(Through the sight of self-surrender, let my prattle become recitation of your name, the movement of my limbs gestures of worship, my walk perambulation around you, my food sacrificial offering to you, my lying down prostration to you; whatever I do for my pleasure, let it become transformed into an act of worship to you.)

Catuṣṣaṣṭyā tantraiḥ sakalamatisandhāya bhuvanaṃ
Sthitastattatsiddhiprasavaparatantraiḥ paśupatiḥ |
Punastvannirbandhādakhilapuruṣārthaikaghaṭanā
Svatantraṃ te tantraṃ kṣititalamavātītaradidam ||

(The Lord of creatures, having created the entire universe with the sixty-four tantras, the chief sources of occult powers remained satisfied. But on your insistence, he introduced into the earth this tantra of yours, which bestows all the four aspirations of men: dharma, artha, kama, and moksha.)

Tava svādhiṣṭhāne hutavahamadhiṣṭhāya nirataṃ
Tamīḍe saṃvartaṃ janani mahatīṃ tāṃ ca samayām |
Yadāloke lokān dahati mahati krodhakalite
Dayārdrā yā dṛṣṭiḥ śiśiramupacāraṃ racayati ||

(Oh! Mother, I bow to the Destroyer who ever remains in your Svadhisthana Chakra adopting the form of fire as also to the great power, whose glance, tender-wet with kindness, protects by cool healing when the angry look of the Destroyer burns the worlds in the great dissolution.)

Taṭittvantaṃ śaktyā timiraparipanthiphuraṇayā
Sphurannānāratnābharaṇapariṇaddhendradhanuṣam |
Tava śyāmaṃ meghaṃ kamapi maṇipūraikaśaraṇaṃ
Niṣeve varṣantaṃ haramihirataptaṃ tribhuvanam ||

(I worship the blue, cloud-hued one who has sought refuge in your Manipura Chakra and adorned by lightning through the effulgence of the darkness-destroying power, shines with the bow of the Indra, studded with various lustrous gems and rains mercy on the three worlds burnt by the Destroyer in the great dissolution.)

Tavādhāre mūle saha samayayā lāsyaparayā
Navātmānaṃ manye navarasamahātāṇḍavanaṭam |
Ubhābhyāmetābhyāmudayavidhimuddiśya dayayā
Sanāthābhyāṃ jajñe janakajananīmajjagadidam ||

(I meditate on the nine-faceted one, dancing the great cosmic dance with the nine moods along with the dance-loving power in your Muladhara. This universe becomes reborn mercifully and possessed of a father and mother thanks to these two inseparable ones.)

Dhunotu dhvāntaṃ nastulitadalitendīvaravanaṃ
Ghanasnigdhaślakṣṇaṃ cikuranikurumbaṃ tava śive |
Yadīyaṃ saurabhyaṃ sahajamupalabdhuṃ sumanaso
Vasantyasmin manye valamathanavāṭīviṭapinām ||

(Oh! Auspicious one, let the cluster of your hair soft and dense as the group of full-blown blue lotuses dispel our mental darkness; the flowers of trees in Indra's garden have come to reside therein with a view to attaining its inherent fragrance, I think.)

Tanotu kṣemaṃ nastava vadanasaundaryalaharī-
Parīvāhasrotaḥsaraṇiriva sīmantasaraṇiḥ |
Vahantī sindūraṃ prabalakabarībhāratimira-
Dviṣāṃ vṛndairbandīkṛtamiva navīnārkakiraṇam ||

(Let the partition of your hair, bearing the sindura, which resembles the ray of the rising sun imprisoned by the cluster of dense, dark, inimical hair, enhance our welfare; it looks as if it is the outlet for the flow of the wave of your facial beauty.)

Arālaiḥ svābhāvyādalikalabhasaśrībhiralakaiḥ
Parītaṃ te vaktraṃ parihasati paṅkeruharucim |
Darasmere yasmin daśanarucikiñjalkarucire
Sugandhau mādyanti smaradahanacakṣurmadhulihaḥ ||

(Your face puts to shame the radiance of the lotus, with its gentle smile, rows of beautiful teeth and fragrance; in it the bee-like eyes of the Destroyer of cupid drink the honey of bliss; small curls of hair spread themselves on it like little bees.)

Vibhaktatraivarṇyaṃ vyatikaritalīlāñjanatayā
Vibhāti tvannetratritayamidamīśānadayite |
Punaḥ sraṣṭuṃ devān druhiṇaharirudrānuparatān
Rajaḥ sattvaṃ bibhrattama iti guṇānāṃ trayamiva ||

(Oh! Beloved of the Lord, these three eyes of yours become tricoloured—red, white, and black—due to your wearing collyrium for adornment. They look like the triad of the three qualities—rajas, sattva, and tamas—intended to create the deities of creation, protection, and destruction dissolved in you at the time of the great dissolution.)

Arālaṃ te pālīyugalamagarājanyatanaye
Na keṣāmādhatte kusumaśarakodaṇḍakutukam |
Tiraścīno yatra śravaṇapathamullaṅghya vilasa-
nnapāṅgavyāsaṅgo diśati śarasaṃdhānadhiṣaṇām ||

(Oh! Daughter of the King of Mountains, the curved space between your eyes and ears creates in everyone the illusion of the bow of cupid, the one with flowers as arrows; as a result, the backward glance from the corner of your eyes, crossing the path of the ears resembles the shot of an arrow.)

Asau nāsāvaṃśastuhinagirivaṃśadhvajapaṭi
Tvadīyo nedīyaḥ phalatu phalamasmākamucitam |

Vahatyantarmuktāḥ śiśirakaraniśvāsagalitaṃ
Samṛddhyā yattāsāṃ bahirapi ca muktāmaṇidharaḥ ||

(Oh! Flag of the lineage of the snowy mountain, let this nose of yours, which resembles the bamboo-stalk, bestow on us early, deserving results. It—like the bamboo-stalk bears pearls inside and due to their abundance, also wears them outside; these being brought out by the breath passing through the left nostril.)

Prakṛtyā raktāyāstava sudati dantacchadaruceḥ
Pravakṣye sādṛśyaṃ janayatu phalaṃ vidrumalatā |
Na bimbaṃ tadbimbapratiphalanarāgādaruṇitaṃ
Tulāmadhyāroḍhuṃ kathamiva vilajjeta kalayā ||

(Oh! Goddess with beautiful teeth, I shall mention an object comparable to your naturally red lips: let the coral-creeper produce a fruit. The *bimba* fruit has derived its crimson colour by the reflection of your lips; hence won't it be ashamed to stand comparison even with a small part thereof?)

Aviśrāntaṃ patyurguṇagaṇakathāmreḍanajapā
Japāpuṣpacchāyā tava janani jihvā jayati sā |
Yadagrāsīnāyāḥ sphaṭikadṛṣadacchacchavimayī
Sarasvatyā mūrtiḥ pariṇamati māṇikyavapuṣā ||

(Oh! Mother, your tongue, red like the hibiscus flower ever recites the auspicious qualities of your husband. Residing on its tip, the crystal white form of the Goddess of Learning seems to turn into crimson like the ruby.)

Karāgreṇa spṛṣṭaṃ tuhinagiriṇā vatsalatayā
Girīśenodastaṃ muhuradharapānākulatayā |
Karagrāhyaṃ śambhormukhamukuravṛntaṃ girisute
Kathaṅkāraṃ brūmastava cibukamaupamyarahitam ||

(Oh! Daughter of the mountain, how can we describe your incomparable chin, which resembles the handle of a mirror, touched in affection with the finger-tip by your father, the snowy mountain and lifted again and again by your Lord, desirous of drinking your lips.)

Bhujāśleṣān nityaṃ puradamayituḥ kaṇṭakavatī
Tava grīvā dhatte mukhakamalanālaśriyamiyam ।
Svataḥ śvetā kālāgurubahulajambālamalinā
Mṛṇālīlālityam vahati yadadho hāralatikā ॥

(This neck of yours, its hairs standing on end, due to the daily embraces by the arms of the Destroyer of Tripura looks like the stem of the lotus which is your face. The necklace of pearls down below, though inherently white, looks dark due to sandal paste containing other perfume ingredients and resembles the stalk of the lotus leaf.)

Nakhānāmuddyotairnavanalinarāgaṃ vihasatāṃ
Karāṇāṃ te kāntiṃ kathaya kathayāmaḥ kathamume ।
Kayācidvā sāmyaṃ bhajatu kalayā hanta kamalaṃ
Yadi krīḍallakṣmīcaraṇatalalākṣārasachaṇam ॥

(Oh! Uma, kindly tell us, how do we describe the attractive beauty of your hands which put to shame, with the radiance of the nails, the grace of the newly-open red lotus at dawn. It is a pity that even by the association with the red colouring on the feet of the goddess of prosperity which play on it, the red lotus cannot equal even one-sixteenth of the beauty of your hands.)

Samaṃ devi skandadvipavadanapītaṃ stanayugaṃ
Tavedaṃ naḥ khedaṃ haratu satataṃ prasnutamukham ।
Yadālokyāśaṅkākulitahṛdayo hāsajanakaḥ
Svakumbhau herambaḥ parimṛśati hastena jhaḍiti ॥

(Oh! Goddess, let this pair of your breasts, their nipples exuding milk at the sight of your children and simultaneously drunk by Kumara and Ganesha dispel our sorrow. Seeing them, the elephant-faced one anxiously and hastily feels his temples with his hand, evoking laughter in you and the Lord.)

Harakrodhajvālāvalibhiravalīḍhena vapuṣā
Gabhīre te nābhīsarasi kṛtasaṅgo manasijaḥ |
Samuttasthau tasmādacalatanaye dhūmalatikā
Janastāṃ jānīte tava janani romāvaliriti ||

(Oh! Mother, Oh! Daughter of the mountain, when his body was enveloped by the flames of the Destroyer's anger, cupid plunged into the deep pond which is your navel; the world considers the resultant line of smoke which arose to be the hair-line rising from your navel.)

Yadetat kālindītanutaratarangākṛti śive
Kṛśe madhye kiṃcijjanani tava yadbhāti sudhiyām |
Vimardādanyo'nyaṃ kucakalaśayorantaragataṃ
Tanūbhūtaṃ vyoma praviśadiva nābhiṃ kuhariṇīm ||

(Oh! Auspicious one, Oh! Mother, this thin line of hair above your slender waist, looking like the minute wave of the dark Yamuna river in the eyes of the wise, also gives the impression that the minute space between your pot-like breasts seems to enter the deep navel escaping from the mutual pressure exerted by them.)

Sthiro gaṅgāvartaḥ stanamukularomāvalilatā-
Kalāvālaṃ kuṇḍaṃ kusumaśaratejohutabhujaḥ |
Raterlīlāgāraṃ kimapi tava nābhirgirisute
Biladvāraṃ siddhergiriśanayanānāṃ vijayate ||

(Oh! Daughter of the mountain, your navel flourishes as the still current of river Ganga, as the bed for the hair creeper supporting the lotus-buds of your breasts, as the fire pit for the flame of cupid's magnetism, as the sport resort of Rati, cupid's wife, and as the entrance to the cave where the penance of the eyes of your Lord attains its goal.)

Nisargakṣīṇasya stanataṭabhareṇa klamajuṣo
Namanmūrternārītilakaśanakaistruṭyata iva |
Ciraṃ te madhyasya truṭitataṭinītīrataruṇā
Samāvasthāsthemno bhavatu kuśalaṃ śailatanaye ||

(Oh! Ideal of womanhood, Oh! Daughter of the mountain, let your waist, inherently slender and strained by the weight of the breasts, gradually bending as if to break, thus in a state similar to that of a tree on a river bank washed away by the floods, be ever safe!)

Gurutvaṃ vistāraṃ kṣitidharapatiḥ pārvati nijā-
Nnitambādācchidya tvayi haraṇarūpeṇa nidadhe |
Ataste vistīrṇo gururayamaśeṣāṃ vasumatīṃ
Nitambaprāgbhāraḥ sthagayati laghutvaṃ nayati ca ||

(Oh! Daughter of the mountain, the King of Mountains took heaviness and expanse from his flanks and gave them as dowry to you. Hence this hip of yours is heavy and expansive; it hides the earth and makes it light.)

Parājetuṃ rudraṃ dviguṇaśaragarbhau girisute
Niṣaṅgau jaṅghe te viṣamaviśikho bāḍhamakṛta |
Yadagre dṛśyante daśaśaraphalāḥ pādayugalī-
Nakhāgracchadmānaḥ suramakuṭaśāṇaikaniśitāḥ ||

(Oh! Daughter of the mountain, it is certain that cupid, who possesses mischievous arrows made two quivers out of your two lower legs to hold twice the number of arrows in order to defeat the Lord, the Destroyer, for at their ends are seen ten edges of arrows, sharpened mainly on the crowns of angels which appear to be the nails of your toes.)

Mṛṣā kṛtvā gotraskhalanamatha vailakṣyanamitaṃ
Lalāṭe bhartāraṃ caraṇakamale tāḍayati te |
Cirādantaḥśalyaṃ dahanakṛtamunmūlitavatā
Tulākoṭikvāṇaiḥ kilikilitamīśānaripuṇā ||

(When your lotus-like feet strike your Lord on the forehead, during love-play, as he pretends to be in love with another and mentions her name and puts His head down in shame, cupid completely gets rid of his long cherished rancour against the Lord for burning him and proclaims his victory through the jingling of your anklets.)

Pradīpajvālābhirdivasakaranīrājanavidhiḥ
Sudhāsūteścandropalajalalavairarghyaracanā |
Svakīyairambhobhiḥ salilanidhisauhityakaraṇaṃ
Tvadīyābhirvāgbhistava janani vācāṃ stutiriyam ||

(Oh! Mother, this praise of words in your honour composed with your own words is like the worship of lights in honour of the sun done with its own rays, the oblation in honour of the moon with the water emanating from the moon stone, and the pleasing of the ocean with its own waters.)

Upadeshasahasri

Upadeshasahasri literally translates to 'a thousand teachings', and is considered the most detailed exposition by Shankara (outside his commentaries) on Vedanta. The work is in two parts, the first in metre, and the second in prose. Its purpose is defined in the very first shloka, viz., to examine the methods and means of self-knowledge and moksha.

Shankara cogently dwells in this work on the importance of knowing one's true self, and distinguishing it from the mind, body, intellect and the ego. The identity between the Atman and Brahman is also expounded upon in detail, with 233 verses in the eighteenth chapter exclusively analysing the Upanishadic mahavakya: Tat tvam asi.

The interesting thing about Shankara's Prakarana texts is that they are not didactic monologues on his philosophical vision, but lively and engaging, guiding the earnest disciple to apply his mind through enquiry and analysis, reasoning and interpretation, and above all through a search for the right spiritual insight.

To provide a sense of the nature of the text, we have taken a short excerpt from the English translation by Swami Jagadananda, published in 1941 by the Ramakrishna Math in Madras (now, Chennai).

Vidyāyāḥ pratikūlaṃ hi karma syātsābhimānataḥ |
Nirvikārātmabuddhiśca vidyetīha prakīrtitā ||

(Accompanied by egoism, actions are incompatible with knowledge. For it is well known here {in the Vedantas} that knowledge is the consciousness, that the self is changeless.)

Ahaṃ kartā mamedaṃ syāditi karma pravartate |
Vastvadhīnā bhavedvidyā kartradhīno bhavedvidhiḥ ||

(Actions have their origin in the consciousness that one is a doer and has a desire of having the result of what one does. Knowledge depends on a thing {its own object and also on evidence}, while action depends entirely on the performer).

Prtyavāyastu tasyaiva yasyāhaṅkāra iṣyate |
Ahaṅkāraphalārthitve vidyete nātmavedinaḥ ||

(It is only one having egoism that may incur sin {by the omission of duties}. A man who has got self-knowledge has neither egoism nor a desire for the results of actions.)

Kṛtakṛtyaśca siddhaśca yogī brāhmaṇa eva ca |
Ya evaṃ veda tattvārthamanyathā hyātmahā bhavet ||

(He who thus knows the reality of the self becomes successful in attaining the goal of his life and becomes perfect. He becomes a knower of Brahman and one with it. One knowing the self otherwise may be said to commit suicide.)

Ātmalābhātparo nānyo lābhaḥ kaścana vidyate |
Yadrthā vedavādāśca smārtāścāpi tu yāḥ kriyāḥ ||

(There is no other attainment higher than that of the self. For that is the purpose for which the teachings of the Vedas, the smritis and the actions {described in the Vedas} are there.)

Yena vetti sa vedaḥ syātsvapne sarvaṃ tu māyayā |
Yena paśyati taccakṣuḥ śṛṇoti śrotramucyate ||
Yena svapnagato vakti sā vāghrāṇaṃ tathaiva ca |
Rasanasparsane caiva manaścānyattathendriyam ||

(Existence-knowledge through which all things in a dream are known is the knower. It is the same entity that is known in a dream by maya. It is the same consciousness through which one sees, hears, speaks, smells, tastes, touches and thinks, respectively called the eye, the ear, the larynx, the auditive organ, the tongue, the organ of touch and the mind.)

Sa gurustārayedyuktaṃ śiṣyaṃ síṣyaguṇānvitam |
Brahmavidyāplvenāśu svāntadhvāntamahodadhim ||

(The teacher should immediately take the disciple in the boat of the knowledge of Brahman across the great ocean of darkness which is within him —the disciple who is of a one-pointed mind and endowed with the qualities of a {true} disciple.)

Satyaṃ jñānamanantaṃ ca rasadeḥ pañcakātparam |
Syāmadṛśyādiśāstroktamahaṃ brahmeti nirbhayaḥ ||

(One becomes free from fear when one knows that one is Brahman which is existence. Knowledge and infinite, beyond the five sheaths consisting of food etc., and which is described in the shruti as not perceivable.)

Bandhaṃ mokṣaṃ ca sarvaṃ yat idmubhayaṃ heyamekaṃ dwayaṃ ca
Jñeyaṃ jñeyābhyatītaṃ paramadhigataṃ tattvamekaṃ viśuddham |
Vijñāyaitadyathāvacchṛutimunigaditaṃ śokamohāvatītaḥ
Sarvajñaḥ sarvakṛtsyādbhavabhayarahito brāhmaṇo'avāptakṛtyaḥ ||

(Having gained a perfect knowledge of bondage and liberation with their cause {viz., ignorance and knowledge, respectively}, having acquired a complete understanding of cause and effects which are objects of knowledge and are {therefore} to be negated, and having properly known the one supreme and pure truth {to be the self} which is beyond all objects of knowledge, known in the Vedantas and taught by the shruti and the teacher, a knower of Brahman stands freed from the fear of being born again, becomes all and all-knowing, goes beyond grief and delusion and has the acme of his life fulfilled.)

Vivekātmadhiyā duḥkhaṃ nudyate calanādivat |
Avivekasvabhāvena mano gaccatyanicchataḥ ||
Tadānudṛśyate duḥkhaṃ naiścalyenaiva tasya tat |
Pratyagātmani tasmāttadduḥkhaṃ naivopapadyate ||

(The pain {due to the identification with the subtle body} comes to an end when one has the discriminating knowledge {that one is the innermost self} like the movement etc., {belonging to the gross body} which are negated {when one knows that one is different from it}. Unhappiness is seen in the self when the mind roams against one's will on account of ignorance. But it is not seen in it when the mind is at rest. It is, therefore, not reasonable that unhappiness is that in the innermost self.)

Brahmjnanavalimala

This work of Shankara is a jewel for its compressed concentration of thought. Its great attraction is its brevity, wherein in just twenty-one verses, we see a delineation of not only the characteristics of the person who has realised Brahman, but also the means to attain it. In the very first verse, Shankara himself says that by hearing this composition but once, a sincere aspirant can attain liberation.

The work has been composed in the anustup metre, which enables it to be easily recited or set to music. The shlokas are particularly helpful in facilitating meditation, where any one of the verses can be used to focus and still the mind.

Sakṛcchravaṇamātreṇa brahmajñānaṃ yato bhavet |
Brahmajñānāvalīmālā sarveṣāṃ mokṣasiddhaye ||

(The work entitled Brahmjnanavalimala, by hearing which just once knowledge of Brahman is attained, enables all to attain liberation.)

Asaṅgo'hamasaṅgo'hamasaṅgo'haṃ punaḥ punaḥ |
Saccidānandarūpo'hamahamevāhamavyayaḥ ||

(Unattached am I, unattached am I, ever free from attachment of any kind; I am of the nature of existence-consciousness-bliss. I am the very self, indestructible and ever unchanging.)

Nityaśuddhavimukto'haṃ nirākāro'hamavyayaḥ |
Bhūmānandasvarūpo'hamahamevāhamavyayaḥ ||

(I am eternal, I am pure {free from the control of maya}. I am ever liberated. I am formless, indestructible and changeless. I am of the nature of infinite bliss. I am the very self, indestructible and changeless.)

Nityo'haṃ niravadyo'haṃ nirākāro'hamucyate |
Paramānandarūpo'hamahamevāhamavyayaḥ ||

(I am eternal, I am free from blemish, I am formless, I am indestructible and changeless. I am of the nature of supreme bliss. I am the very self, indestructible and changeless.)

Śuddhacaitanyarūpo'hamātmārāmo'hameva ca |
Akhaṇḍānandarūpo'hamahamevāhamavyayaḥ ||

(I am pure consciousness; I revel in my own self. I am of the nature of indivisible {concentrated} bliss. I am the very self, indestructible and changeless.)

Pratyakcaitanyarūpo'haṃ śānto'haṃ prakṛteḥ paraḥ |
Śāśvatānandarūpo'hamahamevāhamavyayaḥ ||

(I am the indwelling consciousness, I am calm {free from all agitation}, I am beyond *prakriti* {maya}, I am of the nature of eternal bliss, I am the very self, indestructible and changeless.)

Tattvātītaḥ parātmāhaṃ madhyātītaḥ paraḥ śivaḥ |
Māyātītaḥ paraṃjyotirahamevāhamavyayaḥ ||

(I am the supreme self, beyond all categories {such as prakriti, *mahat*, ahankara, etc.}, I am the supreme auspicious one, beyond all those in the middle. I am beyond maya. I am the supreme light. I am the very self, indestructible and changeless.)

Nānārūpavyatīto'haṃ cidākāro'hamacyutaḥ |
Sukharūpasvarūpo'hamahamevāhamavyayaḥ ||

(I am beyond all the different forms. I am of the nature of pure consciousness. I am never subject to decline. I am of the nature of bliss. I am the very self, indestructible and changeless.)

Māyātatkāryadehādi mama nāstyeva sarvadā |
Svaprakāśaikarūpo'hamahamevāhamavyayaḥ ||

(There is neither maya nor its effects such as the body for me. I am of the same nature and self-luminous. I am the very self, indestructible and changeless.)

Guṇatrayavyatīto'haṃ brahmādīnāṃ ca sākṣyaham |
Anantānantarūpo'hamahamevāhamavyayaḥ ||

(I am beyond the three gunas—sattva, rajas, and tamas. I am the witness of even Brahma and others. I am of the nature of infinite bliss. I am the very self, indestructible and changeless.)

Antaryāmisvarūpo'haṃ kūṭasthaḥ sarvago'smyaham |
Paramātmasvarūpo'hamahamevāhamavyayaḥ ||

(I am the inner controller, I am immutable, I am all-pervading. I am myself the supreme self. I am the very self, indestructible and changeless.)

Niṣkalo'haṃ niṣkriyo'haṃ sarvātmādyaḥ sanātanaḥ |
Aparokṣasvarūpo'hamahamevāhamavyayaḥ ||

(I am devoid of parts. I am actionless. I am the self of all. I am the primordial one. I am the ancient, eternal one. I am the directly intuited self. I am the very self, indestructible and changeless.)

Dvandvādisākṣirūpo'hamacalo'haṃ sanātanaḥ |
Sarvasākṣisvarūpo'hamahamevāhamavyayaḥ ||

(I am the witness of all pairs of opposites. I am immovable. I am eternal. I am the witness of everything. I am the very self, indestructible and changeless.)

Prajñānaghana evāhaṃ vijñānaghana eva ca |
Akartāhamabhoktāhamahamevāhamavyayaḥ ||

(I am a mass of awareness and of consciousness. I am not a doer nor an experiencer. I am the very self, indestructible and changeless.)

Nirādhārasvarūpo'haṃ sarvādhāro'hameva ca |
Āptakāmasvarūpo'hamahamevāhamavyayaḥ ||

(I am without any support, and I am the support of all. I have no desires to be fulfilled. I am the very self, indestructible and changeless.)

Tāpatrayavinirmukto dehatrayavilakṣaṇaḥ |
Avasthātrayasākṣyasmi cāhamevāhamavyayaḥ ||

(I am free from the three kinds of afflictions—those in the body, those from other beings and those caused by higher powers. I am different from the gross, subtle and causal bodies. I am the witness of the three states of waking, dream and deep sleep. I am the very self, indestructible and changeless.)

Dṛgdṛśyau dvau padārthau staḥ parasparavilakṣaṇau |
Dṛgbrahma dṛśyaṃ māyeti sarvavedāntaḍiṇḍimaḥ ||

(There are two things which are different from each other. They are the seer and the seen. The seer is Brahman and the seen is maya. This is what all Vedanta proclaims).

Ahaṃsākṣīti yo vidyādvivicyaivaṃ punaḥ punaḥ |
Sa eva muktaḥ so vidvāniti vedāntaḍiṇḍimaḥ ||

(He who realises after repeated contemplation that he is a mere witness, he alone is liberated. He is the enlightened one. This is proclaimed by Vedanta.)

Ghaṭakuḍyādikaṃ sarvaṃ mṛttikāmātrameva ca |
Tadvadbrahma jagatsarvamiti vedāntaḍiṇḍimaḥ ||

(The pot, wall, etc., are all nothing but clay. Likewise, the entire universe is nothing but Brahman. This is proclaimed by Vedanta.)

Brahma satyaṃ jaganmithyā jīvo brahmaiva nāparaḥ |
Anena vedyaṃ sacchāstramiti vedāntaḍiṇḍimaḥ ||

(Brahman is real; the universe is *mithya* {it cannot be categorised as either real or unreal}. The jiva is Brahman itself and not different. This should be understood as the correct shastra. This is proclaimed by Vedanta.)

Antarjyotirbahirjyotiḥ pratyagjyotiḥ parātparaḥ |
Jyotirjyotiḥ svayaṃjyotirātmajyotiḥ śivo'smyaham ||

(I am the auspicious one, the inner light and the outer light, the indwelling light, higher than the highest, the light of all lights, self-luminous, the light that is the self.)

Stotras

Given his firm commitment to the jnana marga, and his general devaluation of conventional forms of worship, it may come as a surprise to some that Shankara wrote some of the most moving stotras or hymns in praise of several deities of the Hindu pantheon. These are marked by a deep sense of surrender and devotion, and the refrain in all of them is for the almighty to grant him release from the samasaric world of pain and suffering, and birth and rebirth.

We have included in this anthology, Shankara's devotional hymns to Shiva, Vishnu, Bhavani, Annapoorna, Devi (or Divine Mother), and to the rivers Ganga, and the Narmada.

It is interesting that in several of these, Shankara asks for nothing else than for forgiveness for his many transgressions in not paying sufficient obeisance to the deity. The act of seeking pardon, and of accepting his own finitude in contrast to the omnipotent magnanimity of the divine, evokes a deep sense of humility and surrender—both considered invaluable by him in the preparation for understanding the ultimate knowledge of Brahman. At the same time, this very act of total surrender to conventional theism does stand out in stark contrast to the majesty of his own philosophical assertion that knowledge alone is the path to liberation.

The devotional hymns written by Shankara (including the Bhaja Govindam, which for technical reasons is considered a Prakarana text and not a stotra) have achieved great popularity for their lyrical simplicity and transparent sincerity in evoking the blessings and the protection of the divine. They are, even today, sung and recited in millions of homes in India and abroad, and often by those who know very little about Brahman and the remarkable—if austerely uncompromising and aloof—philosophy that will always remain the real contribution of Shankara not only to Hinduism, but increasingly now, to global philosophical thought.

Shivapanchakshara Stotra
(The five stanzas to Lord Shiva)

Nāgendrahārāya trilocanāya
bhasmāṅgarāgāya maheśvarāya ।
nityāya śuddhāya digambarāya
tasmai "na" kārāya namaḥ śivāya ॥

(Here, the first word Nagendraharaya begins with the letter 'na'. In the verse, expressions descriptive of the form of Shiva as well as his true transcendent nature are employed. He wears the serpent-king as a garland, and has the third eye on his forehead; he has the ashes smeared all over his body. He is the supreme Lord, eternal and pure, and is sky-clad. To that Shiva who is in the form of the letter 'na', may this obeisance be!)

Mandākinīsalilacandanacarcitāya
nandīśvarapramathanāthamaheśvarāya ।
mandāramukhyabahupuṣpasupūjitāya
tasmai "ma"kārāya namaḥ śivāya ॥

(That water of the Mandakini serves as the sandal paste for bathing Shiva's body. Mandakini is the Ganga as she descends from heaven. The Ganga that flows along the holy Kedara is named Mandakini. Shiva receives the furious Ganga as she falls in his matted locks; and the water trickles and bathes his body. He is the supreme Lord of Nandi and leader of the troops of attendants in Kailasha. He is worshiped with *mandara* and many other flowers. He is specially praised by uttering the letter 'ma'. To Shiva who is adored in the form of the letter 'ma' may this obeisance be!)

Śivāya gaurīvadanābjabṛnda
sūryāya dakṣādhvaranāśakāya ।

ŚriNīlakaṇṭhāya vṛṣabhadhvajāya
tasmai "śi" kārāya namaḥ śivāya ||

(He is Shiva, the bestower of all that is good. The name itself has 'shi' as its first letter. He is as the sun to the bunch of lotuses that is Parvati's face. The Devi had to re-incarnate herself as the daughter of the Himalayas because in her previous manifestation she had to commit suicide for the misdeeds of her father, Daksha. Lord Shiva destroyed Daksha's sacrifice, not because Daksha had dishonoured Lord Shiva, but because he was responsible for his daugther commiting suicide by falling into the sacrificial fire, not being able to bear the dishonour shown by him to her Lord. Shiva is Nilakantha. Shiva has on his banner the emblem of the bull. The letter 'shi' which is the third in the five-lettered mantra is an indicator of his magnificence. To that Shiva, may this obeisance be!)

Vaśiṣṭhakumbhodbhavagautamārya
munīndradevārcitaśekharāya |
candrārkavaiśvānaralocanāya
tasmai "va"kārāya namaḥ śivāya ||

(Lord Shiva is adored by great ascetics and sages like Vashishth, Agastya, and Gautam, as also by the gods. His three eyes are the sun, the moon, and the fire.To that Shiva who is in the form of the letter 'va', may this obeisance be!)

Yaññasvarūpāya jaṭādharāya
pinākahastāya sanātanāya |
divyāya devāya digambarāya
tasmai "ya"kārāya namaḥ śivāya ||

(In their war with the demons, the gods came out victorious. In the hour of victory, they were overcome by false pride which made them forget the source of their strength, the supreme

Brahman. In order to bring them to their senses, Brahman, the great godhead, appeared before them as a bright column of light spanning heaven and earth; the gods did not know what this Yaksha (spirit) was. The first to be sent on a mission of discovery was Agni. When he was asked by the Spirit to prove his strength, he couldn't even burn a blade of grass. Similarly, Vayu who was the next to go as emissary could not move the blade of grass. Finally, the chief of gods, Indra, was commissioned to solve the mystery. At his approach, the Spirit vanished before him. Then, in the same ethereal region, Indra came across a woman who was shining intensely, Uma the daughter of Himavan. He asked her: 'What Spirit is this?' She replied, 'It is Brahman,' and added: 'It was through the victory of Brahman that you attained glory.' Thus, Parvati became the first devaguru. Shiva, the non-dual Spirit (Moksha) is the supreme reality that was revealed by her to the gods. Lord Shiva wears a braid of matted locks. He bears in his arm the pinak bow. He is the most ancient (sanatana) Being: the shining God. The quarters are his clothing. He appears in the form of the letter 'ya'. To that Shiva, may this obeisance be!)

Dakshinamurti Stotra

Viśaṃ darpaṇdṛśyamānanagarītulyaṃ nijātargataṃ
Paśyannnātmani māyayā bahirivodbhūtaṃ yathā nidrayā |
Yaḥ sākṣātkurute prabodhasamaye svātmānmevādvayaṃ
Tasmai śrīgurumūrtaye nama idaṃ śrīdakṣiṇāmūrtaye ||

(I bow to Shri Dakshinamurti in the form of my guru: I bow to him by whose grace the whole of the world is found to exist entirely in the mind, like a city's image mirrored in a glass.

Though, like a dream, through maya's power it appears outside; and by whose grace, again, on the dawn of knowledge, it is perceived as the everlasting and non-dual self.)

Bījasyāntarivāṅkuro jagadidaṃ prāṅnirvikalpaṃ punaḥ
Māyākalpitadeśakālakalanāvaicitryacitrīkṛtam ।
Māyāvīva vijṛmbhayatyapi mahāyogīva yaḥ svecchayā
Tasmai śrīgurumūrtaye nama idaṃ śrīdakṣiṇāmūrtaye ॥

(I bow to Shri Dakshinamurti in the form of my guru: I bow to him who, by the sheer power of his will, projects outside, like a magician or a mighty yogi, this infinite universe; which, in the beginning, rests without name or form, like the sprout in a seed; and after creation, by the power of time and space imagined through maya, appears to be many, possessed of manifold shapes and hues.)

Yasyaiva sphuraṇaṃ sadātmakamasatkalpārthakaṃ bhāsate
Sākṣāttattvamasīti vedavacasā yo bodhayatyāśritān ।
Yatsākṣātkaraṇādbhavenna punarāvṛttirbhavāmbhonidhau
Tasmai śrīgurumūrtaye nama idaṃ śrīdakṣiṇāmūrtaye ॥

(I bow to Shri Dakshinamurti in the form of my guru: to him whose outward manifestation, though based on the real, appears as illusory, ever-changing in him through the vedic pronouncement 'Tat tvam asi', the boon of immediate knowledge of Brahman; to which attaining, a man returns no more to the realm of birth and death.)

Nānācchidraghaṭodarasthitamahādīpaprabhābhāsvaraṃ
Jñānaṃ yasya tu cakṣurādikaraṇadvārā bahiḥ spandate ।
Jānāmīti tameva bhāntamanubhātyetatsamastaṃ jagat
Tasmai śrīgurumūrtaye nama idaṃ śrīdakṣiṇāmūrtaye ॥

(I bow to Shri Dakshinamurti in the form of my guru: to him whose knowledge, issuing forth through the organs of sense like the glow of a powerful lamp placed in a pot with many holes, vibrates outside in the shape of the thought, 'I know'; whose light it is that illumines the whole of the universe.)

Dehaṃ prāṇamapīndriyāṇyapi calāṃ buddhiṃ ca śūnyaṃ viduḥ
Strībālāndhajaḍopamāstvahamiti bhrāntā bhṛśaṃvādinaḥ |
Māyāśaktivilāsakalpitamahāvyāmohasaṃhāriṇe
Tasmai śrīgurumūrtaye nama idaṃ śrīdakṣiṇāmūrtaye ||

(I bow to Shri Dakshinamurti in the form of my guru: to him who dispels the mighty illusion evoked by maya's play; impelled by which, unseeing, childish, and misguided men continually speak, in error, of body, prana, senses, and even of the fickle mind, as 'I'; though in reality these are all mere emptiness.)

Rāhugrastadivākarendusadṛśo māyā samācchādanāt
Sanmātraḥ karaṇopasaṃharaṇato yo'bhūtsuṣuptaḥ pumān |
Prāgasvāpsamiti prabodhasamaye yaḥ pratyabhijñāyate
Tasmai śrīgurumūrtaye nama idaṃ śrīdakṣiṇāmūrtaye ||

(I bow to Shri Dakshinamurti in the form of my guru: I bow to him who, as a man, in deep and dreamless sleep exists as ultimate truth itself; when outer awareness is obscured, like the sun or moon in Rahu's grasp, and organs of sense are all withdrawn; and who, on awakening, tells himself, 'It was I who slept'; and sees again the objects he saw before.)

Bālyādiṣvapi jāgradādiṣu tathā sarvāsvavasthāsvapi
Vyāvṛttāsvanuvartamānamahamityantaḥsphurantaṃ sadā |
Svātmānaṃ prakaṭīkaroti bhajatāṃ yo mudrayā bhadrayā
Tasmai śrīgurumūrtaye nama idaṃ śrīdakṣiṇāmūrtaye ||

(I bow to Shri Dakshinamurti in the form of my guru: I bow to him who, in his loving-kindness, reveals to his worshippers the eternal Atman, which through the changes of waking, dreaming, and dreamless sleep, through childhood, youth, maturity, and old age, persists as the inexhaustible flow of consciousness, revealing itself in the heart as the ever present sense of 'I'.)

Viśvaṃ paśyati kāryakāraṇatayā svasvāmisaṃbandhataḥ
Śiṣyācāryatayā tathaiva pitṛputrādyātmanā bhedataḥ |
Svapne jāgrati vā ya eṣa puruṣo māyāparibhrāmitaḥ
Tasmai śrīgurumūrtaye nama idaṃ śrīdakṣiṇāmūrtaye ||

(I bow to Shri Dakshinamurti in the form of my guru seated before me, who, as a mortal under the sway of maya, and whether awake or dreaming, perceives that the world is composed of multiple entities, joined in relation to one another as cause and effect, owner and owned, teacher and pupil, sire and son.)

Bhūrambhāṃsyanalo'nilo'mbaramaharnātho himāṃśuḥ pumān
Ityābhāti carācarātmakamidaṃ yasyaiva mūrtyaṣṭakam |
Nānyatkiñcana vidyate vimṛśatāṃ yasmātparasmādvibhoḥ
Tasmai śrīgurumūrtaye nama idaṃ śrīdakṣiṇāmūrtaye ||

(I bow to Sri Dakshinamurti in the form of my guru, beyond whom, for a wise and discerning man, no being exists superior; who has manifested himself in an eightfold form as the tangible and insentient earth, water, fire, air, and ether, as the sun, the lord of day, the moon, of soothing light, and as a living man.)

Sarvātmatvamiti sphuṭīkṛtamidaṁ yasmādamuṣminstave
Tenāsya śravaṇātadarthamananāddhyānāñca saṅkīrtanāt |
sarvātmatvamahāvibhūtisahitaṁ syādīśvaratvaṁ svataḥ
Sidhyetatpunaraṣṭadhā pariṇatam caiśvaryamavyāhatam ||

(This hymn to Shri Dakshinamurti clearly reveals the ultimate truth as the soul of everything that has life; therefore by hearing it and by reciting it a man attains unrivalled lordship, acquiring the eight unique powers of the Godhead.)

Vaṭaviṭapisamīpe bhūmibhāge niṣaṇṇaṃ
Sakalamunijanānāṃ jñānadātāramārāt |
Tribhuvanagurumīśaṃ dakṣiṇāmūrtidevaṃ
Jananamaraṇaduḥkhacchedadakṣaṃ namāmi ||

(I bow to Shri Dakshinamurti in the form of my guru, seated upon the earth by yonder banyan tree; I bow to him who bestows on the sages direct knowledge of ultimate truth; I bow to the teacher of the three worlds, the Lord himself, who dispels the misery of birth and death.)

Citraṃ vataṭarormūle vṛdhaśiṣyaḥ gururyuva |
Gurostu manuṃ vyākhyānaṃ śiśyāstu chinnasaṃśayāḥ ||

(Behold, under the banyan are seated the aged disciples about their youthful teacher; it is strange indeed: the teacher instructs them only through silence, which, in itself, is sufficient to scatter all his disciples' doubts.)

Om namaḥ praṇavārthāya śuddhajñānaikamūrtaye |
Nirmalāya praśāntāya dakśiṇāmūrtaye namaḥ ||

(I bow to him, who is the inner meaning of the sacred syllable Om; to him whose nature is pure awareness; I bow to Sri Dakshinamurti, stainless and serene beyond measure.)

Nidhaye sarvavidyānāṃ bhiṣaje bhavarogiṇām |
Gurave sarvalokānāṃ dakṣiṇāmūrtaye namaḥ ||

(I bow to Shri Dakshinamurti, the mine of eternal wisdom; the healer of those who suffer from the malady of birth and death; who is regarded by all as their own teacher.)

Maunavyākhyāprakaṭitaparabrahmatattvaṃ yuvānaṃ
Varṣiṣṭhāntevasadṛṣigaṇairāvṛtaṃ brahmaniṣṭhaiḥ |
Ācāryendraṃ karakalitatacinmudramānandamūrtiṃ
Svā mārāmaṃ muditavadanaṃ dakṣiṇāmūrtimīḍe ||

(I praise Shri Dakshinamurti, my youthful teacher, who, through silent instruction, reveals the truth of the Parabrahman; who is surrounded by aged disciples, mighty sages devoted to Brahman. I praise the supreme teacher, the essence of bliss, who revels in his own self, the silent one, whose hand is uplifted in the benediction of knowledge.)

Vedasarashiva Stotra

Paśūnāṃ patiṃ pāpanāśaṃ pareśaṃ
Gajendrasya kṛttiṃ vasānaṃ vareṇyam |
Jaṭājūṭamadhye sphuradgāṅgavāriṃ
Mahādevamekaṃ smarāmi smarārim ||

(Him do I cherish, the Lord of living creatures, the almighty one, the slayer of sin, who is adored by all, within whose matted locks the Ganges wanders murmuring: Him do I cherish—Shiva, the great god, the one without a second, the destroyer of lust.)

Maheśaṃ sureśaṃ surārātināśaṃ
Vibhuṃ viśvanāthaṃ vibhūtyaṅgabhūṣam |

Virūpākṣamindvarkavahnitrinetraṃ
Sadānandamīḍe prabhuṃ pañcavaktram ||

(Him do I praise, the Lord supreme, the God of gods, the demon-slayer, who is the spirit pervading all, the Lord of the world, whose body is ash-besmeared; whose three eyes are the sun, the moon, and fire: Him do I praise—Shiva, the ever-blessed, the five-faced one.)

Girīśaṃ gaṇeśaṃ gale nīlavarṇaṃ
Gavendrādhirūḍhaṃ guṇātītarūpam |
Bhavaṃ bhāsvaraṃ bhasmanā bhūṣitāṅgaṃ
Bhavānīkalatraṃ bhaje pañcavaktram ||

(Him do I worship, the King of the holy mountains, the Lord of hosts, the blue-throated god, who dwells beyond the three gunas, the primal cause, the shining one, whose body is white with ashes, who rides on the sacred bull: Him do I worship—Shiva, the five-faced one, whose consort is Bhavani.)

Śivākānta śambho śaśāṅkārdhamaule
Maheśān śulin jaṭājūṭadhārin |
Tvameko jagadvyāpako viśvarūpaḥ
Prasīda prasīda prabho pūrṇarūpa ||

(O Lord of Uma! Shambhu, whose brow is adorned with the crescent moon. O Mahadeva, wielder of the trident, wearer of matted locks.
O Thou who alone pervades the universe, O Thou of cosmic form
O Lord, eternally complete, be Thou propitious unto us, O Lord.)

Parātmānamekaṃ jagadbījamādyaṃ
Nirīhaṃ nirākāramoṅkāravedyam |

Yato jāyate pālyate yena viśvaṃ
Tamīśaṃ bhaje līyate yatra viśvam ||

(Him do I worship, the Paramatman, one and without second, who is the cause of the universe, the primal, spirit formless and actionless, who is attained through the syllable Om: Him do I worship—Shiva, of whom the universe is born, by whom it is sustained, in whom it merges.)

Na bhumirna cāpo na vahnirna vāyur
Na cākāśamāste na tandrā na nidrā |
Na coṣṇaṃ na śītaṃ na deśo na veṣo
Na yasyāsti mūrtistrimūrtiṃ tamīḍe ||

(Him do I worship, who is neither earth nor water, who is neither fire nor air nor ether, who is unvisited by sleep, yet evermore unwearied, beyond both heat and cold, without a home: Him do I worship—Shiva, the formless one, the Trimurti.)

Ajaṃ śāśvataṃ kāraṇaṃ kāraṇānām
Śivaṃ kevalaṃ bhāsakaṃ bhāsakānām |
Turīyaṃ tamaḥ pāramādyantahīnaṃ
Prapadye paraṃ pāvanaṃ dwaitahīnam ||

(In Him do I take refuge, the birthless, the everlasting, the cause of all causes, the transcendental, who is beyond all darkness, the auspicious one, the self-existent, the light of lights, who is without beginning or end: in him do I take refuge—Shiva, the supreme purifier, the one without a second.)

Namaste Namaste vibho viśvamūrte
Namaste Namaste cidānandamūrte |
Namaste Namaste tayoyogagamya
Namaste Namaste śrutijñānagamya ||

(O all-pervasive spirit! Thou whose visible form is the universe! Thee I salute again and again. O Thou who art the embodiment of consciousness and bliss! Again and again do I salute thee. Thee I salute again and again, who art attainable through yoga and self-control; again and again do I salute thee, who art only to be known through knowledge of the Vedas.)

Prabho śūlapāṇe vibho viśvanātha
Mahādeva śambho maheśa trinetra |
Śivākānta śānta smarāre purāre
Tvadanyo vareṇyo na mānyo na gaṇyaḥ ||

(O Lord! O omnipresent spirit! Wielder of the trident! Ruler of the universe! O Mahadeva, giver of happiness! O supreme Lord! O three-eyed Shiva! Serene one! Consort of Uma! Slayer of demons! Destroyer of lust! None but thee should we cherish and honour and adore, O Lord!)

Śambho maheśa karuṇāmaya śūlapāṇe
Gaurīpate paśupate paśupāśanāśin |
Kāśīpate karuṇayā jagadetadekas-
Tvaṃ hansi pāsi vidadhasi maheśvaro'si ||

(O Shambhu, giver of joy! Merciful one! Almighty Lord! Consort of Gauri! Lord of all living creatures! Thou who destroyest the fetters of the world! O King of Kashi! Thou who art alone supreme! Moved by compassion, thou dost create, sustain and destroy this world.)

Tvatto jagadbhavati deva bhava smarāre
Tvayyeva tiṣṭhati jaganmṛḍa viśvanātha |
Tvayyeva gacchati layaṃ jagadetadīśa
Liṅgātmake hara carācaraviśvarūpin ||

(Lord and primeval cause! Slayer of Madana! From thee alone the world has sprung. Compassionate one! Thou who art Lord of all, in thee Shiva, who dost reveal thyself through all things living and all without life! To thee alone does the world at last return.)

Shivanamavalyashtakam

He candracūḍa madanāntaka śūlapāṇe
sthāṇo girīśa girijeśa maheśa śambho |
Bhūteśa bhītabhayasūdana māmanātham
Saṃsāraduḥkhagahanājjagadīśa rakṣa ||

(O Mahadeva! O thou auspicious one, with the moon shining in thy crest! Slayer of Madana! Wielder of the trident! Unmoving one, Lord of the Himalayas! O consort of Durga, Lord of all creatures! Thou who scatterest the distress of the fearful! Rescue me, helpless as I am from the trackless forest of this miserable world.)

He pārvatīhṛdayavallabha candramaule
Bhūtādhipa pramathanātha girīśacāpa |
He vāmadeva bhava rudra pinākadakṣha
Saṃsāraduḥkhagahanājjagadīśa rakṣa ||

(O beloved of Parvati's heart! O thou moon-crested deity! Master of every being! Lord of hosts! O thou, the Lord of Parvati! O Vamadev, self-existent one! O Rudra, wielder of the bow! Rescue me, helpless as I am, from the trackless forest of this miserable world.)

He nīlakaṇṭha vṛṣabhadhvaja pañcavaktra
Lokeśa śeṣavalaya pramatheśa śarva |
He dhūrjaṭe paśupate girijāpate māṃ
Saṃsāraduḥkhagahanājjagadīśa rakṣa ||

(O blue-throated God Shiva, whose emblem is the bull! O five-faced one! Lord of the worlds, who wearest snakes about thy wrists! O thou auspicious one! O Shiva! O Pashupati! O thou, the Lord of Parvati! Rescue me, helpless as I am, from the trackless forest of this miserable world.)

He viśvanātha śiva śaṃkara devadeva
Gaṅgādhara pramathanāyaka nandikeśa |
Bāṇeśvarāndhakaripo hara lokanātha
Saṃsāraduḥkhagahanājjagadīśa rakṣa ||

(O Lord of the universe! O Shiva Shankar! O God of gods! Thou who dost bear the river Ganges in thy matted locks! Thou, the master of Pramatha and Nandika! O Harey, Lord of the world! Rescue me, helpless as I am, from the trackless forest of this miserable world.)

Vārāṇasīpurapate maṇikarṇikeśa
Vīreśa dakṣamakhakāla vibho gaṇeśa |
Sarvajña sarvahṛdayaikanivāsa nātha
Saṃsāraduḥkhagahanājjagadīśa rakṣa ||

(O king of Kashi! Lord of the cremation ground of Manikarnika! O mighty hero thou the destroyer of Daksha's sacrifice! O all-prevasive one! O Lord of hosts! Omniscient one, who art the sole indweller in every heart! O God! Rescue me, helpless as I am, from the trackless forest of this miserable world.)

Śrīmanmaheśvara kṛpāmaya he dayālo
He vyomakeśa śitikaṇṭha gaṇādhinātha |

Bhasmāṅgarāga nṛkapālakalāpamāla
Saṃsāraduḥkhagahanājjagadīśa rakṣa ||

(O Mahadeva! Compassionate one! O benign deity! O Vyomkesha! Blue-throated one! O Lord of ghosts! Thou whose body is besmeared with ashes, thou who art garlanded with human skulls! Rescue me, helpless as I am, from the trackless forest of this miserable world.)

Kailāsaśailavinivāsa vṛṣākape he
Mṛtyuñjaya trinayana trijagannivāsa |
Nārāyaṇapriya madāpaha śaktinātha
Saṃsāraduḥkhagahanājjagadīśa rakṣa ||

(O thou who dwellest on Mount Kailasha! Thou whose carrier is the bull! O conqueror of death! O three-eyed one! Lord of the three worlds! Beloved of Narayana! Slayer of lust! Thou, Shakti Lord! Rescue me, helpless as I am, from the trackless forest of this miserable world.)

Viśveśa viśvabhavanāśaka viśvarūpa
Viśvātmaka tribhuvanaikaguṇādhiveśa |
He viśvahvandya karuṇāmaya dīnabandho
Saṃsāraduḥkhagahanājjagadīśa rakṣa ||

(Lord of the universe! Refuge of the whole world! O thou of infinite forms! Soul of the universe! O thou in whom respose the infinite virtues of the world! O thou adored by all! Compassionate one! O friend of the poor! Rescue me, helpless as I am, from the trackless forest of this miserable world.)

Shivaparadhakshamapana Stotra

Ādau karmaprasaṅgātkalayati kaluṣaṃ mātṛkukṣau sthithaṃ māṃ
Viṇmūtrāmedhyamadhye kathayati nitarām jāṭharo jātavedāḥ |
Yadyadvai tatra duḥkhaṃ vyathayati nitarāṃ śakyate kena vaktuṃ
Kṣantavyo me'parādhaḥ śiva śiva bho śrīmahādeva śambho ||

(Even before I saw the light of this world, my sins from previous births, through which I passed because of desire for the fruit of my deeds, punished me as I lay in my mother's womb. There I was scalded in the midst of the unclean: who can describe the pain that afflicts the child in its mother's womb? Therefore, O Shiva! O Mahadeva! O Shambhu! Forgive me, I pray, for my transgressions.)

Bālye duḥkhātireko malalulitavapuḥ stanyapāne pipāsa
No śaktaścendriyebhyo bhavagunajanitāḥ jantavo māṃ tudanti |
Nānārogātiduḥkhādrudanaparavaśaḥ śaṅkaraṃ na smarāmi
Kṣantavyo me'parādhaḥ śiva śiva bho śrīmahādeva śambho ||

(In childhood my suffering never came to an end; my body was covered with dirt and I craved for my mother's breast. Over my body and limbs I had no control; I was pursued by troublesome flies and mosquitoes; day and night I cried with the pain of many an ailment, forgetting thee, O Shankara! Therefore, O Shiva! O Mahadeva! O Shambhu! Forgive me, I pray, for my transgressions.)

Prauḍho'haṃ yauvanastho viṣayaviṣadharaiḥ pañcabhirmarmasandhau
Daṣṭo naṣṭo vivekaḥ sutadhanayuvatisvādasaukhye niṣaṇṇaḥ |
Śaivīcintāvihīnaṃ mama hṛdayamaho mānagarvādhiruḍhaṃ
Kṣantavyo me'parādhaḥ śiva śiva bho śrīmahādeva śambho ||

(In youth the venomous snakes of sound and sight, of taste and touch and smell, fastened upon my vitals and slew my discrimination; I was engrossed in the pleasures of wealth and sons and youthful wife. Alas! My heart bereft of thought of Shiva, swelled with arrogance and pride. Therefore, O Shiva! O Mahadeva! O Shambhu! Forgive me, I pray, for my transgressions.)

Vārdhakye cendriyāṇāṃ vigatagatimatiscādhidaivāditāpaiḥ
Papai rogairviyogaistvanavasitavapuḥ prauḍhihīnaṃ ca dīnaṃ |
Mithyāmohābhilāṣairbhramati mam mano dhūrjaṭerdhyānaśūnyaṃ
Kṣantavyo me'parādhaḥ śiva śiva bho śrīmahādeva śambho ||

(Now in old age my senses have lost the power of proper judging and acting; my body, though still not wholly bereft of life, is weak and senile from many afflictions from sins and illnesses and bereavements; but even now my mind, instead of meditating on Shiva, runs after vain desires and hollow delusion. Therefore, O Shiva! O Mahadeva! O Shambhu! Forgive me, I pray, for my transgressions.)

No śakyam smārtakarmapratipadagahanapratyavāyākulākhyaṃ
Śraute vārtā kathaṃ me dwijakulavihite brahmamārge susāre |
Jñāto dharmo vicāraiḥ śravaṇamananayoḥ kiṃ nididhyāsitavyaṃ
Kṣantavyo me'parādhaḥ śiva śiva bho śrīmahādeva śambho ||

(The duties laid down by the smriti —perilous and abstruse — are now beyond me; how can I speak of Vedic injunction for Brahmins, as means for attaining Brahman? Never yet have I rightly grasped, through discrimination, the meaning of hearing the scriptures from the guru and reasoning on his instruction; how, then, speak of reflecting on truth without interruption? Therefore, O Shiva! O Mahadeva! O Shambhu! Forgive me, I pray, for my transgressions.)

Snātvā pratyūṣakāle snapanavidhividhau nāhṛtaṃ gāṅgatoyaṃ
Pūjārthaṃ vā kadācidbahutaragahanātkhanḍabilvīdalāni |

Nānītā padmamālā sarasi vikasitā gandhadhūpau tvadarthaṃ
Kṣantavyo me'parādhaḥ śiva śiva bho śrīmahādeva śambho ||

(Not even once have I finished my bath before sunrise and brought from Ganges water to bathe thy holy image; never, from the deep woods have I brought the sacred *bel* leaves for thy worship; nor have I gathered full-blown lotuses from the lakes, nor ever arranged the lights and the incense for worshiping thee. Therefore, O Shiva! O Mahadeva! O Shambhu! Forgive me, I pray, for my transgressions.)

Dugdhairmadhvājyayuktairdadhisitasahitaih snāpitaṃ naiva liṅgam
No liptaṃ candanādyaiḥ kanakaviracitaiḥ pujītaṃ na prasūnaiḥ |
Dhūpaiḥ karpūradīpairvividhrasayutairnaiva bhakṣhyopahāraiḥ
Kṣantavyo me'parādhaḥ śiva śiva bho śrīmahādeva śambho ||

(I have not bathed thine image with milk and honey, with butter and other oblations; I have not decked it with fragrant sandal paste; I have not worshipped thee with golden flowers, with incense, with camphor flame, and savoury offerings. Therefore, O Shiva! O Mahadeva! O Shambhu! Forgive me, I pray, for my transgressions.)

Dhyātva citte śivākhyaṃ pracurataradhanaṃ naiva dattaṃ dwijebhyo
Havyaṃ te lakṣasaṅkhairhutavahavadane nārpitaṃ bījamantraiḥ |
No taptaṃ gāṅgatīre vratajapaniyamaih rudrajāpyairna vedaiḥ
Kṣantavyo me'parādhaḥ śiva śiva bho śrīmahādeva śambho ||

(I have not made rich gifts to the Brahmins, cherishing in my heart, O Mahadeva! Thy hallowed form; I have not made, in sacred fire, the million oblations of butter, repeating the holy mantra given to me by my guru; never have I done penance alone at the Ganges with *japa* and study of the Vedas. Therefore, O Shiva! O Mahadeva! O Shambhu! Forgive me, I pray, for my transgressions.)

Sthitvā sthāne saroje praṇavamayamarutkumbhake sūkṣmamārge
Śānte svānte pralīne prakaṭitavibhave jyotirūpe parākhye |
Liṅgajne brahmavākye sakalatanugatam śaṅkaraṃ na smarāmi
Kṣantavyo me'parādhaḥ śiva śiva bho śrīmahādeva śambho ||

(I have not sat in the lotus posture, nor have I ever controlled the *prana* along the *sushmana*, repeating the syllable Om; never have I suppressed the turbulent waves of my mind, nor merged with the self-effulgent Om. In the ever-shining witness-consciousness, whose nature is that of the highest Brahman; nor have I, in samadhi, meditated on Shankara, dwelling in every form as the inner guide. Therefore, O Shiva! O Mahadeva! O Shambhu! Forgive me, I pray, for my transgressions.)

Nagno niḥsaṅgaśuddhastriguṇavirahito dhvastamohāndhakāro
Nāsāgre nyastadṛṣṭirviditabhavaguṇo naiva dṛṣṭah kadācit |
Unmanyavasthayā tvāṃ vigatakalimalaṃ śaṅkaraṃ na smarāmi
Kṣantavyo me'parādhaḥ śiva śiva bho śrīmahādeva śambho ||

(Never, O Shiva! Have I seen thee, the pure, the unattached, the naked one, beyond the three gunas, free from the delusion and darkness, absorbed in meditation, and ever aware of the true nature of the world; nor, with a longing heart, have I meditated on thine auspicious and sin-destroying form. Therefore, O Shiva! O Mahadeva! O Shambhu! Forgive me, I pray, for my transgressions.)

Candrodbhāsitaśekhare smarahare gaṅgādhare śankare
Sarpairbhūṣitakaṇṭhakarṇayugale netrotthavaiśvānare |
Dantitvakkṛtasundarāmbaradhare trailokyasāre hare
Mokṣārthaṃ kuru cittavṛttimacalāmanyaistu kiṃ karmabhiḥ ||

(O mind, to gain liberation, concentrate wholly on Shiva, the sole reality underlying the worlds, the giver of good; whose head is illumined by the crescent moon and in whose hair the Ganges is hidden; whose fire-darting eyes consumed the god of earthly love; whose throat and ears are decked with snakes; whose upper garment is a comely elephant skin. Of what avail are all other rituals?)

Kiṃ vānena dhanena vājikaribhiḥ prāptena rājyena kiṃ
Kiṃ vā putrakalatramitrapaśubhirdehena gehena kim |
Jñātvaitatkṣaṇabhaṅguraṃ sapadi re tyājyaṃ mano dūrataḥ
Svātmārthaṃ guruvākyato bhaja mana śrīpārvatīvallabham ||

(O mind. Of what avail are wealth or horses, elephant or a kingdom? Of what avail is a son, the wife, a friend, cattle, the body and the home? Know all these to be transitory and quickly shun them; worship Shiva, as your guru instructs you, for the attaining of self-knowledge.)

Āyurnaśyati paśyatāṃ pratidinaṃ yāti kṣayaṃ yauvanaṃ
Pratyāyānti gatāḥ punarna divasāḥ kālo jagadbhakṣakaḥ |
Laksmīstoyataraṅgabhaṅgacapalāṃ vidyuccalaṃ jīvitaṃ
Tasmāttvām saraṇāgataṃ śaraṇada tvaṃ rakṣa rakṣādhunā ||

(Day by day, a man comes nearer to death; his youth wears away; the day that is gone never returns. Time, the almighty, swallows up everything; transient as the ripples on a stream is the goddess of fortune, fickle as lightning is life itself. O Shiva! O giver of shelter to those that come to thee for refuge! Protect me, who have taken refuge at thy feet.)

Vande Devamumāpatiṃ suraguruṃ vande jagatkāraṇaṃ
Vande pannagabhūṣaṇam mṛgadharaṃ vande paśūnāṃ patim |
Vande sūryaśaśāṅkavahninayanaṃ vande mukundapriyaṃ
Vande bhaktajanāśrayaṃ ca varadaṃ vande śivaṃ śaṅkaram ||

(I salute the self-effulgent guru of the gods, the Lord of Uma; I salute the cause of the universe; I salute the Lord of beasts, adorned with snakes; I salute Shiva, whose three eyes shine like the sun, the moon, and the fire; I salute the beloved of Krishna; I salute Shankara, he who bestows boons on his devotees and gives them shelter; I salute the auspicious Shiva.)

Gātraṃ bhasmasitaṃ sitaṃ ca hasitaṃ haste kapālaṃ sitaṃ
Khaṭvāṅgaṃ ca sitaṃ sitaśca vṛṣabhaḥ karṇe site kuṇḍale ।
Gaṅgāphenasitā jaṭa paśupateścandraḥ sito mūrdhani
So'yaṃ sarvasito dadātu vibhavaṃ pāpakṣayaṃ sarvadā ।।

(O Shiva! White is thy body, covered with ashes; white gleam thy teeth when thou smilest! White is the skull thou holdest in thy hand; white is thy club, which threatens the wicked! White are the rings that hang from thine ears; white appear thy matted locks, flecked with the foam of the Ganges! White shines the moon on thy forehead! May he who is all white, all pure, bestow on me the treasure of forgiveness for my transgressions!)

Karacaraṇakṛtaṃ vākkāyajaṃ karmajaṃ vā
Śravaṇanayanajaṃ vā mānasaṃ vā'parādham ।
Vihitamavihitaṃ vā sarvametatkṣamasva
Jay jaya karuṇābdhe śrīmahādevaśambho ।।

(O Shiva! Forgive all the sins that I have committed with hands or feet, with ears or eyes, with words or body, with mind or heart; forgive my sins, those past and those that are yet to come. Victory unto Shiva, the ocean of compassion, the great God, the abode of blessedness!)

Annapurna Stotra

Nityānandakarī varābhayakarī saundaryaratnākarī
Nirdhūtākhilaghorapāvanakarī pratyakṣamāheṣvarī |
Prāleyācalavaṃśapāvanakarī kāśīpurādhīśvarī
Bhikṣāṃ dehi kṛpāvalambanakarī mātānnapūrṇeśvarī ||

(O benign Mother, who pourest out upon us everlasting bliss! Thou, the ocean of beauty! Bestower of boons and of fearlessness! O supreme purifier, who washest away all sins! Thou, the visible ruler of the world, the sanctifier of king Himalaya's line! O thou, the Queen Empress of holy Kashi! Divine Annapurna! Be gracious unto me and grant me alms.)

Nānāratnavicitrabhūṣaṇakarī hemāmbarāḍambarī
muktāhāravilambamānavilasadvakṣojakumbhāntarī |
kāśmīraguruvāsitā rucikarī kāśipurādhīśvarī
Bhikṣāṃ dehi kṛpāvalambanakarī mātānnapūrṇeśvarī ||

(Thou whose apparel sparkles, sewn with innumerable gems; who wearest a golden sari to heighten thine unsurpassable loveliness! Thou on whose comely bosom reposes a necklace of many pearls; who dost breathe forth a fragrance, being anointed with saffron and sandal paste! O benign Mother! Thou whose form is soothing to the eyes! O thou, the Queen Empress of holy Kashi! Divine Annapurna! Be gracious unto me and grant me alms.)

Yogānandakarī ripukṣayakarī dharmārthaniṣthākarī
Candrārkānalbhāsamānalaharī trailokyarakṣākarī |
Sarvaiśvaryasamastavāñchitakarī kāśīpurādhīśvarī
Bhikṣāṃ dehi kṛpāvalambanakarī mātānnapūrṇeśvarī ||

(Bestower of yoga's bliss! Destroyer of the foe! Fulfiller of wealth and of righteousness! Thou who appearest like waves of light, or the radiance of sun and moon and fire! Protectress of the three worlds! Giver of wealth and of all things wished for! O thou, the Queen Empress of holy Kashi! Divine Annapurna! Be gracious unto me and grant me alms.)

Kailāśācalakandarālayakarī gaurī umā śaṅkarī
Kaumārī nigamārthagocarakarī oṅkārabījakṣarī |
Mokṣadwārakapāṭapāṭanakarī kaśīpurādhīśvarī
Bhikṣāṃ dehi kṛpāvalambanakarī mātānnapūrṇeśvarī ||

(O Gauri! O Uma! O Shankari! O Kaumari! Thou who hast thy dwelling in the cave of sacred Mount Kailasha! Thou who dost reveal the meaning of the holy Vedas; who art the very embodiment of the mystic syllable Om; who openest the gates of liberations! O thou, the Queen Empress of holy Kashi! Divine Annapurna! Be gracious unto me and grant me alms.)

Dṛśyādṛśyaprabhūtavāhanakarī brahmāṇḍabhāṇḍeśvarī
Līlānāṭakasūtrabhedanakarī vijñānadīpaṅkurī |
Śriviśvesamanaḥprasādanakarī kāśīpurādhīśvarī
Bhikṣāṃ dehi kṛpāvalambanakarī mātānnapūrṇeśvarī ||

(Thou who bearest the manifold world of the visible and the invisible; who holdest the universe in thy womb! Thou who severest the thread of the play we play upon this earth! Who lightest the lamp of wisdom; who bringest joy to the heart of Shiva, thy lord! O thou, the Queen Empress of holy Kashi! Divine Annapurna! Be gracious unto me and grant me alms.)

Urvīsarvajaneśvarī bhagavatī mātānnapūrneśvarī
Veṇīnīlasamānakuntalaharī nityannadaneśvarī |
Sarvānandakarī daśaśubhakarī kāśīpurādhīśvarī
Bhikṣāṃ dehi kṛpāvalambanakarī mātānnapūrṇeśvarī |

(O Bhagwati! Thou who art the sovereign of the world! O Mother Annapurna! O supreme deity! Ocean of mercy! Thou whose long tresses, falling to thy knees, ripple restlessly like a river's current and sparkle like a blue gem! Mother, ever eager to give us food and bliss and all good fortune! O thou, the Queen Empress of holy Kashi! Divine Annapurna! Be gracious unto me and grant me alms.)

Ādikṣāntasamastavarṇanakarī śambhostribhāvākarī
Kāśmīrā trijaneśvarī trilaharī nityaṅkurā śarvarī |
Kāmākāṅkṣakarī janodayakarī kāśīpurādhīśvarī
Bhikṣāṃ dehi kṛpāvalambanakarī mātānnapūrṇeśvarī ||

(Thou who revealest all the letters, from the first to the last! Mother of the cosmos, gross and subtle, and of its Lord as well! Ruler of earth and heaven and the nether world, who does embody in thyself the waves of creation, sustenance, and dissolution! Eternal, uncaused cause, who art the thick darkness of the cosmic dissolution! Thou who bringest desire to the heart of a man; who dost bestow on him well being in this world! O thou, the Queen Empress of holy Kashi! Divine Annapurna! Be gracious unto me and grant me alms.)

Darvī svarṇavicitraratnaracitā dakṣhekare saṃsthitā
Vāme svādupayodharī priyakarī saubhāgyamāhesvarī |
Bhaktābhīṣtakarī drśā subhakarī kāśīpurādhīśvarī
Bhikṣāṃ dehi kṛpāvalambanakarī mātānnapūrṇeśvarī ||

(Thou who holdest in thy right hand a ladle of gold studded with jewels, and in thy left hand holdest a cup of delicious food! Thou giver of good fortune, who dost fulfill the wishes of thy worshippers and bringest about their welfare with a mere wink of thine eye! O thou, the Queen Empress of holy Kashi! Divine Annapurna! Be gracious unto me and grant me alms.)

Candrārkānalakoṭikoṭisadṛśā candrānśubimbādharī
candrārkāgnisamānakuṇḍaladharī candrārkavarṇeśvarī ।
Mālāpustakapāśakāṅkuśadharī kāśīpurādhīśvarī
Bhikṣāṃ dehi kṛpāvalambanakarī mātānnapūrṇeśvarī ।।

(Thou whose radiance burns a million times more bright than sun and moon and fire; for whom the light of the moon is but the shadow of thy lips; whose earrings sparkle like the sun and moon and fire; who shinest like the sun and moon! Thou, the supreme Empress, who in thy four hands holdest rosary and book and goad and dice! O thou, the Queen Empress of holy Kashi! Divine Annapurna! Be gracious unto me and grant me alms.)

Kṣatratrāṇakarī mahābhayakarī mātā kṛpāsāgarī
Sākṣānmokṣakarī sadā śivakarī viśveśvarasrīdharī ।
Dakṣākrandakarī nirāmayakari kāśipurādhiśvarī
Bhikṣāṃ dehi kṛpāvalambanakarī mātānnapūrneśvarī ।।

(Protectress of the Kshatriya line! Giver of utter fearlessness! Benign Mother of all! Ocean of infinite mercy! Thou, the bestower of instantaneous liberation, the giver of eternal good! Provider of Shiva's welfare! Destroyer of every bodily ill! O thou, the Queen Empress of holy Kashi! Divine Annapurna! Be gracious unto me and grant me alms.)

Annapūrṇe sadāpūrṇe śaṅkaraprāṇavallabhe ।
Jñānavairāgyasiddhyarthṃ bhikṣām dehi ca pārvatī ।।

(O Annapurna! Thou who never lackest for anything, who holdest Shankara's heart in thrall! O Parvati, grant me alms: I supplicate thee for the boon of wisdom and renunciation above all.)

Mātā me pārvatī devī pitā devo maheśvarḥ ।
Bāndhavāḥ śivabhaktāśca svadeśo bhuvanatrayam ।।

(My mother is the Goddess Parvati; my father is Shiva, the Lord whose power none can withstand; their worshippers I own as my kith and kin; and the three worlds are my native land.)

Bhavanyashtaka
(Eight stanzas to Bhavani)

Na tāto na mātā na bandhurna dātā
Na putro na putrī na bhṛtyo na bhartā ।
Na jāyā na vidyā na vṛttirmamaiva
Gatistvaṃ gatistvaṃ tvamekā bhāvani ॥

(No father have I, no mother, no comrade,
No son, no daughter, no wife, and no grandchild,
No servant or master, no wisdom, no calling:
In thee is my only haven of refuge,
In thee, my help and my strength, O Bhavani!)

Bhavābdhāvapāre mahāduḥkhabhīruḥ
Papāta prakāmī pralobhī pramattaḥ ।
Kusaṃsārapāśaprabaddhḥ sadāhaṃ
Gatistvaṃ gatistvaṃ tvamekā bhāvani ॥

(Immersed as I am in the limitless ocean
Of worldly existence, I tremble to suffer.
Alas! I am lustful and foolish and greedy,
And ever enchained by the fetters of evil:
In thee is my only haven of refuge,
In thee, my help and my strength, O Bhavani!)

Na jānāmi dānaṃ na ca dhyānayogaṃ
Na jānāmi tantraṃ na ca stotramantram |
Na jānāmi pūjāṃ na ca nyāsayogaṃ
Gatistvaṃ gatistvaṃ tvamekā bhāvani ||

(To giving of alms and to meditation,
To scriptures and hymns and mantras, a stranger,
I know not of worship, possess no dispassion:
In thee is my only haven of refuge,
In thee, my help and my strength, O Bhavani!)

Na jānami puṇyaṃ na jānāmi tīrthaṃ
Na jānāmi muktiṃ layaṃ vā kadācit |
Na jānāmi bhaktiṃ vrataṃ vāpi mātar-
Gatistvaṃ gatistvaṃ tvamekā bhāvani ||

(O Mother! Of pilgrimage or of merit,
Of mental control or the soul`s liberation,
Of rigorous vows or devotion, I know not:
In thee is my only haven of refuge,
In thee, my help and my strength, O Bhavani!)

Kukarmī kusaṅgī kubuddhiḥ kudāsaḥ
Kulācārahīnaḥ kadācāralīnaḥ |
Kudṛṣṭiḥ kuvākyaprabandhaḥ sadāham
Gatistvaṃ gatistvaṃ tvamekā bhāvani ||

(Addicted to sinning and worthless companions,
A slave to ill-thoughts and to doers of evil,
Degraded am I, unrighteous, abandoned,
Attached to ill-objects, adept in ill-speaking:
In thee is my only haven of refuge,
In thee, my help and my strength, O Bhavani!)

Prajeśaṃ rameśaṃ maheśaṃ sureśaṃ
Dineśaṃ niśītheśvaraṃ vā kadācit |
Na jānāmi cānyat sadāhaṃ śaraṇye
Gatistvaṃ gatistvaṃ tvamekā bhāvani ||

(I know neither Brahma nor Vishnu nor Shiva,
Nor Indra, sun, moon, or similar being
Not one of the numberless gods, O redeemer!
In thee is my only haven of refuge,
In thee, my help and my strength, O Bhavani!)

Vivāde viṣāde pramāde pravāse
Jale cānale parvate śatrumadhye |
Araṇye śaraṇye sadā māṃ prapāhi
Gatistvaṃ gatistvaṃ tvamekā bhāvani ||

(In strife or in sadness, abroad or in danger,
In water, in fire, in the wilds, on the mountains,
Surrounded by foes, my saviour! Protect me:
In thee is my only haven of refuge,
In thee, my help and my strength, O Bhavani!)

Anātho daridro jarārogayukto
Mahākṣīṇadīnaḥ sadā jāḍyavaktraḥ. |
Vipattau praviṣṭaḥ praṇaṣṭaḥ sadāham
Gatistvaṃ gatistvaṃ tvamekā bhāvani. ||

(Defenceless am I—ill, ageing and helpless,
Enfeebled, exhausted, and dumbly despairing,
Afflicted with sorrow, and utterly ruined:
In thee is my only haven of refuge,
In thee, my help and my strength, O Bhavani!)

Devyaparadhakshamapana Stotra

Na mantraṃ no yantraṃ tadapi ca na jāne stutimaho
Na cāhvānaṃ dhyānaṃ tadapi ca na jāne stutikathāḥ ।
Na jāne mudrāste tadapi na jāne vilapanaṃ
Paraṃ jāne mātastvadanusaraṇaṃ kleśaharaṇam ॥

(I know, alas! No hymn, no mantra,
Neither prayer nor meditation;
Not even how to give thee praise.
The proper ritual of the worship,
The placement of the hands, I know not,
Nor how to make thee supplication.
But Mother, this at least I know:
Whoever comes to thee for shelter
Reaches the end of all his woes.)

Vidherajñānena drawiṇaviraheṇālasatayā
Vidheyāśakyatvāttava caraṇayoryā cyutirabhūt ।
Tadetatkṣantavyaṃ janani sakaloddhāriṇi śive
Kuputro jāyeta kvacidapi kumātā na bhavati ॥

(Ignorant of the commands of scripture,
Utterly devoid of wealth,
Shiftless, indolent, am I,
Unable to do as I ought to do.
Numerous, therefore, are the offences
I have committed at thy feet.
Mother! Saviour of all mankind!
Auspicious one! Forgive my sins.
A wicked son is sometimes born,
But an unkind mother there cannot be.)

Pṛthivyāṃ putrāste janani bahavassanti saralāḥ
Paraṃ teṣaṃ madhye viralataralohaṃ tava sutaḥ ।
Madīyoyaṃ tyāgaḥ samucitamidaṃ no tava śive
Kuputro jāyeta kvacidapi kumātā na bhavati ॥

(Here in this world of thine, O Mother!
Many are thy guileless children;
But restless am I among them all,
And so it is nothing very strange
That I should turn myself from thee.
Yet surely it were impossible
That thou shouldst ever turn from me:
A wicked son is sometimes born,
But an unkind mother there cannot be.)

Jaganmātarmātastavacaraṇasevā na racitā
Na vā dattaṃ devi dravinamapi bhūyastava mayā ।
Tathāpi tvaṃ snehaṃ mayi nirupamaṃ yatprakuruṣe
Kuputro jāyeta kvacidapi kumātā na bhavati ॥

(Mother of the world! Thou, my own Mother!
Never have I served thee, never yet
Offered thee gold or precious gems;
And still thy love is beyond compare.
A wicked son is sometimes born,
But an unkind mother there cannot be.)

Parityaktā devāḥ vividhavidhisevākulatayā
Mayā pañcāśīteradhikamapanīte tu vayasi ।
Idānīṃ cenmātastava yadi kṛpā nāpi bhavitā
Nirālambo lambodarajanani kaṃ yāmi śaraṇam ॥

(Bewildered by the rules of conduct,
By the injunctions of the scriptures,
I have abandoned, one by one,

The shining gods; and now my life
Has passed beyond the meridian.
Mother, shouldst thou withhold thy mercy,
Where, then, shall I fly for shelter,
Weak and helpless as I am?)

Śvapāko Jalpāko bhavati madhupākopamagira
Nirātaṅko raṅko viharati ciraṃ koṭikanakaiḥ ।
Tavapārṇe karṇe viśati manuvarṇe phalamidaṃ
Janaḥ ko jānīte janani japanīyaṃ japavidhau ॥

(If one who feeds on the flesh of dogs
Can learn to speak with honeyed words,
A beggar gains uncounted wealth
And so lives long and fearlessly,
Simply hearing thy magic name
Who can describe what must befall
One who repeats it night and day?)

Citābhasmālepo garalamaśanaṃ dikpaṭadharo
Jaṭādhārī kaṇṭhe bhujagapatihārī paśupatiḥ ।
Kapālī bhūteśo bhajati jagadīśaikapadavīṃ
Bhavāni tvatpāṇigrahaṇaparipāṭīphalamidam ॥

(Only by taking thee for spouse
Did Shiva become the unrivalled Lord
He who is naked and uncouth,
Besmeared with ash from the funeral pyre;
Whose hair is matted on his head,
About whose neck are venomous snakes
The Lord of every living thing.)

Na mokṣasyākāṅkṣā bhavavibhavavāñcchāpi ca na me
Na vijñānāpekṣā śaśimukhi sukhecchāpi na punaḥ ।

Atastvāṃ saṃyāce janani jananaṃ yātu mama vai
Mṛḍānī rdrāṇī śiva śiva bhavānīti japataḥ ||

(I do not ask of thee, O Mother!
Riches, good fortune, or salvation;
I seek no happiness, no knowledge.
This is my only prayer to thee:
That as the breath of life forsakes me,
Still I may chant thy holy name.)

Nārādhitāsi vidhinā vividhopacāraiḥ
Kiṃ rūkṣacintanaparairna kṛtaṃ vacobhiḥ |
Śyāme tvameva yadi kiñcana mayyanāthe
Dhatse kṛpāmucitamambaparaṃ tavaiva ||

(Mother, I have not worshipped thee
With proper rituals and the prescribed
Ingredients of sacrifice.
Many are my sinful deeds!
Day and night I have spent myself
In idle talk, forgetting thee.
O divine Mother, if thou canst show
The slightest mercy to one so frail,
It will befit thy majesty.)

Āpatsumagnaḥ smaranaṃ tvadīyaṃ
Karomi durge karuṇārṇaveśi |
Naitacchaṭhatvaṃ mama bhāvayethāḥ
Kṣudhātṛṣārtāḥ jananīṃ smaranti ||

(Durga! Goddess of mercy's ocean!
Stricken with grief, to thee I pray:
Do not believe me insincere;
A child who is seized with thirst or hunger
Thinks of his mother constantly.)

Jagaḍamba vicitramatra kiṃ
Paripūrṇā karuṇāsti cenmayi |
Aparādhaparamparāvṛtam na hi
Mātā samupekṣate sutam ||

(Mother of the entire universe!
If thou shouldst show thy fullest mercy,
Would even that be a cause for wonder?
A mother cannot refuse her son,
Though he have done a million wrongs.)

Matsamaḥ Pātakī nāsti
Pāpaghnī tvatsamā na hi |
Evaṃ jñātvā mahadevi
Yathāyogyaṃ tathā kuru ||

(Nowhere exists, in all the world,
Another sinner to equal me,
Nowhere, a power like thyself
For overcoming sinfulness:
O Goddess! Keeping this in mind,
Do thou as it pleases thee.)

Vishnushatpadi

(Six stanzas to Vishnu)

Avinayamapanaya viṣṇo damaya manaḥ śamaya viṣayamṛgatṛṣṇām |
Bhūtadayām vistāraya tāraya saṁsārasāgarataḥ ||

(Save me from pride, O Vishnu! Curb my restless mind
Still my thirst for the waters of this world's mirage,

Be gracious, Lord! To this thy humble creature,
And rescue him from the ocean of the world.)

Divyadhunīmakarande parimalaparibhogasaccidānande |
Śrīpatipadāravinde bhavabhayakhedacchide vande ||

(I worship the lotus of thy feet, whose honey is the sacred Ganges,
Whose fragrance is knowledge, truth and bliss;
I worship the feet of Lakshmi's consort,
Who overcomes the fear and misery of the world.)

Satyāpi bhedāpagame nātha tavāhaṃ na māmakīnastvam |
Sāmudro hi taraṅgaḥ kwacana samudro na tārangaḥ ||

(Even when I am not duality's slave, O Lord!
The truth is that I am thine and not that thou art mine:
The waves may belong to the ocean,
But the ocean never belongs to the waves.)

Uddhṛtanaga nagabhidanuja danujakulāmitra mitraśaśidṛṣṭe |
Dṛṣṭe bhavati prabhavati na bhavati kiṃ bhavatiraskāraḥ ||

(Bearer of Govardhana! Slayer of the demon hosts!
Almighty one, whose eyes are the sun and moon!
Can anyone doubt, O Lord of the universe!
That the vision of thy form dispels this world's mirage?)

Matsyādibhiravatārairavatāravatā'vatā sadā vasudhām |
Parameśvara paripālyo bhavatā bhavatāpabhīto'ham ||

(Sovereign Lord! With thy manifold incarnations
Ever hast thou protected the universe from harm:
Come to my rescue, then O Lord!
Save me, who am afflicted by the fire of the world.)

Dāmodara guṇamandira sundaravadanāravinda govinda |
Bhavajaladhimathanamandara paramaṃ daramapanaya tvaṃ me ||

(Govinda! Damodara! Thou who art possessed
Of infinite virtues and surpassing charm!
Thou churner of the sea of worldliness!
Be gracious unto me and destroy my extreme fear.)

Nārāyaṇa karuṇāmaya śaraṇaṃ karavāṇi tāvakau caraṇau |
Iti ṣaṭpadī madīye vadanasaroje sadā vasatu ||

(Narayana! Thou art ever compassionate!
I have taken refuge in thy two feet:
May these six stanzas, even as honey bee,
Ever remain on the lotus of my lips!)

Ganga Stotra

Devi sureśvari bhagawati gaṅge
tribhuvanatāriṇī taralataraṅge |
Śaṅkaramaulivihāriṇi vimale
Mama matirāstāṃ tava padakamale ||

(Heaven-born river! Bhagwati Ganga!
Goddess, redeemer of all the worlds!
In ripples thy waters playfully are flowing;
Thou wanderest in Shiva's matted hair,
Grant that my mind, O thou who art stainless!
Ever may dwell at the lotus of thy feet.)

Bhāgirathi sukhadāyini mātaś
Tavajalamahimā nigame khyātaḥ |
Nāhaṃ jāne tava mahimānaṃ
Trāhi kṛpāmayi māmajñānam ||

(Bhagirathi! Mother! Giver of gladness!
The scriptures celebrate the glory of thy stream:
But I, alas! Know nothing of thy glories.
Foolish as I am, do thou redeem me,
Thou, the embodiment of merciful love!)

Haripādapadmataraṅgiṇī gaṅge
Himavidhumuktādhavalataraṅge |
Dūrikuru mama duṣkṛtibhāraṃ,
Kuru kṛpayā bhavasāgarapāram. ||

(Rippling, thou flowest from the feet of Hari,
Whiter than frost or diamonds or the moon.
O Mother Ganga! Take away the burden
Of wicked deeds that weighs upon me;
Bear me across the ocean of the world.)

Tava jalamamalaṃ yena nipītaṃ
Paramapadaṃ khalu tena gṛhītam |
Mātargaṅge tvayi yo bhaktaḥ
Kila taṃ draṣṭum na yamaḥ śaktaḥ ||

(He who has drunk thy refreshing waters
Verily has tasted of the highest;
He, thy worshipper, O Mother Ganga!
Never will be seized by the king of death.)

Patitoddhāriṇi Jāhnavi gaṅge
Khaṇḍitagirivaramaṇḍitabhaṅge |

Bhīṣmajanani khalu munivarakanye
Patitanivāriṇī tribhuvandhanya ||

(Ganga! Jahnavi! Saviour of sinners!
Murmuring, thou flowest on thy broken stones.
Mother of Bhishma! Daughter of Jahnu!
Thou, the almighty conqueror of evil!
Truly thou art blest in all the worlds.)

Kalpalatāmiva phaladāṁ loke
Praṇamati yastvāṁ na patati śoke |
Pārāvāravihāriṇī gaṅge
Suravanitākṛtataralāpāṅge ||

(Like the celestial tree of wishes,
Thou grantest the boons of men's desiring;
He who salutes thee will not grieve again.
Thou sportest, O Ganga, with the limitless ocean;
Wondering, the damsels of heaven regard thee,
Watching with restless, sidelong glances.)

Tava kṛpayā cet srotaḥ snātaḥ punarapi jathare so'pi na jātaḥ |
Narakanivariṇī jāhnavī gaṅge kaluṣavināśinī mahimottuṅge ||

(If, by thy grace, one bathes in thy waters,
Never need one enter a mother's womb:
The sins of a lifetime for all annulling,
The claims of destiny at death dispelling.
Jahnavi! Ganga! The worlds accord thee
Honour and renown for the glory that is thine.)

Prilasadaṅge puṇyataraṅge jaya jaya Jāhnavi karuṇāpāṅge |
Indramukuṭamaṇirājitacaraṇe sukhade śubhade sevakaśaraṇe ||

(Brightly, O Jahnavi, thy waters sparkle:
Thou lookest on thy worshippers with loving glance.
Indra himself, the ruler of the devas,
Bows at thy feet with his jewelled crown.
Giver of happiness! Bringer of good fortune!
Help of thy bondslaves, hail to thee!)

Rogaṃ śokaṃ tāpaṃ pāpaṃ hara me bhagavati kumatikalāpam |
Tribhuvanasāre vasudhāhāre tvamasi gatirmama khalu saṃsāre ||

(Banish, O Bhagwati! All my illness;
Take away my troubles, my sins and my grief;
Utterly crush my wanton cravings,
Goddess, supreme in all the worlds!
Thou, Mother Earth's most precious necklace!
Thou art my refuge here in this world!)

Alakānande paramānande kuru mayi karuṇāṃ kātaravandye |
Tava taṭanikaṭe yasya hi vāsaḥ khalu vaikuṇṭhe tasya nivāsaḥ ||

(Giver of delight to the gods in heaven!
Essence of bliss, adored by the afflicted!
On me shower thy compassionate love.
He who has made thy bank his dwelling
Verily abides in Vishnu's realm.)

Varamiha nīre kamaṭho mīnaḥ kiṃ vā tīre sraṭa kṣhiṇaḥ |
Athavā śvapaco gavyutidīnaḥ na ca tava dūre nṛpatikulīnaḥ ||

(Rather a fish or a turtle in thy waters,
A tiny lizard on thy bank, would I be,
Or even a shunned and hated outcaste
Living but a mile from thy sacred stream,
Than the proudest emperor afar from thee.)

Bho bhuvaneśvari puṇye dhanye devi dravamayi munivarakanye |
Gaṅgāstavamidamamalaṃ nityaṃ paṭhati naro yaḥ sa jayati satyam ||

(Thou, the auspicious ruler of creation!
Daughter of a sage and Mother benign!
Flowing deity! Veritable Goddess!
He who repeats this hymn to Ganga
Surely will succeed in everything.)

Yeṣāṃ hṛdaye gaṅgābhaktisteṣāṃ bhavati sadā sukhamuktiḥ |
Madhuramanoharapajjhaṭikābhiḥ paramānandākaralalitābhiḥ ||
Gaṅgāstotramidaṃ bhavasāraṃ vāñchitaphaladam vigalitabhāram |
Śaṅkarasevakaśaṅkararacitaṃ paṭhatu ca viṣayī tadagatcittam ||

(He who cherishes his Mother Ganga
Wins salvation with the greatest of ease.
This, her hymn, felicitous in rhythm,
Pleasant to the ear, to tongue like nectar,
Never surpassed, the wish fulfiller,
Noble and exalted in mood, was written
In the mind bewitching *pajhatika* metre
By Shankara, servant of Shankara himself.
Foolish mortal, given to enjoyment,
Read it daily for your lasting good.)

Narmadashtakam

Sabindusindhususkhalattaraṅgabhaṅgarañjitaṃ
Dviṣatsu pāpajātajātakādivārisaṃyutam |

Kṛtāntadūtakālabhūtabhītihārivarmade
Tvadīyapādapaṅkajaṃ namāmi devi narmade ||

(Salutations to Devi Narmada. Your river-body illumined with sacred drops of water, flows with mischievous playfulness, bending with waves. Your sacred water has the divine power to transform those who are prone to hatred, the hatred born of sins, you put an end to the fear of the messenger of death by giving your protective armour {of refuge}, O Devi Narmada, I bow down to your lotus feet, please give me your refuge.)

Tvadambulīnadīnamīnadivyasampradāyakaṃ
Kalau malaughabhārahārisarvatīrthanāyakam |
Sumacchakacchanakracakravākacakraśarmade
Tvadīyapādapaṅkajaṃ namāmi devi narmade ||

(Salutations to Devi Narmada. You confer your divine touch to the lowly fish merged in your holy waters, you take away the weight of the sins in this age of Kali; and you are the foremost among all *tirthas* (pilgrimages), you confer happiness to the many fish, tortoises, crocodiles, geese and chakra birds dwelling in your water. O Devi Narmada, I bow down to your lotus feet, please give me your refuge.)

Mahāgabhīranīrapūrapāpadhūtabhūtalaṃ
Dhvanatsamastapātakāridāritāpadācalam |
Jagallaye mahābhaye mṛkaṇḍusūnuharmyade
Tvadīyapādapaṅkajaṃ namāmi devi narmade ||

(Salutations to Devi Narmada. Your river-body is deep and overflowing, the waters of which remove the sins of the earth… it flowing with great force with reverberating sound, splitting asunder mountains of distresses, the distresses which bring our downfall, in the heat of this world, you provide the place of rest and assure great fearlessness; you who gave the place of refuge at your banks to the son of Rishi Mrikandu (Rishi Markandeya was the son of Rishi Mrikandu). O Devi Narmada, I bow down to your lotus feet, please give me your refuge.)

Gataṃ tadaiva me bhayaṃ tvadambu vīkṣitaṃ yadā
Mṛkaṇḍusūnuśaunakāsurārisevitaṃ sadā |
Punarbhavābdhijanmajaṃ bhavābdhiduḥkhavarmade
Tvadīyapādapaṅkajaṃ namāmi devi narmade ||

(Salutations to Devi Narmada. O Devi, after I have seen your divine water, my attachment to the worldly life has indeed vanished.... Your water, which is revered by the son of Rishi Mrikandu, Rishi Shaunaka, and the enemies of the asuras (i.e., devas), your water which is a protective shield against the sorrows of the ocean of worldly existence, caused by repeated births in this ocean of samsara {worldly existence}, O Devi Narmada, I bow down to your lotus feet, please give me your refuge.)

Alakṣyalakṣakinnarāmarāsurādipūjitaṃ
Sulakṣanīratīradhīrapakṣilakṣakūjitam |
Vasiṣṭhaśiṣṭapippalādikardamādiśarmade
Tvadīyapādapaṅkajaṃ namāmi devi narmade ||

(Salutations to Devi Narmada. You are worshipped by lakhs of invisible celestial beings like *kinnaras* (celestial musicians), *amaras* (devas), and also asuras and others; your river-body with auspicious waters, as well as your river-banks which are calm and composed, are filled with the sweet sounds of lakhs of cooing birds; you confer happiness to great sages like Vashistha, Sista, Pippala, Kardama and others. O Devi Narmada, I bow down to your lotus feet, please give me your refuge.)

Sanatkumāranāciketakaśyapātriṣatpadaiḥ
Dhṛtaṃ svakīyamānaseṣu nāradādiṣatapadaiḥ |

Ravīndurantidevadevarājakarmaśarmade
Tvadīyapādapaṅkajaṃ namāmi devi narmade ||

(Salutations to Devi Narmada. Rishis Sanatkumara, Nachiketa, Kashyapa and others who are like the six-footed bee {since they seek the honey of divine communion}, hold your lotus feet in their hearts; and Narada and others also hold your lotus feet in their hearts; you confer happiness to Ravi (Sun), Indu (Moon), Ranti Deva and Devaraja (Indra) by making their works successful. O Devi Narmada, I bow down to your lotus feet, please give me your refuge.)

Alakṣalakṣalakṣapāpalakṣasārasāyudhaṃ
Tatastu jīvajantutantubhuktimuktidāyakam |
Viriñciviṣṇuśaṃkarasvakīyadhāmavarmade
Tvadīyapādapaṅkajaṃ namāmi devi narmade ||

(Salutations to Devi Narmada. You cleanse lakhs of invisible and visible sins with your body, the banks of which are beautifully decorated with lakhs of *sarasas* {cranes or swans}; in that holy place {i.e., in your river-banks}, you give both *bhukti* {worldly prosperity} as well as mukti {liberation} to the series of living beings including animals {who take your shelter}. The presence of Brahma, Vishnu and Shankara in your holy dhama {i.e., river-body} provides a protective shield {of blessings to the devotees}. O Devi Narmada, I bow down to your lotus feet, please give me your refuge.)

Aho dhṛtaṃ svanaṃ śrutaṃ maheśikeśajātaṭe
Kirātasūtabāḍabeṣu paṇḍite śaṭhe naṭe |
Durantapāpatāpahāri sarvajantuśarmade
Tvadīyapādapaṅkajaṃ namāmi devi narmade ||

(Salutations to Devi Narmada. O, I only hear the sound of immortality, flowing down as your river-body, originating from the matted hairs of Shankara, and filling your river-banks. There {i.e., in your river-banks}, everyone, whether Kirata {a mountain tribe}, Suta {charioteer}, Vaddava {Brahmin}, Pandita {the learned and wise} or Shattha {Deceitful} gets purified within the dance of your waters. By vigourously removing *papa* {sins} and *tapa* {heat of the miseries of life} of all animals {including man}, you confer that happiness {born of purification}. O Devi Narmada, I bow down to your lotus feet, please give me your refuge.)

Idaṃ tu narmadāṣṭakaṃ trikālameva ye sadā
Paṭhanti te nirantaraṃ na yanti durgatiṃ kadā |
Sulabhyadehadurlabhaṃ maheśadhāṃagauravaṃ
Punarbhavā narā na vai vilokayanti rauravam ||

(Salutations to Devi Narmada. This Narmadashtakam, those who always recite three times of the day do not ever undergo misfortune, It becomes easy to obtain the great privilege of going to the abode of Mahesh, which is very difficult for an embodied being to attain, and those persons do not have to see the fearful world again {by taking birth}.)

Sharada Bhujanga Prayatashtakam
(The eight stanzas to Goddess Sharada)

Suvakṣojakumbhāṃ sudhāpūrṇakumbhām
Prasādāvalambāṃ prapuṇyāvalambām |
Sadāsyendubimbāṃ sadanoṣṭhabimbām
Bhaje śaradāmbāmajasraṃ madambām ||

(I constantly worship my Mother, Sharadamba. She has pitcher-like breasts. She has a pitcher filled with ambrosia. She has gracious disposition. She confers excessive merits. She has a moon-like face. She has the lips which confers boons.)

Katākṣe dayārdrāṃ kare jñānamudrām
Kalābhirvinidraṃ kalāpaiḥ subhadrām |
Purastrīṃ vinidrāṃ purastuṅgabhadrām
Bhaje śaradāmbāmajasraṃ madambām ||

(I constantly worship my Mother, Sharadamba. Her side-glances are moist with compassion. She shows the gesture of knowledge by her hand. She has the efflorescence of different arts. She looks very auspicious with her necklace of pearls. She is the foremost among women. She is fully awake. She has the {river} Tungabhadra {flowing} in her front.)

Lalāmāṅkaphālāṃ lasadgānalolām
Svabhaktaikapālāṃ yaṣaḥśrīkapolām |
Kare tvakṣamālā kanatpratnalolām
Bhaje śaradāmbāmajasraṃ madambām ||

(I constantly worship my Mother, Sharadamba. She has an ornament adorning her forehead. She is fond of excellent music. She is the one {Goddess} who protects her devotees. She has cheeks known for their beauty. She holds a rosary in her hand. She is the embodiment of radiant and ancient speech.)

Susīmantaveṇīṃ dṛśānirjitaiṇīm
Ramatkīravāṇiṃ namadavajrapāṇim |
Sudhāmandirasyāṃ mudācintyaveṇīm
Bhaje śaradāmbāmajasraṃ madambām ||

(I joyously pray to that (Goddess), my mother, incessantly. She has a well-parted braid of hair. She has excelled the female black deer by her looks. She has the voice of the sportive parrot. Her hand is holding a thunderbolt in a slanting posture. Her face is the abode of nectar. She has an incomprehensible flow of speech.)

Suśānatāṃ sudehāṃ dṛgante kacāntām
Lasatsallatāṅgīmanantāmacintyām |
Smarattāpasaiḥ saṅgapūrvasthitāṃ tām
Bhaje śaradāmbāmajasraṃ madambām ||

(I worship that {Goddess} Sharadamba, my mother. She is extremely calm. She possesses an excellent body. Her locks of hair touch the corner of her eyes. She is shining with her creeper-like body. She is infinite. She is beyond the purview of thought. She was formerly in the company of ascetics who constantly paid obeisance to her.)

Kuraṅge turaṅge mṛgendre khagendre
Marāle madebhe mahokṣe'dhirūdhām |
Mahatyāṃ navamyāṃ sadā sāmarūpāṃ
Bhaje śaradāmbāmajasraṃ madambām ||

(I pray to that {Goddess} Sharadamba, my mother, incessantly. She rides the deer, the horse, the lion, Garuda, the goose, the rutting elephant and the mighty bull on the great navami day. She is always of the form of the *Sama* {Veda} {and of a benevolent disposition}.)

Jvalatkāntivahniṃ jaganmohanāṅgīṃ
Bhajanmānasāmbhojasubhrāntabṛṅgīm |
Nijastotrasaṅgitanṛtyaprabhāṅgīm
Bhaje śaradāmbāmajasraṃ madambām |

(I worship that {Goddess} Sharadamba, my mother, incessantly. She is shining with the radiance of fire. She has a beautiful body stupefying the entire universe. I worship that female bee which wanders in the lotus of my heart. She is shining with the excellence of music and I dance in her praise.)

Bhavāmbhojanetrājasampūjyamānāṃ
Lasanmandahāsaprabhāvaktracihnām |
Calaccañcalācārutāṭaṅkakarṇāṃ
Bhaje śaradāmbāmajasraṃ madambām ||

(I worship that {Goddess} Sharadamba, my mother, incessantly. She is worshipped by the lords—Shiva, Vishnu and Brahma. She bears the mark of a beautiful gentle smile on her face. She has her eyes beautified by the swinging of charming ear ornaments.)

Acknowledgements

1. *The Bhagavadgita with the commentary of Shri Shankaracharya,* translated into English by A. Madhava Shastri, Mysore, 1901.
2. *Atmabodha,* translated by Swami Nikhilananda, Sri Ramakrishna Math, Mylapore, Madras, 1947.
3. *Tattvabodha,* translated by Swami Tejomayananda, Central Chinmaya Mission Trust, Mumbai, 2001.
4. *Vivekachudamani,* translated by Swami Madhavananda, The Advaita Ashrama, Mayavati, Almora, 1921.
5. *Guru Ashtakam,* English translation from the Appendix of *Atmabodha,* translated by Swami Nikhilananda, Sri Ramakrishna Math, Mylapore, Madras, 1947.
6. *Manishapanchakam* (Sanskrit) from Vani Vilas Press; and English translation from http://www.eternalworksofshriadisankara.com/strotras.php
7. *Dashashloki,* translated by Vaidya N. Sundaram from http://sanskritdocuments.org/doc_z_misc_shankara/dashashl.html?lang=sa
8. *Saundarya Lahari,* translated by V. K. Subramanian, Motilal Banarsidass Publishers Pvt. Ltd., Delhi, first edition, 1977.
9. *Upadeshasahasri,* translated by Swami Jagadananda, Sri Ramakrishna Math, Mylapore, Madras, 1941.
10. *Brahmajnavalimala*, English translation from

https://sanskritdocuments.org/sites/snsastri/brahmajnaanaavalimaalaa.pdf

11. ***Shivapanchakshara Stotra,*** English translation from http://www.eternalworksofshriadisankara.com/strotras.php
12. ***Narmadashtakam,*** English translation from http://greenmesg.org/mantras_slokas/devi_narmada-narmadashtakam.php

Index

H

I

K

L

S

Sacchidananda Sivabhinava Bharathi, 2
sacred geography, 18
sadhana, 69
Sadhguru Jaggi Vasudev, 122–124
Saguna upasana, 138
sakshatkara, 191
sakshin, 183–184
salvation, 31, 62
samana, 100
samanvaya (harmony), 68–69
Sama veda, 43, 60–61
samhitas, 60
Samkhya dualism, 70
Sampoornanand Sanskrit University, 14
  establishment of, 16
  John Muir, appointed as first principal, 16
  motto of, 16
Saraswati Library, 16
samyagdarshana (perfect intuition), 191
Sanandana (Padmapada), devotee of Shankara, 20
Sanatana Hindu Dharma, 26, 52
sangha, 86
Sankhya school, 76–78, 140
Sanmatha Sthapanacharya, 141
Sanskrit grammar, 22, 81
Sanskrit university, 22
sanyasin, 32
Saptamata statue, 2
Saraswathi, Jayendra, 45
Saraswathi, Vijayendra, 45–46
Saraswati (the Goddess of Learning), 2, 33, 135
Saraswati (supercluster of galaxies), Indian Scientists discovery of, 144
Saraswati river, 23
Sariraka Sutra, 67
sarovar (sacred tank or pool), 49
sarvapratyayadarshin, 95
satchittananda, 94
Sati, 19
satkaryavada, 196
Satpura ranges, 6
sattva, 77
Saundarya Lahari, 39, 82, 135–136, 138
Saura, 141
Schopenhauer, Arthur, 67
Schrodinger, Erwin, 154, 176
scientific minds, 178
Scientists, 142, 144–145, 147, 150–151, 153–154, 156–159, 165–166, 170, 172, 174, 193
Sechsig, Deussen, 67
self-forgetfulness, 189
self-transcendence, 188
sensory perceptions, 102
Serotonin neurotransmitter, 192
serving a secondary purpose (*parartha*), 80
seven-step theory (*saptabhangi*), 87
shabda (world knowledge), 15
Shabda Advaita philosophy, 81
Shah, Hussain, 18
Shah, Maroof, 39
Shah Miri dynasty, 37
Shaiva, 141
Shaivite, 82